WHATEVER IT TAKES

Life Lessons from *Degrassi* and Elsewhere
in the World of Music and Television

STEPHEN STOHN
with CHRISTOPHER WARD

DUNDURN
TORONTO

Copyright © 2018 Ellipse Media Consulting Corp.

All rights reserved. No part of this publication may be reproduced, stored in a retrieval system, or transmitted in any form or by any means, electronic, mechanical, photocopying, recording, or otherwise (except for brief passages for purpose of review) without the prior permission of Dundurn Press. Permission to photocopy should be requested from Access Copyright.

Cover image: istock.com/kostsov
Printer: Webcom

Library and Archives Canada Cataloguing in Publication

Stohn, Stephen, author
    Whatever it takes : life lessons from Degrassi and elsewhere in the world of music and television / Stephen Stohn with Christopher Ward.

Issued in print and electronic formats.
ISBN 978-1-4597-3998-7 (softcover).--ISBN 978-1-4597-3999-4 (PDF).--ISBN 978-1-4597-4000-6 (EPUB)

1. Stohn, Stephen. 2. Television producers and directors--Canada--Biography. 3. Musicians--Canada-- Biography. 4. Lawyers--Canada--Biography. 5. Television broadcasting--Canada. 6. Cultural industries--Canada. 7. Degrassi the next generation (Television program). I. Ward, Christopher, author II. Title.

PN1992.4.S76A3 2018   791.4502'32092   C2017-907136-X
                                            C2017-907137-8

1 2 3 4 5   22 21 20 19 18

Conseil des Arts du Canada   Canada Council for the Arts   Canada   ONTARIO ARTS COUNCIL CONSEIL DES ARTS DE L'ONTARIO an Ontario government agency un organisme du gouvernement de l'Ontario

We acknowledge the support of the **Canada Council for the Arts**, which last year invested $153 million to bring the arts to Canadians throughout the country, and the **Ontario Arts Council** for our publishing program. We also acknowledge the financial support of the **Government of Ontario**, through the **Ontario Book Publishing Tax Credit** and the **Ontario Media Development Corporation**, and the **Government of Canada**.

Nous remercions le **Conseil des arts du Canada** de son soutien. L'an dernier, le Conseil a investi 153 millions de dollars pour mettre de l'art dans la vie des Canadiennes et des Canadiens de tout le pays.

Care has been taken to trace the ownership of copyright material used in this book. The author and the publisher welcome any information enabling them to rectify any references or credits in subsequent editions.
                                            — *J. Kirk Howard, President*

The publisher is not responsible for websites or their content unless they are owned by the publisher.

Printed and bound in Canada.

VISIT US AT

dundurn.com | @dundurnpress | dundurnpress | dundurnpress

Dundurn
3 Church Street, Suite 500
Toronto, Ontario, Canada
M5E 1M2

Kingston Frontenac Public Library

Feb 2018

39011011946466

Praise for *Whatev*

A breezy read with a very appropriate title … a must-read for anybody who is thinking about getting into a life in entertainment as a career. Stephen did it first, so his book is like a treasure map.
— Kevin Smith, filmmaker, podcaster, and author

Stephen has always been a force pushing and developing Canadian music, film, TV, and entertainment to the world. He is one of our greatest ambassadors, and this book really is a great read and ride through many decades of the Canadian scene. It's a must-read for everyone … so get a copy and get ready for a compelling and informative read like you haven't had in a long time.
— Randy Bachman, just a kid from Winnipeg

Boy genius Stephen Stohn shows us that respect, grace, love, and honour trump the bitchy loudmouth tactics so common inside the dream factory of music and motion pictures. This book is essential reading for future moguls and those planning to go all the way. The man is a prince.
— Bruce McDonald, filmmaker

Remarkably relatable, incredibly inspiring … Stephen Stohn might secretly be the Dos Equis guy.
— Ricardo Hoyos, actor and musician

The honest, insightful, and highly entertaining stories here form a sort of sourcebook for those of us who want to work on becoming better human beings. It's kind of a Zen manual for self-awareness disguised as a great entertainment memoir. And that's why you should read it. You'll not only enjoy yourself, you'll be inspired by it too.
— Bob Ezrin, record producer

Funny, engaging, and poignant, you'll feel like you're being personally mentored by one of Canada's most influential producers and creators!
— Jake Epstein, actor and musician

From his escapades as a young hippie, dharma bum, and aspiring musician to becoming one of the top entertainment lawyers in the most formative period in Canadian music cultural history, Stephen has done, seen, and been a big part of a lot of stuff. Filled with tons of stories and anecdotes, *Whatever It Takes* is a surprisingly fascinating, interesting, and candid read.
— Tom Cochrane, musician

Who knew that mild-mannered Stephen Stohn is the Hunter S. Thompson of Canadian entertainment lawyers?
— Ivan Fecan, media mogul

A must-read for any aspiring entrepreneur.
— Marc Kielburger, co-founder, WE

Stephen's insights into the inner workings of our idiosyncratic television industry should be required reading for anyone who wants to turn their dreams of making TV into a reality.
— Ben Mulroney, TV anchor

This book will motivate you … just as Stephen Stohn has motivated me.
— "Maestro Fresh" Wes Williams, rapper, actor, and motivational speaker

Insightful, humorous, and full of heart, *Whatever It Takes* is not only a must-read for anyone in show business, but also a great learning tool for those looking to make a break into the field. Oh, and it's a hella fun read as well!
— Stefan Brogren, actor and director

As a fan of *Degrassi* and the incredible musical artists mentioned in this book, I enjoyed the behind-the-scenes stories. As an improviser, I related to the impact of working with the right people, keeping positive, and always remembering that failure is a step to success, not a barrier. Read this book for fun and life lessons — you're welcome!
— Colin Mochrie, comedian

I couldn't put it down … a fascinating look at the entertainment world, and a humbling reminder that success is driven by what we learn through our failures.
— Kary Bowser, radio producer and internet blogger

The frontier days of the Canadian music and television industry are not so distant in our past. This book tells a great tale of some of the formative events: early boundary-breaking artists like Cowboy Junkies and k.d. lang to the huge episodic TV success with the *Degrassi* series. When we met Stephen Stohn during our first contract time with Warner Music, he was a gentle, sweet, and a very proper looking lawyer. Had I known he was once a hippie songwriting vagabond, travelling across Europe with only his wits as currency, I would have trusted him more.
— Jim Cuddy, musician

A delightful romp … I laughed out loud and was inspired … the book filled me with trips down memory lane as well as fascinating behind-the-scenes secrets I never knew.
— Miriam McDonald, actor

WHATEVER IT TAKES

CONTENTS

FOREWORD

You don't say no to Stephen Stohn.

Now, is that because he's one of Canada's most noted and powerful lawyers? Is it because he's a titan of the Canadian music industry? Because he's one of Canada's only true media moguls? These are all very good guesses, but no.

You don't say no to Stephen Stohn because everything about Stephen makes you want to say "yes." This is his true and rare gift, his secret superpower, and a large part of why he's achieved so much over the course of his remarkable life.

An old agent of mine used to say, "To get anything made in show business, you have to line up a thousand 'yesses' in a row. And if you get even one 'no' in there, the project is dead." And he's right:

> Do you like this idea? Do you like the writer? Will you pay for development? Do you like the script? Do you like all the subsequent rewrites of the script? Do you want to make the pilot? Do you like the director? Do you like the cast/costumes/sets/score/et cetera/et cetera/et cetera? Do you like the pilot? Do you like all the subsequent recuts of the pilot? Do you want to pay to make more episodes? DO YOU TRUST ME?

And on and on and on…. A single negative response to any of these questions is a potential explosion waiting to turn your entire project into dust.

This is why Stephen is so successful. Because Stephen leads with a "yes" in his heart.

When I met with Stephen — one of those delightful and useless "general meetings," or so I thought — I was happily living in Los Angeles and working on a critically acclaimed HBO show when he somehow convinced me to pack up my life and move back to Toronto to make a TV series he could in no way guarantee would ever be seen outside of Canada. All of my agents and friends thought I was crazy, told me not to do it. Because they hadn't met Stephen. But I had. And just as he's done with countless others before and since, he turned my "no" into a "yes."

Where everyone else saw folly and risk, Stephen saw opportunity and the chance for greatness. And more importantly, he made me see it too. He not only made me feel like this insane decision was the right one for me, but he also made me feel safe, valued … and seen. Stephen, this bastion of serenity and security amid the dark and churning waters of the entertainment industry, would be my partner, my protector, my champion….

Taking that job — meeting Stephen's "yes" with a "yes" of my own — was one of the best decisions I've ever made.

Within the pages of this book, you'll find out how he does it. Through incredible stories and amazing insights covering the many realms of businesses that he's mastered, you'll start to see just how this gentle, wonderful, quiet force of nature has helped to create so many outstanding and successful projects — through his undying positivity and his unwavering confidence in the collaborators with whom he so deftly surrounds himself.

I have learned so much from Stephen — tools and skills I still use daily. I'm so excited for you to learn them, too, and to get to know this man whom I love and respect so greatly. I have the utmost confidence that the techniques and management theories contained within will not only make you better at business ... they'll make you a better person.

So sit back and enjoy the read. I know I did.

Martin Gero, producer and writer
Los Angeles, California
October 2017

Martin Gero is variously the creator, writer, director, and producer of some of televisions hottest series, including NBC's hit drama *Blindspot*, HBO's *Bored to Death*, the Sci-Fi Channel's cult hit *Stargate: Atlantis*, and The CW's *The L.A. Complex*. His most recent series is ABC's *Deception*, just now starting production, in which a Las Vegas magician begins working as a "consulting illusionist" for the FBI when his career is ruined by scandal. Martin lives in Los Angeles.

PRELUDE

My heart sank as I put down the phone and wondered what to do next. After thirty-five years and nearly five hundred episodes, *Degrassi* had been cancelled.

I'd had brave words for the network executive at Viacom in reply to his almost nonchalant, "We've decided to move in a different direction. *Degrassi* is over, but we'd like you to come back to us with some ideas on how to celebrate the fourteen years you've been the top show on our network — something fitting to end the series."

"It's not ending," I'd said. "We believe in what we're doing. We thought you did, too. Our plans for this coming season are just too good to let go. *Degrassi* is going to continue. If not with you, then somewhere else."

He ignored me. "I'll look forward to hearing what you come up with to finish the show. Something grand. A special episode, maybe? Or … how 'bout you talk Drake into doing a two-hour concert special to end it all? Think about it and get back to me."

Click. And that was it. A complete shock. We'd been sure the upcoming season was in the bag. But the television business can be brutal. Despite my confident words, it appeared this was indeed the end.

Mute, I stared out the window and recalled the day thirty-five years earlier when, as a newly minted entertainment lawyer, I had first met my future wife, Linda Schuyler. It was a quick meeting, made quicker by the advice I had given her: "Don't hire me!"

She was holding a small book entitled *Ida Makes a Movie*, and she wanted to buy the rights to turn it into a short television film. The book was out of print, and I suggested that buying the rights should be very straightforward; however, if lawyers got involved it could get unnecessarily complicated. "Here's a form for an assignment of all audiovisual rights of whatsoever nature or kind, now or hereafter known, in perpetuity, throughout the universe," I said (as a young lawyer I couldn't help talking in legal mumbo-jumbo). "Take it yourself to the publisher in New York, offer them a small cash payment, and see what happens." I added that by the time I opened a file for her and issued a bill, the internal cost would be greater than any fee I would charge for the small time involved, so my advice was for free.

I actually didn't hear from Linda again for several years. She had indeed travelled to New York and met with the publisher. Her small payment was accepted, and she had become the proud owner of the necessary rights. She then scrounged five thousand dollars from family and friends, and, with her partner, Kit Hood, proceeded to make the film. It turned out well enough that she was encouraged to make another, *Cookie Goes to the Hospital*; then another, *Irene Moves In*; and then a fourth, *Noel Buys a Suit*. The Canadian Broadcasting Corporation (CBC) agreed to license the four films for broadcast. The licence fees were modest, but Linda's production costs were even more modest, so it was a great fit.

The one question CBC had was: "What do we call the series?" There were four films, each with a different protagonist, and CBC needed one title to market them. Linda had mused in reply, "Well, each film is about kids, and we shot them in and around my friend Bruce Mackey's house while he was at work during the days. He lives on Degrassi Street, so why don't we call the series *The Kids of Degrassi Street*."

A total of twenty-six episodes of *Kids of Degrassi Street* were produced by the time CBC suggested aging up to a tween audience by creating a spinoff series called *Degrassi Junior High*. This would require much higher budgets and more complex financing, and Linda realized that she needed an entertainment lawyer to help guide her through it all. She remembered that nice young lawyer who had given her free legal advice back at the beginning of it all.

From then until now we've worked together, with me at first as the lawyer for the production company until, by 1995, Linda and I had also become producing partners and husband and wife. And as the years have unfolded, *Degrassi* has become the longest-running teen television drama in North America.*

◎　　◎　　◎

I snapped out of my reverie and back into the present moment. It was mid-March 2015 and *Degrassi* was ending. The winter in Toronto had been especially cold that year, and snow drifts still piled high outside our television studios — studios that had been an empty warehouse until twenty years earlier when Linda and I had bought that warehouse, fulfilling a dream and slowly turning it into seven interior stages and an exterior backlot of sets, all spread out over two buildings and five acres we called Epitome Pictures. For more than a decade we had produced the most recent iteration of the *Degrassi* television franchise in those studios, where nearly a hundred cast and crew members were currently standing by, waiting for their work to begin for the year.

How would I tell Linda, and the cast and crew, it was all over?

I closed my eyes, breathed deeply, and imagined myself surrounded by a globe of light, a trick I used to keep calm. Eyes still closed, but still not completely calm by any means, I started to realize there might be a small chance to move forward — to manifest a possible strategy we had already been contemplating for the future.

Could the future be accelerated to now?

---

* In the world, only the British teen soap *Grange Hill* (1978–2008), which aired just over six hundred half-hour episodes, ran longer.

1
WHATEVER IT TAKES

I seem to have gotten ahead of myself. Let's turn back the calendar a bit and start closer to the beginning.

My grandfather Max had always wanted a son. Instead, he had five wonderful daughters in a row and never did hear the magic words, "It's a boy!" — that was, until his fifty-fourth birthday. On that day my mother, the eldest of his five daughters, gave birth to me, the first grandchild.* A boy!

As a result I was the golden child. Apart from the fact that I was extremely shy, until the age of seven my life was pretty much the proverbial bowl of cherries. A good circle of friends. A midtown Toronto public school in a nice neighbourhood, with teachers who cared. Every now and again a new pair of running shoes, which I would immediately scuff up so as not to draw too much attention to myself — but not too much because, as everyone knows, you can run faster than anyone in a brand new pair of PF Flyers.

That all changed in the summer of '55, when my parents decided to move into a larger home. I would be in a new school for grade 2.

---

* As a result, on my sixth birthday, Grandfather Max turned sixty. And on my sixteenth, he turned seventy. He died a couple of years later, or we would have shared a twenty-first and seventy-fifth birthday party.

Yes, it would still be a midtown Toronto public school in a nice neighbourhood, with teachers who cared. But for someone who was very shy, breaking into a new circle of friends was not going to be easy. And over the next several years the bully up the street made it nearly impossible.

I forget his name (or more likely I have repressed it). He wasn't huge, but he was very tough. Not only did he threaten me at every opportunity, but he also coerced the other kids living on my street to do the same. The others obliged with name-calling, insults, and other forms of verbal abuse toward me, and of course social ostracism. Meanwhile the poking, arm-twisting, head holds, tripping, and other means of physical intimidation were delivered by the master bully himself.

I guess I didn't help matters. On top of being shy, I had crooked teeth and then, worse, metal braces. I wore thick glasses and got good marks at school. In an era when it was definitely not cool to be a nerd, I was a nerd in nerd's clothing.

For the next five years or so I ended up spending a lot of time on my own. It was not a happy time. I longed to have friends, but just felt alone and lonely.

My parents were good to me in those years, but they didn't help with the bullying. They would tell me, "Sticks and stones may break my bones but names will never hurt me." That is a lie. Names *do* hurt, as does the fear of broken bones.

Now, there is a good side to spending a lot of time on your own. You learn a bit about yourself, and you get to think a lot about life and the people around you. You also develop hobbies. I fooled around with primitive electronics and built crystal radio sets, starting a lifelong love of radio. My grandfather took me to Toronto Maple Leaf baseball games, starting a lifelong love of baseball. I would spend hours trying to solve logic puzzles, and when I succeeded, I'd try to solve them again but in a more elegant manner, starting a lifelong love of approaching problems from different points of view. And perhaps most importantly,

I took piano lessons and then taught myself how to play the ukulele, starting a lifelong love of music.

So yes, there were good sides to it, but what I remember most was the deep unhappiness of feeling like an outsider. It may seem romantic to be a loner, but believe me, it's not.

One realization really did help back then. Even as those years in junior school unfolded, I could start to look back on it all and realize that no matter what had been happening to me, I was, in fact, surviving. I might not have had the life I longed for, but whatever it took, I was making it through.

As 1960 approached, a corner was turned. I was twelve years old by then and a veteran at being bullied. Times were tough for us financially that year, which meant my parents could no longer afford such a large home, so we had to downsize and move again. I stayed at the same school this time, with one huge change: there was no longer a bully up the street.

I was free.

I don't even remember how I felt on the day we moved. You would think it would have been so momentous an occasion, my journey to freedom, that I would remember it vividly, but that whole period of my life seems shrouded in my mind, and I only remember not wanting to jinx it all, hardly able to believe that I had made it through.

It still took years for me to emerge from the introspective shell I'd cloistered myself in during the bullied years. But emerge I did, and this book is, in effect, a series of stories resulting from that emergence.

Today, when I am so involved in producing the *Degrassi* television series, I can reflect back on how being bullied as a child so profoundly affected me, and how *Degrassi* itself has developed into a thirty-eight-year anti-bullying message spread out over more than five hundred episodes. Embedding that message into the series was not my doing; it is the creators and writers who are responsible for things like that.

But, that *Degrassi* message resonates very deeply within me and is reflected in something I do take some credit for — the theme song for the most recent four hundred episodes of *Degrassi*, written by me and two friends back in 2001.* It starts:

Whatever it takes, I know I can make it through....

---

* Jody Colero, Jim McGrath, and I originally wrote the song in 2001. A revised version was created for the launch of *Degrassi: Next Class* in January 2016, with the help of two additional writers, Shobha Lee and Rob Wells.

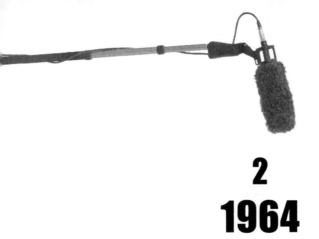

2
1964

In many ways I became a true teenager at the age of sixteen. It was 1964, the year The Beatles invaded America, the U.S. Congress authorized the war in Vietnam, and President Lyndon B. Johnson signed the Civil Rights Act after three civil rights workers were murdered in Mississippi. The average car cost $3,500, and a loaf of bread twenty-one cents.* The first Ford Mustang was produced, and Cassius Clay (later known as Muhammad Ali) beat Sonny Liston to win the world heavyweight boxing championship.

An event that year would forever change my life. Fifty years later I recalled that event in a convocation address I delivered to the graduating students at my alma mater, Trent University in Peterborough, Ontario, on the occasion of my being awarded an honorary doctorate:

> I was lucky enough to discover the kernel, the starting seed, of my real dream at 4:30 p.m. on September 7, 1964. I was attending my very first rock concert, at the old Maple Leaf Gardens in Toronto, and before the main act came on, there were several warm-up acts

---

* Interestingly a 45 rpm single record cost about seventy cents, not hugely different from a download today.

that played two or three songs each with the house lights still up.

Back in those days there weren't the huge stacks of sound equipment and arrays of guitars and drums on stage that we're used to now. I remember each group had their own logos on their drum kits, names like Brenda Holloway, the King Curtis Band, and Cannibal & the Headhunters. They'd play their two or three songs, and then roadies would quickly switch the equipment and the next warm-up act would race on. Near the end was a group called Sounds Incorporated, who had an international hit at the time. They sang their three songs and then left the stage. Their equipment remained, so we figured they would come back to do another few songs. But they didn't come back. It seemed like fifteen or twenty minutes went by with nothing happening. The crowd was getting more and more restive and started chanting, almost to the point of anger and frustration.

Then every light in Maple Leaf Gardens went out. Total blackness. The entire crowd screamed in pandemonium, and suddenly a single spotlight shot onto the Sounds Incorporated drum kit. A roadie raced across the stage and ripped off the front of their bass drum to reveal a new name — The Beatles — and the four lads ran out on stage. We heard almost nothing after that with all the screaming that accompanied their show.

So it was that afternoon I knew what my dream was. I was destined to be a rock star.

Spoiler alert: I never became a rock star. But that day started me on a path through the world of music and television, a path where dreams propelled me (and the extraordinarily talented people who came to surround me) through a series of adventures.

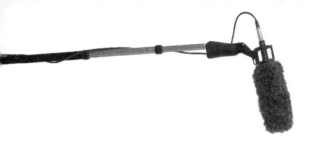

3
THE NEW LENNON AND McCARTNEY

When I first sent some sample chapters of this book to my literary agent, the dapper and insightful Sam Hiyate, he was very supportive. He made some structural suggestions to improve the flow and encouraged me to open up about my personal fears and philosophies in order to give an overall backbone to the unfolding stories.

He was less keen, though, on the following chapters that detail my 1970 travels with Christopher Ward through Europe and beyond. His first response was that no one would believe the stories, that some of them sounded too fantastical to be true. "And even if readers do accept them as true," he went on to say, "they just sound like some random hippie adventures that don't really lead anywhere." Sort of like Ken Kesey's travels in a psychedelic painted school bus, as documented in Tom Wolfe's 1968 book *The Electric Kool-Aid Acid Test* — fine at the time, but not so relevant in 2018.

I think Sam is wrong, and here's why: First, the stories are absolutely true. Second, and more importantly, while it may appear that we were wandering about aimlessly, when I look back, I realize what an important foundation those travels have been for my life. What may appear as aimless was, in fact, a willingness to accept the twists and turns that befell us, not to resist them but to embrace them, and to move onward in a new direction.

This openness and acceptance is celebrated today as being "present in the moment." We weren't being philosophical or Zen-like at the time; we were simply answering the siren call of the zeitgeist of the 1960s — anything was possible if you were truly open to it.

There is no question in my mind that this same sense of being on a mission, acceptance of randomness, and openness to change — honed and reinforced during our travels back in 1970 — led me along the path to where I am today.

Practising openness is difficult for normal, sober, adult humans; we are all imbued with preconceptions and barriers. It becomes easier, though, if we have firmly established and authentic long-term goals, and faith that our choices — even wrong choices — will eventually lead us in the right direction.

Back in 1970 Christopher and I each had our own individual dreams, but they largely coalesced in a mutual goal of becoming rock stars and world-famous songwriters. In our minds, we were the next Lennon and McCartney.

As it turned out, we didn't become what we dreamed of back then, but, remarkably, we came close. Years later Christopher wrote the #1 *Billboard* hit standard "Black Velvet." I co-wrote the *Degrassi* theme song "Whatever It Takes," which has never topped the charts but is heard every day in every country in the world. Together we created some other songs that reached the Top 10, at least on the Canadian charts. Individually, we have each worked with some of the greatest rock stars on the planet, me as an entertainment lawyer and as executive producer of *The Juno Awards* and *Degrassi*, and Christopher as a songwriter and as a VJ/interviewer in the early days of MuchMusic (Canada's version of MTV). And we've been intimately involved in the creation of dozens of songs that have formed the soundtracks to television series such as *Riverdale*, *Instant Star*, and *Degrassi*.

It was that combination of goal setting and openness during our travels that led us to where we are today.

So while the cautions of Sam Hiyate — that the stories of our travels may sound feckless and fantastical — are completely understandable,

I suggest we just settle back and enjoy the ride ... as Christopher and I make our way, in a faded-blue used Volkswagen van, onward toward the Orient....

○   ○   ○

It was January 1970, and a return flight from New York to Luxembourg cost just $319, provided you were willing to fly in a Loftleidir turboprop with a stopover in Reykjavik, Iceland.

Back in those days Loftleidir, now known as Icelandair, was very popular among college students who wanted an inexpensive way to travel to Europe. Known as "the hippie airline," it was more focused on travelling cheaply than travelling comfortably or on schedule. Both Bill and Hillary Clinton were among those who flew Loftleidir to Europe during the 1960s and 1970s, and Hillary is reported to have fondly remembered Loftleidir's slogan from those years, "We are the slowest but the lowest."*

I arrived in Luxembourg, found a cheap hotel, and then set out to purchase a (very) used Volkswagen van, as well as a tent and some other camping equipment. I also spent a long time in a department store arguing and insisting in French that I wanted "*deux maîtresses*," which I was sure meant "two mattresses." It was only later I discovered that I was apparently trying to buy "two mistresses."**

After a few weeks of travelling with some friends, I found myself writing a long letter to Christopher Ward, encouraging him to drop everything and join me.*** Christopher and I had met while we were both students at

---

* For those of you who speak Icelandic, the citation is www.pressan.is/Vidskipti/ Lesavidskiptafrettir/icelandair-hafdi-ahrif-a-samband-hillary-og-bill-clintons--- hitti-ossur-fyrir-stundu-i-usa.

** If you are ever in a similar situation, the French word for "mattress" is "matelas."

*** In the letter, I remember asserting that *Loftleidir* was Icelandic for "Flies Like a Brick," which he found quite amusing.

Trent University. We had become fast friends through our mutual love of music, particularly The Beatles.*

In my letter to him I included a description of our future selves playing songs for a covey of dark Spanish beauties who looked on adoringly. He could not resist.

In our student days at Trent we had performed as a duo for the Trent Folk Club under the self-mocking moniker "Cookies and Milk" — our slogan was "Already a household name!" It seemed to both of us that our sweet Everly Brothers harmonies might meet with some success in Europe. With any luck we could earn enough money playing in cafés to finance and extend the travels.

And so it was that a few weeks later we found ourselves installed together in a campsite just outside of Málaga on southern Spain's Costa del Sol, making new friends as we wrote songs and rehearsed our Cookies and Milk repertoire.

One of our new friends was Peter Kölbl, a retired German army officer who was travelling with his wife and two granddaughters. He helped us by building shelving for the back of the Volkswagen, turning it into something of a camper van. He and his family were also very encouraging of our songwriting and singing, insisting that we play for them every evening.

We had a small cassette recorder that we used for songwriting, and the Kölbls loved asking us to drive around the campsite with our songs playing loudly through the cassette machine, pretending everyone in the campsite was hearing the world-famous musicians Cookies and Milk on the car radio.

We made local friends as well. The salesgirls in the local grocery store (who, I think, pretty much qualified as the "covey of dark Spanish beauties" foreseen in my earlier letter to Christopher) thought my attempts

---

* Shortly after we first met, we found ourselves staying up all night trying to decipher the words fading in the background of the Beatles song "I Am the Walrus," thinking that the words sounded Shakespearean, so reading play after play until discovering the words were indeed from the death scene in *King Lear*.

at speaking Spanish were so funny that they invited us to numerous beachside get-togethers, where Christopher and I would sing songs for them and their friends, and then they would ask me to speak Spanish so they could laugh — a joke that never seemed to get old.

Two California girls, Virginia and Cynthia, also became friends, and it was with them one afternoon that we ventured into the Port of Málaga to do some sightseeing, ending up at a small seaside bar.

Málaga is known for its high-rise hotels and beachside resorts, and its Semana Santa, or Holy Week, draws over five million people annually to its sombre Easter-time parade. But Málaga was also (and still is) a provisioning port for the U.S. Navy. It turned out that the bar we entered was a favoured hangout for U.S. Navy sailors, and as the evening progressed, we struck up a conversation with some of them.

Christopher (right) and me (left) with U.S. Navy sailors after our first concert — on board a U.S. destroyer.

It must have been a bit strange for the sailors — we had long hair while they were very clean-cut — but we were the same age, and we ended up having a long discussion about what it was like to be part of the U.S. military while the war in Vietnam was going on, a war that clearly troubled these particular sailors.

They were also interested in hearing our music, so we pulled out our guitars and played some songs for them in a nearby park. They enjoyed the songs, and our company, and one of them asked if we would consider coming to their ship and giving a concert to the entire crew.

Of course we said yes! The first European concert for Cookies and Milk would be on board a U.S. Navy destroyer!

In today's post-9/11 world, two completely unknown, long-haired musicians would never get close to a U.S. warship, but this was 1970, and we simply sent our Canadian passports ahead to be approved, and a few days later we were on a U.S. Navy tender speeding toward the destroyer with our new friends. And once on board we were treated, if not like stars, then certainly like rising stars, and the several hundred sailors in the ship's mess hall gave our performance a very warm reception.

We sang about a half-dozen songs and an encore, and after our performance our Navy friends gave us a proud and extended tour of the destroyer, ending up in the PX store where we stocked up on months' worth of necessities like soap and shampoo, all at very low prices.

We felt on top of the world, well on our way to becoming the rock stars we dreamed of being. It seemed simple.

It will come as no surprise, but later we were to find out that nothing worthwhile in life is that simple.

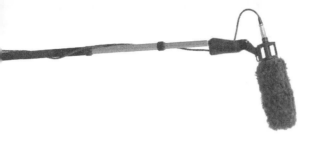

4
JUNIOR WOODCHUCKS

Our journey onward from Spain started shortly thereafter in a bookstore in Torremolinos, a town just southwest from Málaga. We were looking for books that would help translate various languages into English, and found instead something that seemed perhaps even better: *Il Manuale delle Giovani Marmotte*, the Italian version of *The Junior Woodchucks Guidebook*, used by the fictional Disney characters Huey, Dewey, and Louie to get themselves and their uncles, Donald Duck and Scrooge McDuck, out of dangerous situations.

Admittedly, the advice contained in the *Manuale* was somewhat circumscribed for us since it was in Italian. But it had the double merit of teaching us some Italian phrases while also giving us much-needed life information. (To this day I impress myself by using the aviation alphabet set out in the *Manuale* to spell out names and locator numbers when dealing with airlines.)*

Until then we had used excellent Michelin maps for travelling in Spain and France, but we had nothing for countries further east. The *Manuale*

---

* Also called the military phonetic alphabet, it consists of Alpha, Bravo, Charlie, Delta, Echo, Foxtrot, Golf, Hotel, India, Juliet, Kilo, Lima, Mike, November, Oscar, Papa, Quebec, Romeo, Sierra, Tango, Uniform, Victor, Whiskey, X-ray, Yankee, and Zulu.

proved its usefulness at least with rudimentary maps of Europe and Asia, as well as, of course, Italy, to give an overall context of where we might travel.

A plan had been slowly hatching since a visitor at one of our campsite sing-a-longs in Málaga had told us with confidence that a Volkswagen van outfitted like ours would sell for a small fortune in Kathmandu, Nepal. Enough, we were further assured, to enable us to fly back to Luxembourg, buy another van, and repeat the entire trip back to Nepal again. We took in this information as gospel truth.

The *Manuale* crystallized our plan. While details were distinctly lacking, it was clear that once we passed through Italy, we needed to "turn right at the pink country," head through the "blue country" to Turkey, Iran, some other indeterminate but differently coloured countries, and India, and then on to Nepal and the fabled Kathmandu.

So we headed off toward Italy. We were intent on proceeding as directly as possible to Kathmandu, but not so intent as to be oblivious to

Christopher (left) and me (right) in the back of our Volkswagen van, preparing to head to Nepal. Note John and Yoko's War Is Over! If You Want It poster in the back.

the sights along the way. We always stayed in campsites and would get advice from fellow campers about local places to visit — not just the well-known tourist sights, but the out-of-the-way ones as well.

We spent several weeks in Barcelona, where of course we visited Antoni Gaudí's breathtaking Basilica of the Sagrada Família, which had been under construction since the late 1880s (and is still under construction to this day). We spent time in Cannes, home of the famous Cannes Film Festival, a place I would revisit for business purposes dozens of times later on in my career.

In Florence we stayed at a campsite just off the Piazzale Michelangelo, a large public square with a panoramic view across the river to all of Florence. It was there that some magic happened.

After a day of sightseeing I left the others and found myself in the Piazzale, strumming my guitar, singing to myself in the setting sun, when I looked up and saw two young children in wheelchairs listening to me intently. Through some rudimentary hand gestures and some very broken English, I learned from their caregivers that the children were pleading to hear more, but that they had to leave, so it wasn't possible, and asked if I could return tomorrow at the same time.

The next day both Christopher and I came back to the Piazzale at the appointed time, and while the sun reflected on the buildings as it slowly set on the horizon over Florence, we ended up giving a short concert. Our audience consisted not just of our two new young friends, but also of about thirty of their classmates, all in wheelchairs, clapping and singing along. I sometimes wonder if those young children remember our singing together in the Piazzale Michelangelo as fondly as I do.

Our goal of Kathmandu was calling, though, and we headed off the next day. We discovered upon our arrival that the "pink country to the right of Italy" was called Yugoslavia. Our plan was to travel south through Yugoslavia to Greece and then on to Turkey — not the shortest route, but one that avoided Bulgaria, then a hardline communist country.

They were extremely friendly to us in Yugoslavia, even though it, too, was communist (officially it was called the Socialist Federal Republic of

Yugoslavia, led by the dictator Marshal Tito). One morning we awoke to find flowers anonymously placed on the windshield of the van, wishing us good luck in our travels. And the doctor in Belgrade who gave us cholera shots actually had a paperweight replica of the Toronto City Hall on his desk, then relatively new.

Emboldened by the friendliness, we abandoned our plan to travel south through Greece and decided, after all, to travel the much shorter route through Bulgaria. The next day we headed to the Yugoslav-Bulgarian border near Sofia, arriving at about eight o'clock at night. It was a cold and mountainous border point, with snow on the ground even in April.

Unfortunately, the Bulgarian border guards were not nearly as accommodating as we had hoped. They insisted on speaking to us in French. That was not too much of a problem since all Canadians are taught at least rudimentary French. We were intermittently interviewed for a couple of hours, during which time they made it clear they did not intend to let us enter Bulgaria. After a while we twigged that they actually spoke and understood English, and were making us speak in French while they covertly listened to the English conversations between us, thinking we might betray some sinister purpose. We just kept smiling and responding politely until the lead guard informed us of their decision: it would be improper to let us enter Bulgaria because our long hair and blue jeans would be a bad influence on the Bulgarian people.

In one last Hail Mary shot, in halting French I thanked the guard politely for his thoughtfulness and consideration and asked whether he would nevertheless give us a seven-hour visa. We would head straight through Bulgaria and, within seven hours, could leave by sunrise at the far-side border with Turkey. Since it was under the cover of night, the Bulgarians would not see us and, thus, would not be negatively influenced.

Amazingly he said yes — with the proviso that we would have a seven-hour visa only. We had to reach the other side of Bulgaria by dawn.

We were off, pedal to the metal, which in the case of the van was not that fast at all (luckily so, since the roads were often cobblestone and they shook the van dramatically).

In our race to head off we hadn't thought about what might happen to us if we overstayed our visa. Several miles into Bulgaria though, the reality of our situation started to sink in. We were in a hardline communist country, we had long hair and blue jeans, and we had no map. Despite the enormity of its usefulness, the *Manuale* contained nothing whatsoever about Bulgaria. And worse, while there were road signs, they weren't in English — they were in a language and alphabet we didn't comprehend at all.*All we really knew was that we had better keep heading east as fast as we could and hope to hit the Turkish border, or when our seven hours were up, we could be in some deep trouble.

In the middle of the night we found ourselves in the centre of a small city in the mountains, somewhere in the middle of Bulgaria, going around and around the town square. There were two main roads going out of the square in addition to the one we had just arrived on. Christopher was driving, and I was the navigator. It was an eerily beautiful moment, almost as if time itself was stopping while we circled. No one was about apart from us, the town lights were low and yellow, and if our hearts weren't pounding with adrenalin we might have well appreciated the old architecture and quaintness of the city.

But we had a choice to make, and we had to make it quickly. There was a sign on one of the roads that began with a symbol somewhat like a *B*. *B* sounded to us like *border*, so that road pulled us. And yet, as we circled the square one final time I found myself saying, "Take the other road!" It's hard to say why. In the moment it was just something instinctive. It was the more southerly of the two roads, and maybe I thought if the worst came to the worst it would be warmer and closer to Greece than the more northerly route. And why would the Bulgarian word for *border* start with a *B* anyway?**

---

* Turns out it was called the Cyrillic alphabet. Note to the editors of *Manuale delle Giovani Marmotte*: In your next edition please consider a page comparing the Cyrillic alphabet to the English alphabet, or at least to the Italian one. It would be much appreciated. Thank you.

** It doesn't.

But at the time it was simply a decision that had to be made; at least we would be on our way getting wherever we were going. Christopher turned to the southern road unhesitatingly.

As the hours passed by, slowly the sky ahead of us started to lighten. We were indeed heading east.

We were still in mountainous terrain, but after another hour we started heading downhill, and I remember that strangely peaceful pre-dawn moment as we rounded a curve in the road. There before us in the rising sun lay a long flat plain that started from the base of the mountains — and a lineup of cars that unmistakably marked the border into Turkey.*

Twenty-four hours later found us relaxing in the sun outside the famed Blue Mosque in Istanbul. Though it was still only mid-morning, the temperature was already nearing 40°C (around 100°F) — but it was a dry heat, very comfortable, and a stark contrast to the snowy cold of our Bulgarian mountain ride. Just a few weeks earlier we had been in a campsite in the south of Spain, and now here we were in Turkey, gateway to Asia, looking out over one of the Muslim world's most revered holy places.

The Blue Mosque (more properly known as Sultan Ahmet Mosque) was built in the early 1600s and is still a working mosque. We had been concerned, lest our long hair and blue jeans might inadvertently cause offence, but after taking off our shoes, we were welcomed inside. Along with hundreds of others, we silently marvelled at the stunning interior, dominated by blue tiles, and at the light shining in through the mosque's many windows onto the hundreds of prayer carpets on the floor.

We then made the short walk over to another of Istanbul's tourist attractions, the infamous Grand Bazaar. Over five hundred years old, it is one of the largest covered markets in the world, a sprawling labyrinth attracting hundreds of thousands of shoppers daily to its over four

---

* We found out much later that the northerly route from Plovdiv, the city in the middle of Bulgaria, led to the Black Sea port city of Burgas. Not a place we wanted to be heading.

thousand shops. You enter by one of its four large gates, and then can quickly become lost.

In the Grand Bazaar we inadvertently learned the art of haggling since we were running low on money. We needed to visit an American Express office to cash some traveller's cheques before continuing much further, so as various shopkeepers offered us "Turkish first quality" rugs, sheepskin coats, hookahs, and the like, pleading with us that their price was the absolute lowest, we would walk away proclaiming truthfully that we didn't have that much money. Still, they believed we were simply negotiating and kept chasing us, offering cups of tea and further discussions, and lowering their prices until the goods were barely a tenth of the "special price" they had first been offered for "only you wonderful Canadians" whom "we have come to love so dearly."

One younger shopkeeper begged us to tell him what he needed to do to make the sale, and we found ourselves looking around covertly before saying, "We would like to buy some hashish."

To this day I still have dreams of that time in the Grand Bazaar, of following the shopkeeper to a small café deep in the heart of the market, where about a half-hour later another young Turk approached us. During that half-hour we had time to come up with a strategy, albeit a strategy with feeble underpinnings.

We genuinely didn't have any money, and even once we had cashed some traveller's cheques, we had absolutely no idea what hashish would cost, nor what amount would be appropriate. We had no intention of crossing any borders with the hash, and we planned on being in Turkey for, at most, a couple of weeks, but how could we describe this small amount? And how could we ensure the quality of what we were purchasing so that we weren't just being ripped off by something fake? We also knew we should be haggling but had no context within which to even begin the discussions. Missing completely from our strategy was any glimmer of realizing what complete fools we were. What if the young Turk was actually a police officer?

Years later the novel and feature film *Midnight Express* would graphically describe a harrowing tale of what could happen to any foreigner involved in drugs in Turkey in the early 1970s. None of that crossed our minds.

As the young Turk approached, we had our strategy in place. "We're really interested in buying a kilo," we said, "but first we want to buy just a small amount to test the quality." We thought investing him in a possibly larger sale was a brilliant way to ensure the quality, and hopefully a decent price. A swap was quickly arranged for the next day. Not in the friendly confines of the Bazaar, with thousands of people about: we were to walk to the fifth floor of a nearby apartment building with the Turkish equivalent of twenty American dollars, where we would meet the compatriots of the young Turk.

It was while we were walking up the five flights of stairs the next day that the first doubts started to creep in. What if the compatriots didn't

Yes, that's me in the campground in Istanbul, Turkey, flashing the then-ubiquitous peace sign.

believe us? What if they never intended to sell us hash? What if they really just wanted to threaten us, rob us, and leave our knife-ridden corpses festering in some dark recess of the hallways of this increasingly dark apartment building?

Our hearts pounding, we knocked on the door of the designated apartment, and spent several very nervous minutes there until emerging back into the daylight twenty dollars lighter, but without any knife wounds. No festering. No police officers. And duly holding an aluminum foil packet containing a "test sample" of Turkish hashish.

We were alive. And free. And it turned out we had more than enough high-quality hash to keeps us both stoned every day for the rest of our stay in Turkey — a stay that turned out to be much longer than we had anticipated.

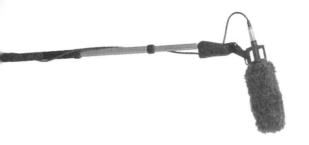

5
THE PLAYBOY CLUB

Music is truly a great communicator.

It was easy to make friends in the various campsites we stayed in. We'd just pull out our guitars and sing a few songs, and before long people would straggle by and introduce themselves.

It was May 1970. We were staying at Camping Florya Turist Park, pleasant accommodations for a campsite, inexpensive, and a relatively short train ride into Istanbul proper for sightseeing each day. One of our fellow campers was particularly entertaining. He was from Iran and claimed to have just returned from teaching the Shah of Iran's daughter how to ski.*

He taught us some handy Turkish phrases and customs, including how to tell fortunes from the coffee grounds remaining in a cup of coffee. He also told us a joke that he found hilarious, about a young man denying he'd gone to Turkey to pursue a particular young lady, but denying it by nodding his head upward and making a clicking noise — the way a Turk would indicate "no." No matter how many times he retold the joke and explained it to us, we never got it, though we did spend a good half-hour practising nodding our heads upward while clicking our tongues.

---

* If true, this would have been Princess Yasmin Farahnaz Pahlavi, who would have been seven years old at the time.

Some of his stories sobered us greatly, though, and made us seriously reconsider our travels eastward, cautionary tales such as two young American girls who wandered into the wrong side of Tehran late at night in miniskirts, and who were hung for their brazen behaviour; culverts filled with human feces beside the roadways; a family that had pushed one of their many children into the path of an American luxury car so they could feed the other hungry mouths with the payoff.

While we didn't necessarily believe these gruesome tales, we didn't disbelieve them either. They led to intense discussions between Christopher and me about the pros and cons of continuing, discussions that led to a perhaps typically Canadian compromise: we would head onward for at least a while, to the capital city Ankara, in central Turkey, then up to Samsun on the southern edge of the Black Sea, before deciding whether or not to head further into the Kurdish-controlled area of eastern Turkey.

With some trepidation we found ourselves entering Asia for the first time on a ferry crossing the Bosphorus.* Hitching a ride with us was Randy Holden, whom we'd also met at the Florya campground. Until a few months earlier he'd been the lead guitarist of the San Francisco psychedelic rock group Blue Cheer, and now he was heading to visit his parents, who lived on the U.S. Army base near Ankara.

At the time Ankara was ostensibly a modern city of some two million people, but it had only very recently introduced a new innovation called "traffic lights" at its intersections. Very few of the Turkish drivers seemed to understand the need for or concept of traffic lights, and at any moment one or more of them might charge at high speed through a red light.

Regardless, we made our way safely through Ankara to the U.S. Army base, dropped off our friend, and got directions to the mess hall, where we talked our way into giving a performance for the troops the next evening. It helped a great deal that we could tell them we were seasoned performers who already had a history of performing for troops, on board a U.S. destroyer no less.

---

* The first bridge crossing the Bosphorus would not open until three years later.

Our hope was to earn a little bit of money before the trip ahead, or at least to be invited to the PX store, where we could stock up inexpensively on some more supplies. But our performance the next evening marked the absolute low point of our self-styled *Cookies and Milk World Tour*. We played on a small raised platform in front of some folding chairs to only a few dozen attendees, and we quickly learned a harsh music business lesson: it is one thing performing before a captive audience in cramped quarters on a ship, but quite another in a cavernous mess hall, fluorescent lights throughout, and a sparse audience with lots of choices about where they might otherwise be better spending their time.

There were some boos and catcalls, and even laughter. Clearly the sweet Everly Brothers harmonies that went over so well in the campsites had little appeal here.

At least we got a meal out of it, and the sergeant in charge consoled us by politely acknowledging it was a very tough crowd and suggesting we might have a more appreciative audience in the city proper. He recommended we try out at two clubs in particular, Club M and Club 123.

But we were in no mood for further tryouts and possible further disappointments. We were on a mission to Kathmandu, and it seemed certain the universe intended us to leave Ankara sooner rather than later.

As it turned out, how wrong we were.

Regardless, the next morning we were up early, eager to leave Ankara behind. We travelled north all day on a dusty but relatively well-maintained road with almost no traffic, passing miles and miles of fields and sheep, and looking forward to reaching the little town of Samsun on the Black Sea by late afternoon. Then, just as we were entering Samsun, the van broke down. Something snapped, and it ceased to operate completely.

At first this seemed like just another van adventure — a new fan belt, perhaps, and we'd be on our way. A few locals headed over to us, and we got out of the van to explain our predicament. But the few locals didn't speak any English, or any other language we knew, and the few Turkish phrases we did know (consisting mainly of *please, thank you very much*, and *coffee*, plus nodding upward while clicking our tongues) weren't getting us anywhere.

Rapidly the few locals surrounding us became a few dozen locals, and the few dozen locals became a few hundred locals. Furthermore, while they were not overtly aggressive, they seemed to have a completely different standard for personal space. In North America, being closer than about a half a metre (a foot-and-a-half) to someone else is usually reserved for intimate contact such as hugging, whispering, or touching. And even that half-metre distance is general reserved for people who are family members or close friends.

The Samsunites, though, felt very comfortable standing right in our faces, barely fifteen centimetres (six inches) away, and staring curiously at us. It was most unnerving. We didn't want to make any sudden movements or do anything that might be offensive to them, but we couldn't help feeling threatened, and were becoming quite concerned with finding a way to communicate that we were friendly — even if our long hair and cowboy hats looked very strange to them — and that we needed help.

I had the idea of moving slowly toward the side of the van and opening up the door. They were eager to see inside, and crowded close around, but I was able to reach our guitars, and then they understood that we meant to play for them.

Sure enough, as the sun set over the Black Sea, we gave one of our strangest concerts ever, singing country songs to several hundred Turks who may never have heard such music before.

Our Western music is based on a twelve semitone scale, of which only eight notes are predominant in each key signature. On the other hand, Turkish music is much more fluid, using all twelve semitones and more, some quarter-tones in between, in a progression that, when combined with highly rhythmic percussion, leads over the course of a typically long piece to a frantic climactic release — in other words, something very different from our concept of the "hook" or chorus being led up to, repeated, and layered in various ways over a short pop or country song. All in all, what we were singing must have seemed extremely odd and discordant to them.

Still, whether they really liked the music or not didn't seem to matter in the least. They smiled and cheered and talked eagerly among themselves. We had found our way to communicate to them. We were friendly. We were Westerners, and maybe even famous? But in any event, we were legit.

Several songs in, there was a commotion within the crowd, and a passage opened up allowing a new person, some sort of leader, or perhaps the mayor, to come forward and approach us. After some trial and error, we established that he spoke some German, and since Christopher had studied German for a year in high school, we were able to convey more or less what had happened to the van, and soon some aspiring mechanics arrived to try to analyze the problem.

Meanwhile we were taken to the kitchen of a local restaurant, where we were presented with food, as the locals crowded around to stare at and laugh with us. Politely, we tried to eat everything that was given to us, trying not to imagine what it was we might be eating.

After dinner we got the good and bad news. The van was fixed, but only temporarily. There was something very wrong with the transmission, and there was no saying how long the temporary fix would last. We realized then that, like it or not, we were going to have to return to urban civilization to deal with the van.

The next morning the beautiful pale blue sky was cloudless as we slowly made our way back to Ankara, past the same seemingly endless fields and sheep we had passed in the other direction just the day before. About halfway back, the clutch snapped and we found ourselves once again stranded beside the road.

We waited and waited. No cars drove by, and despite the beauty of the day our sense of adventure was becoming frayed. We started arguing about whose fault it was that we were in this predicament.

Finally, two Turks on a motorcycle appeared. It took a while for us to understand that they intended to drive one of us to a local town for help, made the more confusing since there didn't appear to be any room on the motorcycle. But the motorcycle had a sidecar, so our two Samaritans rode together on the bike itself while Christopher, who won (or was it lost?) at rock-paper-scissors, rode as a passenger in the sidecar.

The sidecar was very loosely attached to the motorcycle, so his ride must have been extremely bumpy and somewhat terrifying.* And the local town must have been quite far away because it seemed like hours before a cloud of dust signalled Christopher's return, hunched in the sidecar, with some rescuers.

By then I was sitting on a fence post, playing my guitar and happily singing my heart out to an audience of two: a young shepherd boy, and a solitary sheep, both looking on in awe.

With tremendous goodwill, our rescuers jerry-rigged a way to get us and the van, hobbled and locked in second gear, to Ankara. As had everyone in Samsun, they refused our repeated offers of any sort of payment, and they seemed genuinely pleased just to have the opportunity to help. We knew enough to say *teşekkür ederim* (thank you very much) over and over as we slowly pulled away and waved goodbye to our rescuers.

As we waved goodbye also to the shepherd boy and the solitary sheep, the boy saluted back. To this day I've wondered what the boy thought had happened. In some ways it must have been like two Martians appearing suddenly and singing some strange Martian melodies to him before disappearing, never to be seen again. The power of music!

◦   ◦   ◦

Sometimes it's important to move forward with strength and purpose toward a particular goal; and sometimes it's important just to go with the flow and let the universe unfold in its own mysterious way. Wisdom is

---

* Christopher: "It's hard to overstate how bumpy and terrifying it was. Imagine an amusement park ride that you were convinced was going to break free at any moment and plummet you to your death."

probably knowing the difference between the two. But is it wisdom? Or providence? Or just luck?

Our grand adventure had been cut short even as it was barely beginning. Christopher and I arrived back in Ankara a day after we had set out for Nepal, with both our van and our hearts broken down. The previous day had already been an extraordinary adventure, yes. And maybe driving to Nepal through very dangerous territories had always been a pipe dream, and perhaps we had avoided potential tragedy by being forced to return. Yet we were understandably despondent.

Over the next few days we found a garage to fix the transmission on the van. It was going to take weeks to repair and would cost a lot of money — money we did not have. We recalled the advice given by the sergeant at the U.S. Army mess hall a few days earlier and sought out Club M and Club 123 to audition for possible gigs.

The reaction in both clubs was the polar opposite to our disastrous one-night stand at the army base. Club M in particular, though it was a little grotto of a place, seemed to fill with cheering Turks in dark suits and black moustaches when we played. Each afternoon we played first one club then the other, making enough to stay at a grungy campsite, eat meagrely, and more importantly make a down payment on the repairs to the van.

Late one day, as we finished our performance at Club M, a small, rotund gentleman in the conventional dark suit and black moustache, came up to us and said simply, "Mustafa will see you now." We thanked him for his interest and suggested that, whoever this Mustafa was, he could see us tomorrow at one of our performances. But the gentleman responded firmly, "No, you don't understand. Mustafa will see you now." We tried again to demur until he looked straight at us and said, "Now."

We followed the man out of the club, where the rear door to a black Mercedes limousine opened and we were gestured inside. While it seems, in retrospect, highly sketchy for us to have entered the limo, our curiosity had been piqued, and it all turned out very positively. A young man, around our age, handsome and charismatic, introduced himself as

Mustafa Satir. We were to find out that he was a well-known and powerful figure in Ankara, and his picture was routinely in the gossip columns of local newspapers, usually with a beautiful woman on his arm. His father was a former deputy prime minister of Turkey and remained one of the most respected politicians in the country.

Mustafa loved music and had formed his own rock band. He had heard of our success at the clubs and had a proposition for us. Would we join his band as back-up singers and, at the same time, teach him to sing better? He would pay us for our troubles. Further, Mustafa was a part-owner of another venue in Ankara: the Playboy Club. He invited us to perform there.

We just grinned. There was no need to mention that we didn't really know anything at all about the mechanics of singing. If he wanted vocal coaches, well, we would be vocal coaches. And if he wanted back-up singers, we could certainly do that. On top of that, our eyes shone at the thought of the Playboy Club. In our naïveté, we wondered to ourselves whether Miss April or Miss May might drop by as part of some world tour of Playboy Clubs.

From then on, each afternoon Mustafa would arrange to have us driven to an extraordinary building known as the Çankaya Köşkü (the Pink Villa), a pink-coloured palace that, at the time, was used as a second residence for the president of Turkey, as well as housing various governmental offices.*

Mustafa found an unused room on the second floor of the western wing of the Pink Villa and had secured permission to convert it into a rehearsal space for his band. The view outside the windows was spectacular. Although situated in central Ankara, the compound was in a park-like setting spread out over several hundred acres.

---

* The Pink Villa was originally renovated to be the home of the founder of the Republic of Turkey, Mustafa Kemal Atatürk, who was personally involved in its design. It was restored to its original design in 2001, and since then it has served only as a presidential residence.

Intent as we were on earning a living and paying for the repairs to the van, we were largely oblivious to the irony of it all. Although we were living the most meagre of existences, eating the cheapest foods, and sleeping in a tent in a truly decrepit campsite, here we were working closely with the rich and famous, soon to be spending evenings in the Playboy Club and afternoons working on music in a beautiful palace that was a part of Turkish history!

Sometimes the universe does indeed work in mysterious ways.

Our first task in the rehearsal space was to coach Mustafa in the lyrics and pronunciation of various songs. He'd sing the song, and we'd tactfully correct him. We thought we should be imparting some breathing and phrasing techniques, but we didn't actually know any, other than "breathe from the belly," which he seemed pleased enough with. So we mostly focused on the lyrics. I remember a couple of songs, such as "God Bless the Child" for which he had replaced the original Billie Holiday lyric of "And rich relations may give crusts of bread and such" with "And rish dilations may give custa neppa sush" — we praised him for singing probably the only song in the history of pop music to include the real English word *dilations*.

We gradually discovered, though, that we weren't particularly cut out to be back-up singers. Mustafa protested at first, but then he realized it, too. As his singing got better and better, our afternoon sessions gradually petered out.

Mustafa would still often ask us to spend time with him in the evenings. We were invited to high art parties. The art consisted mostly of pornographic images being flashed on the walls of a gallery while people clad only in cellophane milled about — all of which we found simply awkward. Once he asked us to drive him about town in his Mercedes while he made out with a woman in the back seat.

Another time he careened around Ankara with us in his Mercedes and got stopped by the police. You will recall that Ankara had only recently installed traffic lights, and it took an egregious flaunting of the law to get stopped. As the policeman approached, book in hand,

MUSTAFA SATIR'IN SEVGİLİSİ SEVDA
NUR ŞARKICI OLUYOR ...

Daldan dala konup, herkese mavi boncuk dağıtan dansöz SEVDA NUR, son sevgilisi MUSTAFA SATIR 'a özenip şarkıcı olmayı kabul etti.

SEVGİLİSİ İLE PROVA YAPIYOR

Devamlı sevgili değiştirerek isminden bahsetti - ren dansöz SEVDA NUR, İzmirli bir gazinocunun cazip teklifine dayanamayarak şarkı söylemeyi kabul etti. Fuarda bir gazinoda çalışacak olan SEVDA NUR, sevgilisi MUSTAFA SATIR'la devamlı prova yapmakta ve kendisini şarkıcılığa hazırlamaktadır.

GÜNDE DÖRT SAAT ÇALIŞIYOR

Kendisine özel hoca tutan sanatçı günde dört saat çalışmak - ta "Sahneye çok değişik bir kıyafetle çıkacağım"demekte- dir. Daha şimdiden kendine hepsi de birbirinden mini çe-

DOKTORLAR"İFLAH ETMEZ,,DEMİŞLERDİ AMA

TEK AKCİGERLE SAATLERCE

A typical Ankara newspaper from the 1970s, including a picture and story about the celebrity Mustafa Satir, who became our benefactor and bandmate.

we were quite worried, but Mustafa's lack of concern was evident. He rolled down the power window slowly. As soon as the officer saw who was driving, he stopped in his tracks and began immediately backing away, smiling unctuously and repeating, "Ah, Mustafa, Mustafa." Mustafa roared with laughter, obviously enjoying the opportunity to display his power for us.

As the days progressed we were starting to feel much more comfortable in our new lifestyle, until our first performance at the Playboy Club took some wind out of our sails.

The performance itself went fine. We were singing while patrons were eating dinner, and little was expected of us. We drew polite applause, and that seemed to be fine with the Club manager.

But as it turned out, while the Club had lots of Playboy bunny logos on the walls, and other Playboy signage, to our keen disappointment we never saw any actual Playboy bunnies anywhere. In fact, there weren't any female staff at all.

We initially put the absence of bunnies down to some strict Muslim religious observance. Perhaps, we thought, it was a serious violation of some local custom for women to be lauded for superficial attributes by being publicly displayed in scanty costumes. (I wish I could claim that our reaction arose from our own deep-seated and highly-evolved sense of concern for women's rights, but the reality at the time was that we were simply two confused, young, red-blooded Canadian males, who had it in our heads that an appearance by Miss April or Miss May was an actual possibility.)

On the bright side, our financial situation was improving. We were able to eat at the Club, and while we weren't being paid a fortune, we were able to upgrade our living quarters to the Turist Otel, a small but relatively clean hotel close by. We still couldn't afford to have the van back, but we were learning to make our way about Ankara using a kind of shared taxi called a dolmuş.* I recall us observing that if you were standing by the road and casually scratched your head, five dolmuş would fly across three lanes of traffic to pick you up.

We were also making some new friends. There was a nine-piece band (including a three-piece horn section) that performed after us each night at the Playboy Club. They were truly talented musicians, all music school graduates. We got to know the band leader, Şanar Yurdatapan, who became quite a well-known, respected composer and musician in Turkey.

The band was called Şanar ve Onlar (loosely, "Şanar and the Others"), and their arrangements were very inventive. I recall a particularly impressive rendition of "Hello Dolly," with background chanting, and they were able to cover even the most complex North American hits, including songs by bands such as Chicago, and Blood, Sweat and Tears.

---

* The name derived from the Turkish word for "filled," since each dolmuş tried to be filled with riders. A dolmuş with empty seats might slow to a crawl in the hopes of picking up a few more riders, but once filled it would travel at an extraordinary rate of speed.

We became friends with two of the members of the band, Gemil and Nadir, who spoke at least some broken English.

We would normally leave the club each night while Şanar ve Onlar were still playing. One night Gemil and Nadir suggested we stay until midnight, when "the show" would begin. We didn't understand what "the show" was until midnight arrived and a stripper appeared.

Her act consisted of dancing around a giant red rocket ship while she removed her clothing. Once we saw the show, it hit us: any faint hopes we may have still hung onto, that the lack of Playboy bunnies had to do with local customs or religious observances, were immediately dashed. We were forced to acknowledge that the club was a knock-off, not in any way related to the real Hugh Hefner Playboy empire. Neither Miss April nor Miss May were going to make a surprise appearance.

I think that was one of those coming-of-age moments. Still, as they say, we had our health. And our new friends. And we were making music, a lot of it. When we weren't rehearsing with Mustafa or performing at the club, we were writing songs.

Our set at the club was expected to last an hour, but with a shortage of Cookies and Milk songs in the candlelight-and-wine genre, we had to improvise. We had our core of light country rock songs with sweet harmonies — songs from The Everly Brothers, The Flying Burrito Brothers, Poco, The Byrds, and so on — and we always wrapped up our set with the Roy Rogers and Dale Evans classic "Happy Trails." We had some of our own songs as well, but we still didn't have enough for the full hour, so in the middle of the set we would break for my solo performance.

Now, I am not the greatest guitar player or the greatest singer. This is not false humility on my part; I'm not that well-coordinated, and my voice is thin. But I did have a couple of saving graces: I could play virtually any song by ear, and whatever my voice may have lacked in tone, at least I sang on key. There are some songs that just work well with particular voices. For my voice, those songs included the Burt Bacharach/ Hal David hit made famous by Dionne Warwick, "Walk on By"; Gerry and the Pacemakers' "Don't Let the Sun Catch You Crying"; and George

Harrison's "You Like Me Too Much" from the *Help!* album. To those I added a nonsense feel-good song I'd written many years earlier on the ukulele. In the middle I'd blow through my pursed lips to improvise a trumpet solo — at least, in my mind it was a trumpet solo! It undoubtedly sounded more like a very lame kazoo, but the song always brought a smile to people's faces even though the lyrics were at best impressionistic, and at worst meaningless:

Button up, button up, Button Up Little Clover*
As we ambled down the parkside back in memory lane
'Member now, 'member now how I loved it when your
Smile it caught my eye and we were standing in day
You know, you know what a feeling as we ran the rods
Together down New Orleans way
Feelin' so we could happen once again

And I'd finish with the Chris Montez song, "Call Me."**

After a while we loosened up a bit. You'll recall that we had bought some hashish in Istanbul's Grand Bazaar, and once we had a few performances under our belt, we started to play our nightly set happily stoned. When it came time for my solo performance, I'd imagine in my hash haze that I was in Las Vegas with a forty-piece orchestra behind me. By lowering the key of the songs, I could make my voice sound more like a crooner. I'd read somewhere that one of Frank Sinatra's techniques was to sing slightly behind the beat so that a subconscious anticipation would

---

* I have no idea why someone would give their former lover a pet name like "Little Clover." Paul McCartney famously wrote a song called "Scrambled Eggs," and it was only later that he revised that lyric to make it "Yesterday." So maybe it's not about making sense, just about getting the melody right!

** Not to be confused with the Blondie song of the same name. The one I sang was written in 1965 by Tony Hatch, originally for Petula Clark, but became a standard easy-listening hit that same year when covered by Chris Montez.

build up in the listener's ear. So I'd delay key phrases, and as the nights wore on the delays became longer and longer:

Don't be afraid, you can …
(pause … pause … wait for it … wait for it …)
Call me!

Sometimes I'd speak the words, and mime speaking on the telephone; other times I'd slur the words in a cross between Dean Martin, Wayne Newton, and Sean Connery ("I will always shtay by you"). Christopher would be laughing offstage, by the entrance to the kitchen. I couldn't look in that direction, I just focused on being my true, polished Las Vegas self.

In between songs I'd talk to the audience, Vegas-style. "Hey, is anyone out there from Ankara? Love you, love you!" If no one understood what I was saying, then I'd know the lyrics didn't matter. I'd launch into the Ian & Sylvia classic "Lovin' Sound," but instead of singing the proper lyrics as an ode to the power of love, I'd sing it as an ode to a dog named Baron that belonged to one of my favourite professors at Trent University — a reference that would have been challenging for the average Turkish diner to appreciate. As our stint at the Playboy Club continued on, I added vastly more egregious lyrics over this really sweet melody, all the while with a choirboy smile on my face. When the end of the song came, I'd smile broadly as the polite applause came, bow slightly and pretend to try to stop the applause, then thank the imaginary orchestra, and call Christopher back on stage.*

All good things must come to an end, and our end came more abruptly than we'd expected. Suddenly it was July, and apparently in the summer everyone in Ankara, or at least everyone who might spend their

---

* The song was written by Ian Tyson. Years later I worked with Ian for a while as his lawyer, but could never bring myself to tell him how I'd massacred his beautiful song. I hope he's not reading this.

nights in clubs listening to music, departed the city and headed to the coast. The Playboy Club, like most other clubs, shut down until the fall.

Şanar and the boys were heading out for the summer season to a resort in Izmir and suggested we meet them there, where they'd hopefully be able to help us get a gig, and we could all hang out on the Aegean coast. Sounded good to us.

The timing was perfect. We'd finally made enough money to get our beloved van back. We parked it happily by the Turist Otel and went upstairs to start packing. But when we came downstairs later that evening, while the van was still there, its wheels were not. We were mystified until some street urchins came rushing up to tell us in a mixture of Turkish and English, and through much waving and shouting, how some horrible thieves had stolen our wheels. Fortunately, they thought they knew who the perpetrators were and — for a fee — they could help us. For the equivalent of ten dollars and an extra dollar tip for being such excellent and brave "detectives," we got our wheels back.

It could have been worse, and we had to admire their brazen entrepreneurial spirit, warped as it may have been (at least from our point of view).

Our exit was marred by one last misadventure. We'd filled the bathtub, washing clothes in preparation for leaving in the morning for Izmir, and there was a leak that caused water to drip down to the foyer below. The manager came upstairs to confront us, insisting that we were somehow responsible for the leak and needed to pay for its repair. This was contrasted with the way he then left the room backwards, bowing and saying, "Yes, yes, my dear Mr. Stohn, I love you, I love you, Mr. Stohn." He returned many times, each time equally insistent in his demand and equally unctuous in his departure.

We knew we had no responsibility for the leaky pipes in the hotel, but we weren't sure how to get past the manager in the lobby below. We waited until his lunch hour, when only his wife would be at the front desk, and then made our break. His wife followed us and planted herself imperiously in front of the van to prevent our departure.

Something came over me, and I leaped out of the driver's seat to confront her and screamed, for whatever reason, in Spanish. "¡San Bernardo es una montaña en el norte de Italia!" I shouted, pointing toward the sky. "¡Es también famosa por la producción de cobre!" *

I continued to rant similarly, and wave my arms wildly, as if a demon had possessed me and I was speaking in tongues. In fact, my words were completely meaningless, phrases I'd been forced to memorize as part of my high school Spanish lessons that had suddenly flooded back to me in that moment of high adrenalin.

The manager's wife was so transfixed by this bizarre display that she stepped out of the way, so I jumped back in the van and stepped on the gas.

Yes, we were constantly looking over our shoulders wondering if the Ankara police would be coming after us. And we were heading away from our original destination of Nepal, back toward the West. But we'd had a couple of months of even greater adventure than we'd ever hoped for. Now we were back on the road.

---

* "Saint Bernard is a mountain in northern Italy! It is also famous for the production of copper!"

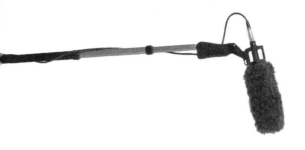

6
ALL GOOD THINGS ...

Arriving in the Turkish seaside city of Izmir, we sought out our friends from Şanar ve Onlar and began the search for a club to perform in.

Our efforts were for naught. To our chagrin, we struck out completely.

The boys in the band took pity on us though; they put us up in a spare room in their apartment and even paid for our food and gasoline. When we tried to offer any form of payment, they insisted that we were guests in their country and, in their Muslim religion, it was their honour and duty to assist us. All they asked in return was for us to chauffeur them to the seaside for afternoon swimming.

We had no intention of continuing to live off the kindness of our friends. When it became clear that we were not going to earn money in Izmir, we decided to take the opportunity, while we still had at least a small amount of cash, to leave Turkey and head back in the direction of Luxembourg, where we could make some money by selling the van and, perhaps, find some cafés to perform in en route. If worst came to worst, we still had our return tickets from Luxembourg back to North America on the "hippie airline," Loftleidir.

When we let them know of our plan to leave, at first they remonstrated with us to stay. When they understood why we needed to head back to Europe, however, they organized a get-together, which we assumed was simply a fond farewell dinner.

A farewell dinner it was, but much more. Our hosts used the occasion to reveal to us something quite startling.

Christopher and I had been aware for some time that in the middle of the night some of the band members routinely left the apartment for several hours at a time. We had asked about where they went, but they pretended not to understand our questions. We had never pressed for an answer; rather, we guessed it would be impolite to insist. Maybe they had girlfriends they were secretly visiting, and modesty, pride, or perhaps some Muslim custom kept them from talking about this. But the truth was not so straightforward.

As we sat around the table at our "farewell dinner," one of the band members we didn't know well showed us the front page of the daily Izmir newspaper, saying, "That's us." At first we didn't understand what he meant. It was simply a Turkish newspaper with (we assumed) the news of the day. This front page showed an overturned vehicle in flames.

"You asked us where we go in the middle of the night," he continued. "That's us." We still didn't quite understand until he pointed to the picture of the vehicle in flames. Long story short: by day and evening they were students and musicians, but by night they were a Marxist-Leninist cell. The vehicle in question was an American car; our hosts had found it and torched it.

We continued to press, still not fully comprehending. "But that doesn't make any sense! We are staying in your apartment. You are giving us food and gas and being wonderfully kind hosts and friends. We are from North America, and yet you burn American cars?"

The boys in the band (or at least those who were part of the cell) tried to explain that they were involved in what they saw as a fight against fascism and imperialism. They believed these forces were inherent in the current Turkish government, which was aided, abetted, and perhaps even directed by the United States.*

---

* This was not just a local matter either. We came to realize that we had been oblivious to bloody clashes between workers and security forces elsewhere in Turkey. This cell was part of a much larger movement to introduce a socialist consciousness in the universities and to join the peasants in a revolutionary struggle. Indeed, several days later, as we retraced our journey through Istanbul, we found that martial law had been imposed there.

This was a rude — or perhaps necessary — awakening for us. We saw ourselves simply as dedicated musicians, completely uninvolved in politics or revolutions, and yet here we were face to face with both. Events were unfolding in a way we had, naively, never expected.

Meanwhile, the band members seemed to feel it was important for us to understand their viewpoint, and they asked us to stay an extra day so that they could take us on a short trip to show us what motivated them. Early the next morning we drove toward the hills outside of Izmir, stopping after a couple of hours at the outskirts of what we came to realize was a village made almost entirely out of mud. The sun was beating down from a brilliantly blue sky, and it all seemed quite peaceful and beautiful, almost idyllic.

Our friends began, all of them pitching in to the extent their English permitted: "You can see that the people living here are happy enough, but beneath it all life is a constant struggle. They live the simplest possible existence — in mud huts. They often go hungry and, worse, their children often go hungry. You are seeing this village at its best. Its worst comes by January when the rains return in full force ... and this village will be entirely wiped out." That gave us real pause. It was hard to imagine. "But the people living here are used to losing their homes. This will all be rebuilt by the spring when the rains end."

Then came the real point of it all. "We understand how capitalism could be a wonderful thing. But capitalism doesn't work when you struggle to put food on the table for your family; capitalism doesn't work when your home is washed away every year; capitalism doesn't work when you must live in a mud hut."

And that was that. They weren't expecting anything more of us. It was important to them that we knew what they were doing and why they were doing it, but having made us aware, they were content to bid us a fond farewell.

Looking back on this time, I mostly remember the kindness of our Muslim friends, a kindness which was even more striking in its contrast with the more violent side of their lives that was revealed only at the end of our visit. I also think of the mud village and the lesson our friends had been imparting to us: be careful not to assume that your own views and beliefs are applicable to others who live in completely different circumstances.

The revelations of that day opened our eyes to the superficiality of our own approach to life. Being stoned, singing nonsense lyrics in nightclubs, or worrying about the clutch in the van was trivial in comparison with the struggle for survival of families in a mud village, or the passion of revolutionaries battling what they felt was injustice.

It's not that we came away from Izmir discarding our dreams of success in the entertainment world. Simply, we started to realize that rather than escaping through drugs and travel, there were more rewarding ways to focus whatever talents we had.

The next day — not that much older, but seemingly wiser — we said goodbye to Şanar, Gemil, Nadir, and our other friends in the band, and headed off in the direction of Istanbul and ultimately Luxembourg, making our transition back toward urban Western civilization.

The transition was not that easy. We felt like failures as we started our journey back to Luxembourg. We had earned enough in Ankara to get the van repaired, but not much more. Our inability to find work in Izmir meant that once we left Turkey, we were pretty much broke.

Our grand plan of reaching Kathmandu had ended five thousand kilometres (three thousand miles) short. We had experienced great, almost wondrous adventures, but bottom line: we had failed.

On top of that, Christopher and I started to seriously get on each other's nerves. We had been travelling together for many months, and it put severe strain on our friendship. Our cash situation made the strain worse.

We left Turkey through the border to Greece with just enough money to make our way to Thessaloniki. There we spent several hours outside a hospital planning to sell our blood to help pay for our onward journey. Local religious beliefs at the time restricted Greeks from giving blood themselves, leading to a "red market" price of about $20 per pint. We were nervous about the hygienic standards of the hospital, though, and also worried that they might take far more than a pint from each of us. We also felt very unsettled by the small crowds of local Greeks who clustered around us, pleading with us to direct our blood to their particular relatives.

At the last moment we met a young American couple who were hitchhiking to Germany. They were willing to pay for gas and meals if we would drive them there, and we were very relieved to keep our blood and head at once toward Germany.

Unfortunately, our relief was relatively short-lived.We did make the drive to Germany, ending up in Cologne, but there we faced the ultimate humiliation of having to find the Canadian consulate so that we could request that our parents wire some money. Our previously unshakeable confidence in our own self-sufficiency and invulnerability came to an ignominious halt.

During the five days we waited for the wires to arrive, we lived on the kindness of a Canadian consular official who, out of his own pocket, loaned us the equivalent of five dollars per day so that we could eat. We slept in the van and bathed daily in the Rhine, and each day our total food intake consisted of a shared loaf of bread, some strawberry jam, and a large tomato, with a small piece from a chocolate bar for dessert.

Because we had no money, Christopher and I were forced to spend even more time together. Our daily excursions consisted mostly of checking in with the consulate every few hours to find out if our money was in. It became easy for each of us to blame the other for the predicament we were in.

When the wires finally did arrive, we had only enough cash to head back to Luxembourg, where we would wait out the next available return flight to Canada. This unexpected end to our travels, hot on the heels of several weeks of scrimping for our daily existence, led to even more bickering and hostility between Christopher and me.

We drove straight to the Luxembourg airport where, remarkably, we found an impromptu but very lively market in one of the parking lots. Departing travellers were selling camping equipment and other useful supplies to incoming passengers. Even cars and vans were for sale, and within a few hours we had sold the van, the mattresses, the tent, and all our other camping supplies, giving us enough money to stay in Europe for another month at least.

Christopher was determined to stay on in Europe for a while, but I was equally determined to return to Canada as soon as possible. To my mind, our friendship had deteriorated to worse than nothing; the appeal of the nomadic lifestyle had completely faded. Christopher was the better man of the two of us: he was much more forgiving and willing to try travelling together for at least a little longer, but I had reached the end of my rope, and as I boarded my Loftleidir flight home, leaving Christopher behind, I found myself very much looking forward to never having to speak with him again.

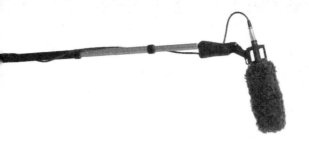

7
KILLING GROUND

During the critical hours following an oxygen tank explosion that crippled the Apollo 13 moon mission, NASA Flight Director Gene Kranz is said to have exclaimed, "Failure is not an option!" The crisis required emergency jerry-rigging of the carbon dioxide removal system to enable the crew to return safely to Earth.*

I have come to believe that the reverse is true, that failure is an unacknowledged virtue. If you're not failing, then you're not pushing the envelope of possibilities. In other words, "Failure is not an option, it's a necessity."

At the time it occurred, I was completely unaware of the Apollo 13 drama. The "Houston, we have a problem" six-day odyssey — followed by a billion people on radio and television and driving banner headlines in newspapers around the world — had occurred back in April 1970 while Christopher and I were making our way from Málaga to Yugoslavia. Staying in campsites along the way, we remained blissfully unaware of any events happening elsewhere in the world. It was not until years later that I found out about the Apollo 13 crisis.

---

* He never actually said it. The line was created by a screenwriter for the *Apollo 13* feature film (though Kranz liked the quote so much that he later used it as the title of his autobiography).

Meanwhile, later that year I had faced my own brand of failure as we limped back to Cologne; as we wired home for money; and as I boarded the flight back to Canada, never coming close to the intended goal of Kathmandu.

More failure was just around the corner.

The year started robustly enough. Over numerous beers in the Pilot Tavern in midtown Toronto, two friends — Peter O'Brian and Chris Dalton* — and I hatched a plan to produce Canada's first large-budget commercial feature film. Or rather, Peter and Chris hatched the plan — since they had at least a smattering of knowledge about filmmaking — and I hitched along for the ride. For me this plan built upon the world view that Christopher and I had forged while travelling in Europe. The thought that three novices could produce a major feature film was illogical and nonsensical on its face, but in the zeitgeist of our European travels — that anything was possible if you were truly open to it — the thought seemed eminently rational.

> **Peter:** The Pilot Tavern was our home base. We were in our early twenties, drinking lots of beer ... I don't think Stephen was as much as Chris and I were ... I hope he regrets that! We had an office just down the street from the Pilot.** The ground floor was a cinema and I remember *Mon Oncle Antoine* played there. The Don Shebib film *Goin' Down the Road* played at the New Yorker Cinema

---

* Chris's later career included producing over four thousand TV commercials and running five different commercial production houses, one of which being Dalton/Fenske & Friends. Peter went on to produce more than a dozen feature films, including *My American Cousin* and (working with Phillip Borsos) *The Grey Fox* and *One Magic Christmas*, winning some nineteen Genie Awards in the process. Peter is currently the chair of the educational broadcaster TVO.

** The Pilot Tavern has since moved, but at the time it was located on Yonge Street just south of Bloor. The next street south of Bloor was Charles Street, where we had our offices on the second floor.

further down the street, and we were totally inspired by
this idea of a home cinema of our own culture.

While a small number of feature films had been produced in Canada prior to the 1970s, they were of the lower budget variety and not intended to compete directly with Hollywood offerings. The National Film Board (NFB), an agency of the Canadian government, had become one of the world's largest film studios, but was primarily known as a leading producer of world-class documentaries, animation, and experimental films.*

Peter and Chris felt the time was ripe to build on the skills of Canadian filmmakers, skills that had been honed over many years by National Film Board projects, but to shift focus toward a commercial feature film. They had found a book by someone named Ellis Portal, a book they thought would make a great action drama, particularly suited to and focused on Canada, but commercial enough to attract a Hollywood distributor and a Hollywood-level budget. The book, called *Killing Ground*, tells the story of Lt. Colonel Alex Hlynka, who returns to Canada from peacekeeping duty overseas to find that separatists have gained power in Quebec. The separatists have begun to take steps to foment revolution, and ultimately civil war. In response, the United States decides to invade Canada.

We later found out that the real name of the author was Bruce A. Powe. He had been inspired to write *Killing Ground* by an actual war games scenario that he had access to during his tenure with the Canadian government. The scenario had been prepared by the armed forces, and, fearing retribution for using this confidential scenario, Powe had written the book under the pseudonym Ellis Portal.**

---

* Over the years the NFB has produced over thirteen thousand productions, winning over five thousand awards, including twelve Academy Awards.

** Powe's pseudonym choice was not entirely random. If you travel south on the Yonge subway line in Toronto, on the right-hand side you will see a sign reading "Ellis Portal" identifying the tunnel entrance to the Bloor subway stop, the same stop that you would have exited from back then to visit the offices of the publisher of the book.

Our first step was to seek out the publisher of *Killing Ground* to find out if the motion picture rights were available. They were.

Next, we contacted a lawyer friend of Peter's family, George Miller. And at the same time, we set about planning how to raise the necessary money to make a down payment on the motion picture rights, as well as to pay for George's advice.

Back then the internet had not yet been invented, and of course there was no Google. Nor were there any practical film courses, or at least not in Canada. Fledgling filmmakers like ourselves had almost nowhere to turn to find out about the process of developing a feature film. Peter and Chris had some experience in low-budget television commercials, but little beyond that. And none of us had any real idea of what would be involved in raising the development money we would need.

First things first, though, we needed to make some money to keep us afloat. Through a friend of a friend, Peter and Chris successfully secured a contract to create some radio commercials.* The revenue from those commercials allowed us to eke out a living over the summer of 1971 while we devoured every book we could find that had anything to do with filmmaking.

George Miller helped by encouraging me to read a set of law books called *Entertainment, Publishing and the Arts*, which provided sample agreements and commentaries for all aspects of filmmaking. We routinely bought the trade newspaper *Variety* and read every article intently. We also bought a series of self-help books describing how to be a successful salesperson, from which we learned about the process of "getting to yes" and the potential roadblocks of "closing the deal."

We figured we would need about ten thousand dollars to get to the stage where the *Killing Ground* project would be shown to be viable, or not, and decided to seek out ten friends, or friends of friends, willing to invest one thousand dollars each. We prepared a budget and a synopsis for these

---

* We created the brand line "Summer is here ... in Becker country!" for what ended up being a campaign of several commercials for a chain of convenience stores.

62

potential "Phase I Investors," figured out what share of the revenues they would be entitled to, and then set about coming up with a list of prospects.

Before approaching anyone, Peter, Chris, and I held mock meetings, where one of us would pretend to be the potential investor, and the others would make the pitch. The most difficult part was always when we got to the point of asking for a cheque. We were much better at talking the project up, at "getting to yes," but we were more reluctant to "close the deal." We practised over and over and pushed through until we were more comfortable asking for the cheque, but we were stymied as to how we would end the meeting, even if we were successful. We didn't want to be overly effusive in our thanks; on the other hand, we wanted to show our true appreciation of their involvement. After much going back and forth we decided that if the potential investor said "yes," our response would be "That's grand!" It was a bit of a play on words, since the investment they were making was indeed for a "grand," but to us it seemed like the right tone!

Amazingly, ten friends did indeed support us by becoming Phase I Investors. To this day I remember those individuals fondly. They supported us for our passion rather than our actual experience, and they did so knowing full well that their investment was highly risky and might yield little or no return.

In later years I've come to respect the power of passion. It can overcome a lot of obstacles. True passion has nothing to do with making money; it's about making something happen that you strongly feel needs to happen, and if your passion is true, the dollars often seem to follow.

The Phase I development financing could only take us so far; we needed to save on expenses at every opportunity. George Miller helped, both by providing some initial free legal advice and also by insisting that I use my new-found knowledge gleaned from the *Entertainment, Publishing and the Arts* books to prepare first drafts of the agreements we needed, thus cutting down on the legal time he needed to spend. I worked as hard as I could, drafting and re-drafting, and of course I made many egregious errors, but as we worked together, he gradually became my first true mentor, forever urging me to "Make it simpler, make it simpler!"

I'd had no intention of becoming a lawyer, but I found myself enjoying the challenges George threw at me. He was a great believer in "Throw the baby [namely me] into the ocean and see if he can swim!"

As a quid pro quo for some of his free legal advice, he would sometimes ask me out of the blue to do things like, "Go to the such-and-such tavern and find out their proper legal name. I want to sue them." I, of course, would remonstrate that they would never tell me what their proper legal name was, and he would reply, "That's fine, just do it!" (I solved that one by putting on a well-worn jacket to make myself look like a harried government bureaucrat, getting a clipboard with some official looking paper on it, marching straight up to the bartender, and asking to see their liquor licence. She complied immediately, and I copied down the legal name on the licence, complimented her on how the licence was correctly displayed, lamented that other establishments were not equally fastidious, and retreated while wishing her a good day.)

George helped us incorporate a company called Muddy York Productions Ltd. The name was a reference to an early nickname for the City of Toronto, which was originally incorporated as York in 1793, and was known for its often-impassable muddy streets. (We were amused when people who wanted something to do with a film company would look us up in the phone directory and call and ask for Mr. York, as if Muddy York were a real person — I suppose like the famed blues musician Muddy Waters.)

We paid ourselves fifteen dollars a week each so that we could live, barely.

Peter: I think it was fifteen dollars a week plus a certain stipend — we all went out for lunch at a place across the street called Brothers, where they had things like the hot hamburger sandwich, which is a hamburger on white bread with gravy and canned peas and fries and a lot of salt. I think the company paid for these meals, and at the end of the day there was beer money.

We went to many meetings and didn't always understand entirely some of the terms that were being used, but we read every word of *Variety* every day until —Eureka! — we discovered what the terms meant. And we were passionate about what we were doing.

Peter and Chris started writing the initial screenplay. We didn't want anyone to know that inexperienced filmmakers had created this draft, so we invented a supposedly well-known Hollywood veteran writer named Charles Young, put his name on the screenplay, and talked reverently of his scriptwriting prowess.*

At the same time, we needed to raise more development financing, and we thought of approaching Robert "Bobby" Laidlaw, a wealthy philanthropist, and a friend of both Peter's and my grandparents.** At the time, he was in his eighties. After my grandmother helped set up a meeting, Peter, Chris, and I visited him at his mansion in Roche's Point, north of Toronto.

> **Peter:** We got ushered in … a butler opened the door to this mansion and we went into this big room with sun coming through tall windows that looked onto a garden. He [Laidlaw] said, "What do you want?" So we started doing the pitch, and we went on for about twenty minutes before we realized he was sound asleep. We stopped and then wondered if maybe he was actually dead. We debated what we should do, in front of him, like a scene in a movie. Suddenly he woke up and said, "I'll give you forty thousand dollars" and went back to sleep. Out of

---

* The offices we rented in midtown Toronto were at the corner of Charles and Yonge Streets, so "Charles Young" was based on the location of our office, in the same way that Bruce W. Powe based "Ellis Portal" on the location of his publisher's office.
** Through the Laidlaw Foundation, which Robert Laidlaw formed in 1949, he made major contributions to leading health care, educational, and cultural institutions, including the Hospital for Sick Children, Upper Canada College, the University of Toronto, the National Ballet School, and the National Ballet of Canada.

the forty thousand we were able to develop the film to
the point where it was viable for financing.

As the screenplay took shape, we reached out to potential actors and directors. We got a letter of interest from John Vernon, a Canadian actor well-known for starring in many Hollywood movies and TV series, including Canada's first successful English-language TV drama called *Wojeck* — it starred Vernon as a crusading coroner. We hired a real writer, acclaimed novelist and playwright Timothy "Tiff" Findley, to work on the second draft of the screenplay.* Then we secured a letter of interest from British director Ken Hughes. He'd produced, directed, and written dozens of feature films, the best known at the time being *Chitty Chitty Bang Bang*.

As more and more talented people came on board, we started to make inroads into securing production financing. We hired a production manager who helped us create a detailed budget for the film, just over two million dollars. This is a lot for any young filmmakers, but it was a particularly large amount back in the early 1970s.

We kept meeting with potential production financiers. We were still neophytes, but every day we were learning more. Slowly we gathered together more and more of the necessary funding, including a two hundred thousand–dollar commitment from Paramount Pictures for distribution rights. This was heady stuff. Yes, it was only one-tenth of the production budget, but it gave confidence to the other financiers standing by.

The real breakthrough came when we secured interest from renowned Canadian actor Christopher Plummer. At the time, he was probably best known for his role as Captain Georg von Trapp in the musical film *The Sound of Music*. Since then he has won numerous accolades for his work, including an Academy Award, two Emmy Awards, two Tony Awards,

---

* In his life, Tiff wrote twelve novels, two short story collections, two memoirs, and four plays. In addition to receiving the Order of Canada and winning the Governor General's Award for fiction, Tiff was named by the French government a Chevalier de l'Ordre des Arts et des Lettres.

a Golden Globe Award, a SAG Award, and a BAFTA Award. Peter and Chris met with him in London.

> **Peter:** David Niven Jr., who had some sort of "our man in London" role with Paramount, set up a meeting with Christopher Plummer at the Connaught Hotel in London. Plummer was impressed enough with our pitch that he put one foot up on the bar and yelled, "And now off to Muddy York!" loudly in front of everybody. Of course, the bar patrons had no idea what he was yelling about.

That led to a letter of interest from James Coburn, the legendary American actor who had been featured, often as a "tough guy," in some seventy features films including the likes of *The Magnificent Seven*, *Hell Is for Heroes*, *The Great Escape*, *Charade*, and *Our Man Flint*.

We were on top of the world, on the verge of creating Canada's first great feature film, and still in our early twenties.

We learned a golden lesson in doing all this: if you work hard, surround yourself with people who are brighter and more talented than you are, and actually listen to them and give them full credit when due, you can accomplish almost anything.

"Almost anything" is the operative phrase here. Six weeks before we were to start formal production of the *Killing Ground* project, it all came tumbling apart.

A key portion of our financing, six hundred thousand dollars, was coming from British sources represented by an investment adviser named Robert McGuirk. A larger than life character who talked in a southern drawl, and dressed somewhat like Colonel Sanders, McGuirk had impressed us with his business acumen and lengthy stories about the industry. He'd insisted we pay him some upfront fees, which he characterized as necessary to "cover his out-of-pocket expenses" while he got his investors lined up. We'd done so gladly, as we could sense the financing coming together and production of *Killing Ground* tantalizingly just ahead on the horizon.

Only, we found out in the weeks just prior to production, there were no investors. We, and the U.K. accountants we had hired to help us secure this financing, had been completely taken in. We had paid McGuirk for nothing. We scrambled, and scrambled some more, to no avail. Slowly but relentlessly everything we'd struggled for and accomplished over three years came completely and irretrievably unravelled.

Our *Killing Ground* project was over. It was a heart-crushing disaster.

As I said at the beginning of this chapter, I've come to think that the reverse of the Gene Kranz idiom is true: failure is an unacknowledged virtue. If you're not failing, then you're not pushing the envelope of possibilities. But there was no telling that to the young Stephen Stohn in his early twenties, the young Stephen Stohn who had just had his heart ripped out, who alongside his friends had been riding a crest of superstardom, about to change the entertainment industry in Canada, and become mega-moguls, only to see all their dreams disappear completely.

There was no point telling young Stephen Stohn what a wonderful experience he'd had. That he still had his health. That it just wasn't meant to be. No, that young Stephen Stohn just wanted to crawl into the deepest, darkest, most miserable hole he could find and never come out again.

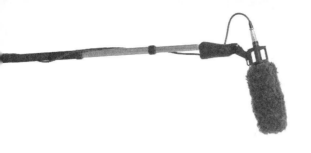

8
"MY LAWYER"

To make ends meet after the *Killing Ground* disaster, I got a job working part-time in George Miller's law office. A tall, rumpled lawyer who smoked too much, George could easily have been on the front cover of a vintage *Saturday Evening Post* magazine as Norman Rockwell's version of the kindly country practitioner. He was, in fact, a successful urban lawyer with a varied practice including entertainment law.

The year was 1974, before photocopiers had been popularized. In order to make multiple copies of legal documents, secretaries would insert several sheets of paper into a manual typewriter (electric typewriters were not yet in wide use either) with sheets of carbon paper in between. The skill of a typist who could churn out a perfect page was highly valued. I wasn't a typist myself, but I was a good proofreader and could help by checking the typists' work, and by sorting and filing their documents.

George had higher ambitions for me. "You should apply to law school," he said. After some considerable remonstrations on my part, I did exactly as he suggested.

When my application to the University of Toronto Law School was accepted a year later, George congratulated me heartily, and agreed that I could continue working in his law office while going to school, but on one condition: "Stever, you must promise me that law school comes first.

If I ever ask you to do something and it conflicts with your studies, just let me know so that we can make sure that law school always come first."*

I'm sure George meant it when he said that — or did he?

○   ○   ◎

It was 8:30 a.m. on a cold rainy day in November of my first year in law school. There was a paper I needed to write, a class I needed to attend. I had to grab some stuff from the office, pop on the subway, and be back to school by 9:00 a.m.

The conversation started with George saying, "Stever, I need a quick something." And it continued:

> **Stephen**: George, remember that conversation we had? I've got to pull out the card now, I've got to write this paper, prepare for exams, do all this stuff. I have to exercise the "law school always comes first" card!
> **George**: Good for you Stever. Now, here's a briefcase, and inside is everything you need. Just go to Courtroom 14B in Old City Hall and adjourn a case for me.
> **Stephen**: George, I just can't. I'm playing the card.
> **George**: There is no card. You're going to court. I can't go, and you have to appear in Courtroom 14B.
> **Stephen**: I've never been in court, what do I do?
> **George**: It'll all work out. Just tell them you're a student and you don't know what you're doing. Just adjourn it.

---

* I'm not that fussed about what people call me, for the most part it's simply "Stephen." Two exceptions include George, who had the habit of referring to me as "Stever," and impresario Garth Drabinsky, whom, despite his troubles, I grew quite fond of; he called me "Stevie." Oh, and Kevin Smith refers to me as "Stohner," which I choose to take as an extreme compliment.

It was very upsetting. I walked along, trying to get to the subway, and it was raining. I opened the briefcase, and there was only one thing inside, a little green slip. The slip said, "Accused: Frank Drew. Crime: Assault with a Dangerous Weapon Causing Grievous Bodily Harm."

This was a real criminal case! I started hyperventilating. I didn't know the client. I didn't know anything whatsoever about the case. All I had was this little green paper claiming that on such and such a date he attacked such and such a person, causing Grievous Bodily Harm. This guy could go up the river for five or even fifteen years!

As I made my way to Old City Hall I memorized what I'd say, running through it over and over. You know how when you get really stressed you need something to hang on to? Well, what I hung on to was, "If it pleases Your Honour, my name is Stephen Stohn. I'm a student with the law firm of Miller & Charlton, who are acting for the accused in this matter, Mr. Frank Drew. My principal, George Miller, is unavailable to attend this morning, but he has asked if we could please adjourn this matter to another day." I kept practising that in my mind, thinking at the same time, "If I'm really lucky, it'll be on first thing … and I can salvage the rest of this godforsaken morning."

Old City Hall was jammed with people — people who knew what they were doing. The place bustled with clerks, judges, police officers, and ordinary citizens. I found Courtroom 14B and saw the list outside the door. Hallelujah, right up near the top was the name Frank Drew. So I turned around and called his name up and down the corridor. Again and again I called. But he wasn't there, it was 9:00 a.m., and I was getting increasingly agitated.

Things quieted down inside the courtroom and a bailiff came outside and chanted "Frank Drew, Frank Drew," looking for the accused. At that moment this guy came rushing up and I yelled, "Frank?" He said, "Yes!" and I replied, "I'm Stephen." We were just in time. I grabbed him by the arm, and we went in to stand in front of the court.

The judge nodded to me, and I started, "If it pleases Your Honour, my name is Stephen Stohn. I'm a student with the law firm of Miller &

Charlton who are acting for the accused in this matter, Mr. Frank Drew."
I was about to continue asking for the adjournment, my hand resting
confidently on Frank's shoulder, when he said, "I'm not Frank Drew."

My life flashed before me. All I could think of was contempt of
court. I'd seemingly tried to impersonate an accused, or some such thing.
Whatever it was, it was bad. I managed to garble out something along
the lines of, "What my colleague meant to say was Mr. Drew has been
delayed this morning. We were hoping for an adjournment." The judge
obviously knew I was in trouble, and said something like, "We'll put this
matter down until later this morning and hopefully Mr. Drew will be in
attendance by that time."

We went outside, and I found a pay phone to call George and say,
"George, you don't understand, this is horrible. I've gone before a judge;
I had the wrong client." He roared with laughter. I was so angry with
him that at that moment I hated George Miller. "No, you're staying right
there," he told me, amid guffaws of laughter.

"George, be reasonable. There is no client. Frank Drew is not here,"
I said.

At that moment the door to Old City Hall opened, and a guy came
in, old and unkempt looking, but haloed in the light. "Are you Frank
Drew?" I asked.

"Yes."

We sat down, and I explained that I was a mere student, not a lawyer.
How I didn't know anything about the case. How I was a peon. There'd
already been a mix-up, and we had to go in and adjourn the case to another
day when George was available. Frank smiled and responded simply, "No.
There's no way we're adjourning this case. We're fighting it today!"

This was not good. Over and over I tried talking sense into Frank.
We had a few hours to kill. As a result of the mix-up we were at the bottom of the morning's list, and I tried to use the time to point out to Frank
how important it was that he have a real lawyer represent him.

We got to know each other a bit over those few hours, Frank starting to tell me about himself. He obviously had a weak bladder, as he

kept going to the restroom, and I used one of those restroom exits to call George. "He's insisting on going forward with the case today. You have to come down here!" George just said, "Don't listen to him. You're going to adjourn the case." Easy for George to say. This just made me red in the face. George was safely back at the office, not here on the front lines.

When Frank came back we got into more conversation, but as we were talking it slowly dawned on me that Frank didn't have a weak bladder at all. He was slurring his words, getting drunker and drunker. He'd been going to the restroom to drink, as he then admitted, a mickey of rye. I became even more upset, thinking how before even becoming a lawyer I was probably guilty of so many different forms of contempt of court.

Suddenly, it became all about me, me, me, and how my career was going to be over. I explained to Frank, "You have no idea how this is affecting me."

Frank just put his hand confidently on my shoulder, and said, "Don't worry Stephen, I've been through this many times." He paused and looked me in the eye. "Here's what you do. Understand this will work. Whatever they say, put your feet together, your hands behind your back, look down and don't say anything. Just be really, really humble."

"Ummmm, that's really not going to work here," I replied.

So, Frank was an interesting guy. It turned out the "Dangerous Weapon" that had caused such "Grievous Bodily Harm" was in fact a broom handle that had delivered a black eye and a swollen arm. Particularly as he drank more, he became more loquacious, but he also started making less sense. And as his words washed over me, I started to realize I did have control over my own life, and it didn't matter what Frank said. My job was to go in there and ask for an adjournment, and that was exactly what I was going to do. No matter what.

Finally it was 12:30 p.m., time for the last case of the morning. "Frank Drew, Frank Drew," the bailiff chanted. I was propping Frank up a little bit as we entered the courtroom. He wasn't falling down, but was trying to walk very purposefully to prove he wasn't drunk. Which was delusional.

The moment arrived. If there were drums in the court, the drums would have rolled. "If it pleases Your Honour, my name is Stephen Stohn. I'm a student with —" The judge interrupted. "We know who you are Mr. Stohn. Who is your client *this* time?" There was laughter in the court.

I was so petrified I blanked completely. The jig was up. The judge had my number, and I had no idea what to say or do. There were probably so many different protocols, so many different proper ways to proceed, but I had nothing. The single thought that suddenly came through my mind in that moment of blackness were those experienced words of Frank Drew himself, from only an hour or so earlier: so, I put my feet together, put my arms behind my back and I looked down and tried to be really, really humble.

There was a long pause. I knew I was supposed to answer the question, that I had to do or say something, but I was rooted in complete inaction, and humbleness — until I became aware that someone else had started speaking, someone who knew what he was doing. It was the Crown Attorney saying, "Your Honour, our witnesses have failed to appear this morning, and with Your Honour's consent we'd like to withdraw the charges against Mr. Drew." Somehow I managed to recover my voice enough to croak, "That would be acceptable to the defence, Your Honour."

So Frank and I walked out of the courtroom together, both free men. As we got to the door, Frank threw his arms around me and cried, "My lawyer!"

I've never been back in a courtroom since, and I never will.

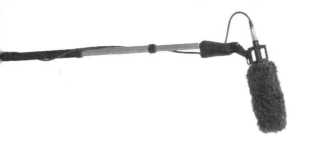

9
LOST IN A LOVE SONG

While I was still in law school, someone from the past returned to my life.

I was in Peterborough at an informal reunion of friends from Trent University, on one of those fine fall days that Canada is famous for, brisk but sunny, the leaves on the trees bursting with colour. Someone mentioned that I must be pleased to know that Christopher Ward was also coming over to the reunion.

No! I did not want to see Christopher.

But suddenly there he was, heading toward me, guitar in hand. I made some polite conversation before turning to get away. He stopped me. "Stephen, maybe you can help me; I've been offered a recording deal by WEA." WEA was short for Warner Elektra Atlantic, now Warner Music. "I hear you're in law school, could you maybe help me negotiate the contract?"

"Not me," I replied. "I'm not a lawyer yet, but I could ask George Miller, who should be able to help you." He thanked me, and once more I turned to get away.

He stopped me again. "Would you like to hear the song WEA wants to record as the single?" I was trapped. I could only listen to the song, as any polite Canadian would, before finally making my escape.

It seemed to take ages for him to tune the guitar and then finally to start singing the song. I was fidgeting, while others at the reunion circled around and hushed so that we all could listen in. As Christopher started playing, though, I found myself being quite drawn in. It was a simple country song, but it spoke to the heart, and when the final chorus ended, I would have been glad to hear it again. Indeed, everyone in the room clapped and encouraged an encore.

As I was finally able to leave, I found myself saying to Christopher, "That really was a very beautiful song. I've got to go, but well done. I understand why WEA wants to sign you to a contract."

He looked me straight in the eye and said, "You idiot!" I was stunned at his rudeness and, in my anger, now felt fully justified in immediately walking out. Then he added, "You wrote the song!"

I didn't know what he meant until he reminded me of a song called "Must Have Lost My Way" we'd written together during the month that he and I performed songs nightly at the Playboy Club in Ankara, Turkey. At that time the lyrics had centred around a traveller who was starting to wonder exactly what he was travelling toward, and who was increasingly thinking about the girl he had left back in his hometown. So there were phrases like "lost in memories," "I don't seem to know my mind," and "looking for something to find."

Christopher had completely rewritten the lyrics, changing the traveller into a lover who was lost in reverie while listening to a song on a jukebox (although there were still travelling references), and calling the song "Lost in a Love Song."

He reminded me that it was during our travels in Europe and Turkey that I had been key to his learning the art of songwriting, and he recalled a conversation between us, in a campsite in Spain early in our travels:

Christopher: What's a "middle eight"?

Stephen: The middle eight bars of a song, also called the bridge. You know, the "I don't want to sound complaining" section of "Please Please Me."

Christopher: Right.

Stephen: Or the "And when I touch you" part of "I Want to Hold Your Hand." They liked that one so much they used it twice.

Christopher: I think we need one of those.

At the time, I had been writing songs for a few years, while Christopher was just getting started. He hadn't really grasped the structural side of the craft back then, so his songs had tended to ramble a bit (maybe he'd been listening to Van Morrison's *Astral Weeks* too much — if that's possible.)

Christopher: Stephen had an innate grasp of chord structure and how a melody could develop over the course of a song for a greater emotional payoff. I was the attentive student. I was also the designated lyricist. So a songwriting partnership was struck. Old school style, or Elton and Bernie style, where there's more or less a strict division of labour, rather than The Beatles' tendency to write chunks of songs, at least like they did in the early days. I think "Lost in a Love Song," originally called "Must Have Lost My Way Now," with the too-clever second line "Looking for something to find," was the first real song that we wrote together. And it was the first of many, as my debut album contained almost exclusively Stohn/Ward co-writes.

Fairly soon thereafter, George did work with Christopher to sign the deal with WEA, though George insisted that I learn about recording contracts by being the front man in the negotiations. The experience taught me a lot about an important element of negotiating: bargaining power. Namely, that we had none. Try as I did, I was able to make almost no changes to the standard agreement. Gary Muth was the head of A&R (Artists & Repertoire) for WEA at the time:

The label from Christopher's and my first release. At the time, I had never been to Burbank, or even Los Angeles, but imagined it was like the picture on the label — streets lined with beautiful palm trees leading to a wondrous future — which, it turns out, it sometimes is.

Gary: In those days you basically took the deal that the record company gave you. There was hardly any negotiating … with anybody. The actual contract was printed, and you'd write in some percentages, and that would be it. The artists were glad just to be in the studio. I remember talking with Andy Kim about his early days and he said, "We didn't care about the paper, all we wanted to do was get in the studio." *

---

* Andy had a long and extremely successful career, including hit songs such as "Rock Me Gently," which reached #1 on the *Billboard* chart in 1974. But his most successful song was for The Archies — "Sugar, Sugar" was the top song of the year in 1969.

Despite the one-sided negotiations (or, more to the point, lack of negotiations), Christopher signed the deal, and the first single released was indeed "Lost in a Love Song." It was a minor hit on the Canadian country charts, enough to get Christopher's contract extended to record a full album. The royalties from the song were enough for Christopher and I to share a season ticket package for the Toronto Maple Leafs hockey club — seated in the highest possible row, furthest from the ice surface, in the greys, but season tickets nonetheless.

More importantly, it meant Christopher needed to write more songs. The person I'd thought I never wanted to see, ever again, was a friend once more. And we were going to write an album together.

◦   ◦   ◦

Over the next six months Christopher challenged me to come up with some more melodies that he could then add lyrics to. It was slow work, particularly with everything else going on in my life. By June we still hadn't made enough progress, so I decided to head up alone to our family cottage in beautiful Georgian Bay and do nothing but write. The cottage was rustic. It had no electricity, but did have a wonderful view of the sunsets across the bay and out to Lake Huron. More importantly for my purposes, it also had a sturdy old Heintzman upright piano.

In those days the most important radio station in North America was CKLW at 800 on the AM dial, known as "The Big 8 in the Motor City." The transmitters were actually located in Windsor, Ontario, but it billed itself as a Detroit radio station. It beamed into almost thirty U.S. states and was the number one radio station in eight of those states. For inspiration, I set up a portable radio on the piano, listened to CKLW, and watched the beautiful sunsets. As a fun visualization, I imagined hearing the song I was working on being broadcast over the Big 8.

I concentrated on melodies, not trying to make any sense of the words. We didn't know at the time that this was a common practice among song-writers, and that those original nonsense words are called "dummy lyrics."*

There were several song fragments and one song that resulted from that first cottage writing sojourn. The song started with a monotonous duotone back and forth melody to the dummy lyric:

Sun is sinking in the silence the surfers shout
Summer moon is a diamond in the house

and ended with the chorus

Surfin' is gone now, surfin' is over

repeated over and over. It was an homage to Brian Wilson and The Beach Boys, and I imagined it starting with a sound like a circus calliope droning back and forth, before breaking out into an unexpected melody, straining sixth and ninth notes against root chords until the tension released into the chorus.

I was thinking of the time at the end of the summer, at sunset on the last day of surfing, a bittersweet time when a wonderful season has produced lasting memories, but it has now ended. It didn't matter that I knew nothing of surfing; neither did Brian Wilson! Christopher later rewrote the lyrics to describe the bittersweet uncertainty of blooming love — that wonderful time when, in one moment, you know that the person you love truly loves you, and in the next you are ravaged by doubts and are convinced that it's all over. So the opening lyric became

---

* Christopher: "Stephen has a melodic gift and I truly believe that if he had wanted to pursue a career as a professional songwriter, it would have been his. Instead, he helped birth thousands of songs with his work on behalf of so many artists. But as for his lyric capabilities, let's recall that he once referred to himself in a song as 'the Mississippi Mudpie.' Enough said."

Love will linger in a moment of breathless night
Summer moon is a diamond in the sky.

The chorus became the beautifully evocative

Once in a Longtime
Love is a sweet dream
Gone with the night wind
Once you believe it....

It was nearly eighteen months later when we went into the studio and recorded the song. There were some truly great session players on the track including Steve Ferrone from the Average White Band on drums, Randy and Michael Brecker on horns, and Peter Appleyard on vibes. Moe Koffman, Doug "Dr. Music" Riley, Guido Basso, Sandy Torano, and Jack Waldman also contributed. The great Jack Richardson (of The Guess Who fame) produced the session. The string section came from the Toronto Symphony Orchestra.

We were still working on other songs for the album when WEA decided to immediately release "Once in a Longtime" as a single. The weekend it was released, I was once again on my own at the cottage, and I tried listening to some of the smaller radio stations to see if our song might start to get some airplay. Unknown artists almost never got played right away on the big radio stations like the Big 8 in Detroit, or 1050 CHUM in Toronto. They always waited for smaller radio stations to take a chance, to see if the audience liked it. But no such luck. None of the small stations had started to play the song.

I sat down at the piano, looked out at the sunset, and switched the radio to the Big 8 for some inspiration. My mind had drifted away as they rambled on about the Detroit weather and traffic, so it took a while to register — the song intro the announcer was talking over sounded awfully familiar. Then the lyrics started in: "Love will linger in a moment of breathless night...." I jumped up and down and danced all around the cottage, and I cried.

The rush of adrenalin that came every time we heard the song on the radio was intoxicating. In the end, "Once in a Longtime" wasn't the big worldwide hit that we hoped it would be, but it did reach the Top 10 across Canada.

We made good use of that adrenalin. While the radio airplay and sales were rising, we channelled our energy into writing more songs to complete the album.

As head of A&R at WEA, Gary Muth had secured small offices for his department in the midtown Yorkville area of Toronto, far away from the rest of WEA, which was located in the industrial suburbs. The offices were on the second floor of a two-storey Victorian brick building. The ground floor housed an answering service that, coincidentally, was the service that Christopher and I and many of our friends used.*

Gary had a back office, complete with a piano, that he offered to Christopher and me to use for our songwriting. It was particularly handy for me, since the University of Toronto Law School was only a short walk away.

Gary: Stephen wasn't a lawyer at the time; he was still a student. He would always drop by after his classes and do his work in the back office. And Christopher used to rehearse with his band in the basement. It was a dirty, grotty basement that years before had been a nightclub. The ceilings were so low that Christopher referred to it as "Club Quasimodo."

One day, Gary called us into his front office to deliver some difficult news. "It's going well," he said. "There's some really great songs. But … I just don't hear a hit single." The upshot was that until we created a single, we wouldn't be going into the studio to record the full album.

---

* An "answering service" was an early version of voice mail; your phone calls were answered by live operators who connected directly with your home telephone.

Coming out of the meeting we were despondent. Partly to vent frustration and partly as a weak attempt at gallows humour, Christopher said sarcastically, "Well that's simple. Stephen, you're heading up to the cottage this weekend. Why don't you come back Monday with a hit for us?" I played along, saying, "Will do. But you have to accept two conditions." The first condition was easy enough for Christopher to accept, the song would end with him sustaining a note that was at the very top of his range, ultimately to be surrounded by swirling strings, horns, and drums when produced.

The second condition was just a joke. I suggested that midway through the song, it would arbitrarily shift upward in key by a halftone. Christopher choked at this, as I knew he would. That kind of key change was, in his mind, a sleazy songwriter trick to imply something new and creative in the melody when in fact there was really nothing new or creative at all. "No! That sounds like Barry Manilow!" he cried. "Exactly." I responded. "Take it, or leave it." And with that we laughed and headed our separate ways for the weekend.*

Then something almost miraculous happened.

Having set the goal of creating a hit single, I worked furiously on a melody all weekend long. Yes, the melody started out low and gradually worked its way upward until it hit a high, sustained note at the end. And yes, the key arbitrarily shifted upward by a halftone coming out of the middle eight.**

When I got back from the weekend and played the song for Christopher, he loved it. All of it. He even swallowed the halftone upshift. And he immediately set about creating lyrics. The opening lines reflect the loss you feel when love goes sour:

---

* It was indeed one of the hallmarks of Barry Manilow's style. In fact, in "Can't Smile Without You" he raised the key by a halftone four different times during the song, to my mind a stunning achievement.

** You can listen to "Maybe Your Heart" on YouTube at www.youtube.com/watch?v=2E1VgsoS6i4. The halftone upshift occurs at about the 2:15 mark, and the high sustain with swirling strings starts around the 2:45 mark.

How I've fallen from your favour
The sweet love you've taken away
The sound of goodbye
Echoes all through the night
And I must wait, through lost days....

This led to the chorus:

Maybe Your Heart will be broken in two ... like mine.

More to the point, once Gary Muth heard the song, he loved it, too, and we were given the immediate go-ahead to record the full album, with emphasis on "Maybe Your Heart" as the new single.

The song was a big success — Top 10 across the country, and #1 in various centres, including (of all places) Quebec City. It got a lot of airplay throughout Canada, including on the Big 8 in Detroit and CHUM in Toronto. People related to the song, and we heard numerous stories from people we didn't even know about how "Maybe Your Heart" affected their lives, like having to pull their car over to the side of the road when they heard the song because it made them cry.

While I credit the success of all our songs to Christopher's lyrics, Christopher has always been very celebratory of my melodies (this mutual admiration is probably why our partnership worked so well).

Christopher: For a few years our work was heard a lot on Canadian radio, and I think it was the soaring melodies that made that happen. I couldn't have written a melody like "Once in a Longtime" or "Maybe Your Heart," but they were a joy to sing. Those songs still sound good to me, and when I hear one on the radio, it always makes me happy.

Once again we had visualized some things, and they had in many ways come true. Neither "Once in a Longtime" nor "Maybe Your Heart" made it onto the *Billboard* charts. In that sense, their success was limited. But they had been recorded and released, and had met with at least some national success.

This visualization thing seemed to be working, at least in part.

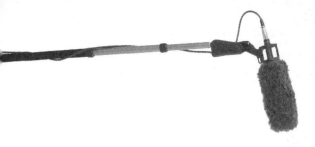

10
IT STARTED AS A JOKE ...

Chris Dalton, Peter O'Brian, and I thought that our *Killing Ground* feature film would be the first truly successful large-budget film in English-Canadian history. While we were busy failing at producing it, other Canadian filmmakers were rising to the fore.

Most notably, in the early 1970s Toronto filmmaker Don Shebib directed the landmark docudrama *Goin' Down the Road*, an artistic and commercial success that received national and international distribution. At the same time in Quebec, Claude Jutra directed the acclaimed *Mon Oncle Antoine*, considered one of the best — if not the best — Canadian films of all time.*

The Canadian government was interested in building on these successes. In 1967 it had created the Canadian Film Development Corporation (or CFDC, now known as Telefilm Canada), giving it an initial budget of ten million dollars to help develop a commercial feature-film industry. But many of its films went unseen by Canadian audiences.

The government decided that encouraging private investment in films would be a useful adjunct to their CFDC initiative, and so in 1974

---

* The "Top 10 Canadian Films of All Time" is a list compiled by the Toronto International Film Festival, ranking what are considered the best Canadian films. *Mon Oncle Antoine* has routinely been placed at the top of the list.

it amended the Income Tax Act to allow investors to deduct from their taxable income 100 percent of their share of the costs of feature films that were certified as Canadian.

Tax lawyers and accountants soon realized that the investors' "share of the costs" of a film could be much more than their actual investment, since non-investors (like distributors paying distribution advances and funding agencies such as the CFDC) could cover a lot of the costs of the film. Structured in the right way (usually through a limited partnership), investors could write off more than they invested and potentially make a profit even if the film was not successful.

This resulted in a massive increase in investment in Canadian production and marked the beginning of what became known as the "tax-shelter era." Like ducks to water, investors took to Canadian film, and there arose strong demand for certified Canadian films. Peter, Chris, and I were happy to help address that demand.

We had failed in producing a big-budget feature film but had learned a lot along the way. Working with George Miller, we created a limited partnership that would underwrite the $115,000 cost of a feature film based on a stage play called *Me*. The limited partners (the investors) would put up forty thousand dollars, and we would fund the balance with assistance from the CFDC.

John Palmer and Martin Kinch had worked as directors at Toronto Free Theatre, where *Me* had some success. We optioned the film rights and engaged John as a director while Martin, along with Barry Pearson, adapted the play to film. One of the attractive features of the play was that it was set in a very limited number of locations, making it less costly to shoot.

I was in first-year law school at the time, but filming would take place during the summer. In fact, George Miller was moving his law offices that summer, and his previous office remained vacant during the exact time we proposed to be filming. He graciously allowed us to use the space, and we transformed it into a mini-studio for our four-week shoot.

Our $115,000 budget was a comedown from the two-million-dollar one we had set for *Killing Ground*. Still, the *Me* production gave each of us a crash course on all the day-to-day realities of working on a film set.

In the end, though, as a work of commercial art, perhaps the best that can be said about the film *Me* was that everyone tried their best, and we all learned. And it got completed — on budget and on time.

There was only one review for the film version of Me, and it came from overseas, from the *London Evening Standard*. The film critic took a shine to *Me*'s rough edges, calling it "one of the most important films to come out of North America." Ironically it never came out *in* North America — we were never able to find a distributor for it, so it never got released to the public.

As a pure investment, it was a success. The limited partners wrote off the $115,000 cost against income taxes they would otherwise have paid, thus saving $57,500 or more in taxes (they were all in a 50 percent or higher tax bracket). Since their investment was only $40,000, this represented at least a $17,500 profit; in other words, a 43.75 percent return on their investment.

This set the stage for the following summer when, using a similar limited partnership arrangement, we notched up our success level a bit by not only producing but also finding a distributor for *The Clown Murders*.

The most notable aspect of *The Clown Murders* was undoubtedly that it was one of the first films John Candy ever appeared in, and one of only three dramatic films he ever starred in.*

John was a joy to work with. The production budget was still very low — $175,000 — so all the actors, including John, were paid minimum scale. Years later I ran into him at a Second City reunion and started to introduce myself, not sure he would remember me. But he immediately interrupted and said, "No, no, I remember you very well indeed. You are the last person I ever worked for scale for!"

The plot for *The Clown Murders* was relatively straightforward. Four men kidnap an old girlfriend on Halloween night as a joke to ruin a

---

* The other two were *JFK* (1991) and *Cool Runnings* (1993).

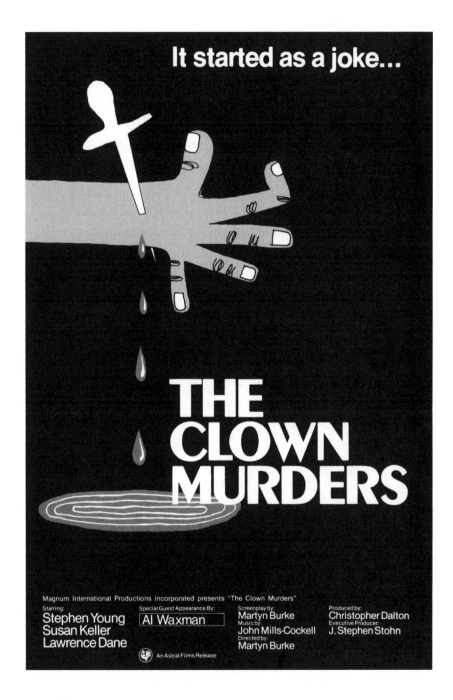

The original poster for *The Clown Murders*, notably, does not include a credit for John Candy, as this was one of his first forays into the world of feature film.

real estate deal, only to have a very real clown-masked killer stalk them, seeking revenge. The poster featured a stylized hand with a knife running through it, and the log line "It started as a joke ..." Indeed, while it was intended to be a horror film, it did have some unintentionally comedic moments.

I was proud of the production values that we achieved on *The Clown Murders*. There's no question it had serious flaws, but we were gaining more experience.

On the night it was released, I paid my admission and walked anonymously into one of the theatres it was being shown in, the Odeon Hyland at Yonge and St. Clair in Toronto. I'd prepared for the screening by drinking several glasses of straight Scotch with some friends at the nearby Fran's restaurant. Evidently I hadn't prepared well enough; as we walked into the theatre, we encountered patrons leaving an earlier screening, one of whom, a complete stranger, yelled out at me, "Don't waste your time or your money, it's horrible!"

Nevertheless, I sat through the screening, with some measure of pride at seeing my name roll by in large letters. It may have been a flawed film, but how many people get to see their name in lights on the big screen?

To give a flavour for the reaction to *The Clown Murders*, here is one of the user-generated reviews from IMDb.com. The writer pithily sets out some high and low points:

Not only is this film boring, but it is also quite stupid. But, yet, still good. The only reason to see this film is because it stars John Candy. He does an okay job of acting, I guess, but the story itself does little to hold your interest. It bores you and indulges you with a hard to follow story of characters that all seem to turn on each other for no apparent reason in the end. Now, this film is really, really slow and could put the world's biggest insomniac to sleep.

Other IMDb.com reviews were even less enthusiastic. As an example:

This movie is really quite pathetic. It is a movie about a murderer. The plot is confusing and jumps around so much it is hard to follow. The only reason to actually watch this movie is because John Candy is in it.... There is an embarrassing scene where John's character has a nervous breakdown, and he is seen rolling in the mud in his underwear, blubbering like a baby. The movie aside, I thought John pulled that scene off quite well.

At any rate, if you are a real John Candy fan, then you have probably already seen this movie. If you are not a fan, don't waste your time.

I was twenty-eight years old at the time, and in my final year of law school. At this relatively young age, I had three films under my belt: one that was never made, one that was made but never released, and one that was made and released, but flopped.

Still, as they say, I had my health, and soon I would have my law degree. With the experience I'd had in the movie industry, as well as two Canadian Top 10 songs under my belt, I was set to start attracting clients to my forthcoming entertainment law practice.

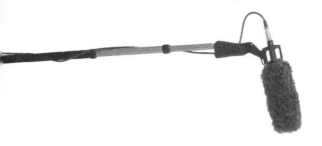

11
THE YOUNG LAWYER

My early entertainment law career started straightforwardly enough, working with George Miller in his small law office. George and I worked together on feature-film files, and gradually I became a specialist in using limited partnerships to fund films, using the capital cost allowance rules under the Income Tax Act that I described earlier, namely that investors could write off 100 percent of the cost of the film in the year they made their investment.

With my love of songwriting and music, I wanted to build up a music law practice as well. It helped that I had written songs that achieved some success; it gave me some credibility in attracting music-oriented clients, one of which rose to the fore — a fledgling but influential indie label called Ready Records, headed by two inventive and hard-working entrepreneurs, Angus MacKay and Andy Crosbie. They became more than clients — we were friends embroiled in all aspects of the music business.

Angus and Andy were always trying different approaches to the business and constantly asking questions about the best way to proceed. If I ever felt I was in over my head, and if George didn't know the answer, we would hire a U.S. entertainment lawyer to provide necessary advice; I would manage the relationship with the American lawyer, not billing for my time, but gaining valuable knowledge and experience. As time went on and I became more proficient, we relied less and less on outside legal help.

Ready Records grew and grew. They were best known for the group Spoons, who had multiple hit albums (their most popular single being "Nova Heart"), but Ready also signed important local acts like Blue Peter, Colin Linden, The Extras, and many others. Working with Angus and Andy provided a solid foundation for what eventually became an extensive music law practice.

Meanwhile, my first artist client was Billy Bryans, then the drummer for Downchild Blues Band (he also co-produced the band's hit single "Flip, Flop and Fly"), and ultimately a co-founder of The Parachute Club.* Gradually more musicians became clients, by the mid-1980s including artists such as Tom Cochrane, Honeymoon Suite, Glass Tiger, 54-40, Blue Rodeo, Randy Bachman, The Northern Pikes, and The Pursuit of Happiness.

So my practice was expanding nicely until one day the film side of the practice changed dramatically. In 1982 the federal government suddenly announced new Income Tax Act provisions, effectively ending the use of capital cost allowance for tax shelter purposes in the production of feature films.**

At first this was devastating. A major portion of my legal practice became non-existent. Almost overnight, feature films virtually stopped being produced in Canada.

---

* In the summer of 1982 Billy was offered the chance to play at the first Toronto International Film Festival. His new group, Mama Quilla II, was on hiatus at the time, so he and bandmate Lorraine Segato formed a one-off band for the occasion, adding several other local musicians. Their performance was a success, and the "one-off band" continued under the name The Parachute Club, going on to record several worldwide hit albums and singles, including "Rise Up."

** The capital cost allowance for feature films was reduced to 50 percent in the first year. In other measures, the top income tax bracket was reduced substantially (reducing the incentive for tax shelters generally) and loans taken out to invest in tax shelters would no longer be tax deductible.

It shook me. For the first time I considered joining a larger law firm, where working on a wider variety of files and projects could help buffer the ups and downs of individual entertainment projects.

Until then I'd been leery of working at a major firm. I was afraid that the corporate culture would be antithetical to many of my music and film clients — that long-hairs in jeans and T-shirts in the reception areas would be frowned upon by the high-powered litigation and mergers-and-acquisitions types in pinstripe suits. And I'd worried the large-firm drive for billable hours would dilute my focus on pure entertainment law, where the bills were usually smaller, and even then sometimes difficult to collect. In fact, years earlier when I was graduating from law school, George Miller had tried to insist that I work at a major firm, whereupon I had replied bluntly, "I will never, ever, work at a large law firm!"

Long story short: to the absolute contrary of that unequivocal assertion to George Miller, I became a partner in 1985 at McCarthy & McCarthy (now McCarthy Tétrault LLP or, more colloquially, simply "McCarthys"), which was, at the time, the largest law firm in Canada.*

Peter Grant, the brilliant communications lawyer who had taught one of my courses at law school, ultimately drew me into McCarthys. I discovered that my fears about corporate culture proved completely unfounded. McCarthys embraced having an entertainment lawyer in the firm. They embraced having unconventional-looking clients in the waiting area. The lawyers at McCarthys liked me, and I liked them. And thanks to Peter Grant's guidance and influence, I ended up working with lawyers who became lifelong friends, friendships lasting long after our McCarthys time together, including Roma Khanna (until recently the president of MGM's Television Group and Digital in Los Angeles), Ian MacKay (now the president of the Canadian music rights collective Re:Sound), John Morayniss (now the president of the hugely success-ful production company eOne Television), and most of all, Graham

---

* I take comfort in Oscar Wilde's belief that "consistency is the last refuge of the unimaginative."

Henderson (now the president of Music Canada, the industry association representing the major music labels).

In effect, I transitioned from one friend and mentor, George Miller, to another, Peter Grant. Peter introduced me to an entirely new way of thinking. By then I was used to negotiating a myriad of individual agreements, like recording contracts, actor agreements, option agreements, and film-financing agreements; these were individual day-to-day agreements on the micro level. Peter introduced me to macro thinking — what were the issues and problems that the film industry, the recording industry, and other entertainment industries were facing on the national and global level. This was interesting in and of itself, but it also gave me a far better appreciation of the day-to-day agreements I was negotiating: I came to more fully understand the business pressures that each party was facing.

In the process, I became a mentor myself, as I worked with Graham Henderson to teach him the basics of negotiating, working well with clients, and of course entertainment law. Really, I was simply passing along, as best as I could, things that had been passed to me from my mentors. It seemed like such a natural thing to do. Graham was very appreciative.

Graham: At first, Stephen was quite mysterious to me. I knew he was an entertainment lawyer. I didn't quite know what that meant. He had clients like Honeymoon Suite and Killer Dwarves, and he was this friendly, bright, funny, very passionate guy who clearly loved what he was doing, and who was interested in teaching, not just dumping stuff on you. I've got a very inquisitive mind and I was willing to learn. That was the beginning of it.

I remember having these meetings in the boardroom. He would come in and sit down and walk through whatever it was — recording contracts, songwriter agreements, merchandising agreements — explaining step by step. He taught me how to mark-up contracts, writing little comments in the margin, and underlining things you don't like … that took a lot of time and he did not bill that time to the clients. I also learned: now I've got to get on the phone and call these people … and he coached me on how to interact with the institutional lawyers, like the record company, the merchandising company.

In the music business, there's a couple of different schools. There's the screaming school which seems to dominate — it certainly did then — where you scream, yell, and hope that you get what you want because of your bargaining power. And then there's another school, which Stephen is in, that's almost like "love them to death." So I start phoning all these lawyers, all of whom had dealt with Stephen at one point or another and I keep encountering comments like this:

"So Stephen won't be doing this deal with me?"

"No."

"That's too bad. I love Stephen."

I started to realize there's a reason, and it's that Stephen is thoughtful, collegial, based on the idea that there are long-term relationships here that need to be developed and paid attention to and fostered and nurtured. You don't yell at the guy on the other end of the phone, even if sometimes you really want to because they're yelling at you.

Graham and I became very close over those years. We worked on many files together, but we also had fun. We worked so well together that when it came time to leave McCarthys in 1996, we formed our own entertainment law firm, called at the time Stohn Henderson LLP, and had the chance to work together building up our own offices. The firm continues to this day, though Graham left a number of years ago to become one of Canada's most effective lobbyists, working for record companies to improve their rights in the face of an onslaught of technological challenges. As I approach my seventh decade, I no longer spend too much time at the firm — but it's thriving, with seven lawyers doing only entertainment law at what is now known as Stohn Hay Cafazzo Dembroski Richmond LLP.

But back to the early days at McCarthys — a confluence of three important events occurred around that same time.

The first was a federal government reaction to the devastation it had caused in the film industry following the 1981/1982 changes to the Income Tax Act, which had gutted the financing of films. Francis Fox, the Liberal federal minister of communications, issued a new National Film and Video Policy in 1984, under which the Canadian Film Development Corporation was transformed into Telefilm Canada, and given a new mandate not only to support feature films, but also to actively support the production of television series. Telefilm was to administer a thirty-five-million-dollar Canadian Broadcast Program Development Fund to jump-start a television production industry in Canada.

The second event was that a former client resurfaced. As I previously recounted, Linda Schuyler and I first met in 1979 when, as a young lawyer just recently called to the bar, I had given her some free legal advice to help her purchase rights for a short film. Unbeknown to her or anyone at the time, that short film turned out to be the first of *The Kids of Degrassi Street*. About seven years later we met again.

In the interim, she and her producer/director partner Kit Hood had produced twenty-six short films collectively known as *The Kids of Degrassi Street*, featuring the lives of primary school children, with each episode focused on a particular issue facing a particular child. The Canadian Broadcasting Corporation (CBC) was keen on a new format that would use similar storytelling techniques, but would age up to junior high school and feature an ensemble cast of characters with interweaving storylines. *Degrassi Junior High* was born.

CBC ordered a first season of thirteen episodes of *Degrassi Junior High*, with an overall budget close to four million dollars; but the licence fee from CBC would only cover a portion of that budget. The rest of the financing would largely come from a combination of a licence fee from PBS in the United States (through its flagship station WGBH Boston) and, vitally, investment by Telefilm Canada out of its new Canadian Broadcast Program Development Fund.

Linda and Kit needed the help of an entertainment lawyer, and she remembered my having helped her years earlier. I became the lawyer for Linda and Kit's production company, Playing With Time, Inc.

> **Linda:** Until then I had done all the business side of it myself. As time went on I had to get more and more proper about things, and one day I thought "I'm in too deep." And it came to me, "Remember that lovely young man who said to me, 'Maybe we'll work together in the future. This first meeting is free.'" My partner at the time was Kit Hood, and I said, "I think we should go back and get the advice of Stephen Stohn. I trusted him; he was a straight shooter, and I didn't think he was out for himself in any way." So Stephen took over the legal side of things, and more and more the business affairs side also.

The third in the confluence of important events that occurred around this time was the return to Canada of the soon-to-be mogul Ivan Fecan (pronounced *Fet-san*).

Ivan was a powerhouse even back then. He would eventually become the head of the entire Bell Media empire in Canada, but at the time he had left a job at CBC Radio to work in the United States for Brandon Tartikoff, the NBC programmer behind such monster hits as *Cheers, L.A. Law, The Cosby Show,* and *Seinfeld.*

Ivan learned a tremendous amount about programming working with Tartikoff as his mentor. CBC had been sorry to see him leave in the first place; now they wanted him back, enough that they offered him the job of heading up their English-language TV network. Ivan jumped at the chance.

In one of his first meetings in his new job back in Canada, he called Linda into his office with some news. "I really like *Degrassi Junior High*. Right now we're broadcasting it Sunday afternoons, but I have good news for you. We're moving it to prime time on Monday evenings."

"No, you're not!" said Linda, "You can't do that. We're not ready for prime time!"

Ivan was bit taken aback and replied, in essence, "Why don't we pretend that you're the producer, and so you produce the show; and I'm the broadcaster, so I decide when and where to broadcast it...."

Linda called me in a panic. "He's going to ruin our show! He wants to move it, and it won't work."

"Hold on," I said, "I know who Ivan Fecan is. Peter Grant talks in glowing terms about him. He's a genius. He's worked with Brandon Tartikoff." I paused, and then added, "Sometimes you just have to let go ... you have to hitch your wagon to a star. Ivan is a star. Hitch your wagon to him!"

Linda called Ivan back and said she'd go along with him, but only if he promised he wouldn't cancel the show when his gambit failed, that he'd order more episodes and move *Degrassi Junior High* back to Sunday afternoons where it belonged.

Now, contractually, Linda didn't have a leg to stand on. CBC held the broadcast rights, and she had no say in when they broadcast it. But Ivan just laughed and agreed, and he moved the show to Monday evenings at 8:30 p.m., immediately following the NBC sitcom *The Fresh Prince of Bel-Air* starring Will Smith.

Ivan knew what he was doing. The ratings on both *The Fresh Prince of Bel-Air* and *Degrassi Junior High* turned out to be in the millions.

The *Degrassi* franchise, or should I say the prime time *Degrassi* franchise, was up and running.

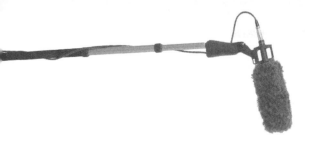

12
PATSY CLINE AND
K.D. LANG

At around the same time I began working as the lawyer for *Degrassi*, my career as a music lawyer was also beginning to flourish.

Someone came into my life in a place called Albert's Hall, a place whose name conjures up visions of a grand concert hall, worthy of mention in a Beatles song. But the Albert's Hall I'm talking about is a small, crowded space on the second floor of the Brunswick House, a tavern in the university district of Toronto. Despite — or maybe because of — its reputation for more than a century of drunken revelries, wet T-shirt contests, and police raids, the Brunswick House also attracted many eclectic musical acts.*

It was a Tuesday in the fall of 1984 when I got a call from my friend Jody Colero, himself an eclectic musician, to say I "must" go see a young singer playing that week at Albert's Hall. "I won't say anything more," he said. "Just go and see for yourself."

I assured Jody I'd go, but I hadn't gotten around to it yet when two days later I got a similar call from Christopher Ward. "Stephen, I can't describe the music properly, but you'll love this young woman called k.d.

---

* Ye Olde Brunswick House, as it was also known, was founded in 1876 and operated as a tavern continuously until 2016. The space now operates as a drug store.

lang playing at Albert's Hall. It's country, but it's not country. I don't know what else to say … it's mesmerizing."

Again I promised to go, but I still hadn't made it there when the phone rang at eight thirty on Saturday evening. I was settling down to a restful glass of wine after a nice dinner at the end of a hectic week. The caller was one of my law colleagues, Nancy Reason, whose husband Liam Lacey was the rock critic at the *Globe and Mail*. "Stephen, we're here at the Brunswick Tavern. You live just four houses away. We're holding a seat for you, and if you're not over here in five minutes, we're coming over there and breaking your legs!"

Five minutes later I was sitting with Nancy and Liam. Also in attendance was Richard Flohil, the legendary Canadian folk promoter, known for his passion for authentic music and for the artists who make authentic music; he'd seen k.d. perform in Edmonton and was the one who had promoted her to Albert's Hall.

I don't think there was room for more than eighty of us, sitting around cramped tables, craning our necks toward a tiny stage in the corner.

It was truly a life-altering moment; k.d. was sensational.* The song that I really remember from that night was "Johnny Get Angry," a cover of a frivolous Top 40 single, in k.d.'s hands laden with irony arising from its "ode to macho" lyrics:

Johnny Get Angry
Johnny get mad
Give me the biggest lecture I ever had
I want a brave man

---

* I refer to her here as "k.d." as that is how she has been known for a long time; but back in those early years she was often simply "Kathy" to us.

I want a cave man
Johnny show me that you care, really care for me *

She wore square glasses and was throwing herself around in this tiny corner of the room, whooping, dancing, lurching within inches of the audience, and singing with an incredibly powerful voice. In the middle of the song she suddenly screamed and threw herself to the ground, and the music stopped completely. We all gasped, in shock, as she remained immobile for what seemed like an eternity but in reality was probably about thirty seconds. Suddenly she leaped up and finished the rest of the song to raucous relief and applause.

She closed with Patsy Cline's "I Fall to Pieces," which is exactly what almost everyone in the audience did when she left the stage. Later I learned of k.d.'s real passion for the late, legendary country singer Patsy Cline, and of k.d.'s conviction — which I was prepared to completely embrace — that she was the reincarnated spirit of Patsy Cline.**

I didn't introduce myself. I was simply taken by the performance, and very grateful for the people who got me there, because I knew at the time it was a seminal moment ... in her career, and in the world of music.

On Monday morning I got into the office at 9:00 a.m. and immediately called up the A&R directors of the major record companies in Canada, as well as Canada's largest independent label, Quality Records, and left identical messages for each of them saying exactly the following words:

---

* Johnny Get Angry
  Words and Music by Hal David and Sherman Edwards
  Copyright © 1962 BMG Rights Management (U.K.) Ltd. and Keith-Valerie
  Music Corp., a division of Music Sales Corporation (ASCAP) and Casa
  David Music. Copyright Renewed. All Rights for BMG Rights Management
  (U.K.) Ltd. administered by BMG Rights Management (U.S.) LLC. All
  Rights Reserved. Used by Permission.
  Reprinted by Permission of Hal Leonard LLC.
** Hence the name of her band at the time, The Reclines.

"I have seen the future of music ... and her name is k.d. lang."

I followed with, "The music is phenomenal; it can't be categorized in any way. It's not country; it's not pop; it's just a brand new way of expressing something extraordinarily universal in a mesmerizing way. I have no vested interest in this. I'm not her lawyer. I'm not her manager. I've never met her. But this has to be on your radar."

About three weeks later, I got a call from Larry Wanagas, and I was nervous to return the call because the message was, "I'm k.d. lang's manager. I hear you've been calling record labels on behalf of my client." When I called him back, the first words out of my mouth were, "Please understand I wasn't trying to represent anything to anyone. I just wanted to express my enthusiasm for a genuine talent and that's it!"

But his reply was upbeat. "I'm delighted that you did, and I'd like to come in and meet you. Could you help us move her career forward?"

That was the start of a relationship that lasted more than a decade.

Larry: It all started with a number of people seeing k.d. at the Edmonton Folk Festival in the summer of '84. Sylvia Tyson was delayed, so k.d.'s set got extended by half an hour. Sylvia's band was at the side of the stage watching the extended set by k.d., and she tore it up. Richard Flohil was also at that show, and talked Derek Andrews into giving us a rare booking in Toronto at the time, a full week at Albert's Hall. The first night was okay busy, but after that you couldn't get into the venue: people lined up on the stairs, out the door and down the street. It was amazing, thrilling, unexpected. It couldn't have gone any better. It basically opened the doors for us for everything that followed.

As Larry and I got to know each other, I discovered how he and k.d. had connected. He owned a recording studio in Edmonton and a bluegrass band had been recording there when one of the fiddle players asked if he could rent the studio to audition and rehearse his band. Larry obliged, and meanwhile the fiddle player had run an ad in the *Edmonton Journal* looking for a female country swing singer. An eighteen-year-old Kathy Dawn Lang answered the ad several days later and walked in the door.

Larry: We heard her sing "Last Cheater's Waltz" (a song made popular by Bob Wills and the Texas Playboys). She was immediately hired. The guy rehearsed the band, and they did a first show at Devil's Lake Corral, north of Edmonton; k.d. sang great. After the show, he paid everyone and then said, "Thanks, that's it." Turns out he was doing it all as an anniversary gift to his wife! All that work auditioning, rehearsing, it was a lot of work for one show. I was sitting there with k.d. and she said, "Well, what am I going to do now? I thought I was in a band!" I said, "Come and see me at my studio on Monday, I've got a few ideas," and that led to fifteen years of working together.

There was a period of some months in early 1985 when there was genuine interest from various labels in Canada, but they admitted they were confused about how to market k.d.'s music. While the songs were not mainstream pop, they weren't country either; they seemed to defy categorization.

Larry, himself, was unsure of what direction to take. He had never managed an artist before and wasn't even sure if he was the right man for the job of managing k.d. I encouraged him by saying something that I believe to this day, that finding a good manager is harder than finding a record deal or a publishing deal, and that the best manager for a particular artist is not necessarily the one with the most experience, or the biggest roster, or the biggest Rolodex.* Rather, I told Larry that I look

---

* A Rolodex is a rotating holder of index cards, used to store information on business and personal contacts, back in the days before contacts apps and personal computers and smartphones.

for three essential qualities in a manager: (1) honesty, (2) business sense, and (3) complete conviction that the artist is one of the best talents ever to arrive on Earth.

Larry qualified on all three counts.

> **Larry:** k.d. wasn't interested in the business side; she was driven simply by her music. And as for me, Stephen gave me peace of mind. I'd never done any of this stuff before. I was certainly confident in my ability to recognize talent. I was confident in her ability. But I had never worked in the business. It really was a boost in confidence for me to know that Stephen was part of the team.

We talked about the best way to proceed, about the merits of signing with a label in Canada versus signing directly to one of the major record labels in the U.S. It might seem like an obvious choice — the U.S. labels would have much more money and marketing clout — but I don't think it is. In many cases it is better to sign with a local label that is more invested in your success and, in that way, to have the dedicated attention that your home country can provide, rather than possibly getting lost in the shuffle of a major U.S. label with hundreds of acts on their roster.

However, in k.d.'s case I felt it was imperative to sign with a major international label. Her music not only deserved, but required, the focus of a major marketing machine that was able to transcend the obvious difficulty of categorizing her music, and to develop a cross-format campaign that would ideally propel her music outward from the U.S. toward Canada and elsewhere. I worried that even if a local label achieved some success in Canada, it would be misinterpreted as "regional" or "quirky" in the world market and might never expand outside of Canada unless a major international label was already invested in her career.

The head of A&R at CBS Records in Canada, David Bendeth, offered a possible way forward. He was determined to sign k.d., at least to an initial development deal. We didn't want a development deal, we were determined to have a full multi-album commitment. And, of course, David represented the Canadian arm of CBS only, whereas, we wanted the backing of the international arm. David was passionate about the project, though, and determined to garner commitment from his New York office. We had many discussions about different approaches to take, while he worked to whet the appetite of his New York counterparts. After several weeks, it became clear that the New York office of CBS was truly interested in k.d., but to seal the deal they would need to see her on stage. Larry worked with Richard Flohil and, aided by the imprimatur of interest from CBS, as well as Richard's extensive network of contacts, a showcase set at the Bottom Line was arranged.

The Bottom Line is one of New York's fabled venues. A big barn of a place with a large stage against the centre of one wall, it could hold several hundred customers. While hardly an intimate atmosphere, it somehow managed to be a homey, welcoming environment, with devoted staff, unobstructed views, and a strict no-smoking policy even in its early days.* Pictures of some of the thousands of artists who had performed there were on its walls, artists as diverse as Eric Clapton, Barry Manilow, Lyle Lovett, Peter Gabriel, The Turtles, Ravi Shankar, Chuck Mangione, The Violent Femmes, Bruce Springsteen, Laura Nyro, Tony Orlando, and Pete Seeger; the list goes on and on.

At the time, k.d. was on a cross-Canada tour, and Larry was in Edmonton, so we all made our ways separately to the Bottom Line for k.d.'s showcase on May 2, 1985.

The stage at the Bottom Line was many times bigger than the tiny corner of Albert's Hall, and k.d. not only sang her heart out but also threw herself over every inch of the expanse. The set was everything we could have hoped for. Near the end k.d. was so carried away in her performance that she jumped onto the stage-side table where the CBS executives were sitting, gyrating as she sang so that her sweat flew onto them. They loved it.

---

* It opened its doors in 1974 and closed in 2004. Archive recordings of most of the performances at the Bottom Line are available via www.bottomlinearchive.com.

When we all got together after the set, the CBS executives pressed for a meeting, either right away or early the next morning. However, k.d. was in the middle of her tour and had to fly back immediately to Canada. A meeting was arranged for three weeks later.

CBS offered to pay for our travel to the meeting, but Larry and I insisted on covering the costs ourselves so that we would maintain our independence. Exciting as this all was, we didn't want to feel even slightly beholden to any record company until a deal was signed.

Three weeks later found the three of us (Larry, k.d., and me) flying into New York on the morning Boston–New York Shuttle after a midnight lobster dinner and meeting with the folks at Rounder Records. (As the pre-eminent independent folk/rock label, Rounder was also keen to sign k.d., but understood our desire to sign with a major label.) As we travelled, k.d. and I were seated together, and it was the first time I really got a chance to speak with her, just the two of us.

My impression at the time was of a surprisingly shy young woman, who nevertheless emanated a directness and power, whose words were completely unfiltered to the extent they almost seemed not to be coming from her but rather from some incredibly wise entity who was directly tapped into the inner workings of our universe. To put it a different way, it was almost as if she were merely a physical embodiment through which the music was releasing itself into our world.

Even to a business-minded lawyer like myself, it seemed natural to think of her as what she believed she was, the reincarnated spirit of Patsy Cline. It wasn't that she was pretending to be Patsy, but it really seemed like she was being deeply driven by a muse of some sort. I would later think of that muse as the "timeless mind"; others might think of it as God or the collective unconscious or even the Force, but for k.d., if that muse were to have a name, Patsy was it.

Our meeting at the "Black Rock" headquarters of CBS in midtown Manhattan was set for 12:30 p.m., and we expected a short in-office meeting followed by lunch at one of the great restaurants in the area.

We were ushered in, and the CBS executives immediately started talking about potential big-name producers, so clearly there was a deal to be made. This was extraordinarily exciting. As a young lawyer, here I was in this rarefied atmosphere talking with people who were very interested in signing this unique talent I represented. The meeting went on until about 2:00 p.m., when we were ushered out with an "our people will be in touch."

We were surprised, since we'd been invited for a 12:30 p.m. meeting, that we hadn't been offered anything to eat. To polite Canadians, it seemed rude. So rude, in fact, that in the elevator going down to the lobby k.d. turned to me and said, "I will never sign with CBS!"

I immediately remonstrated, "It's not personal! They are New Yorkers; their sense of time is different from our sense of time. Yes, they invited us over the lunch hour, but it just wouldn't occur to them to stop working to grab a sandwich. It's just the way they are; we can't hold it against them!"

"I will never sign with them," she replied, and then she paused and added, "Patsy wouldn't want me to."

To which there is no reply.

I do remember that we went across the street to a deli and had something to eat. It would have been salad for k.d., and probably burgers for me and Larry. We talked it all through and k.d. recognized what I was saying. This was a real opportunity. There'd be real money and a chance to get her music out with a very prestigious record label.* But she stopped the conversation, put her hand on my shoulder, looked me straight in the eye and reassured me, "Stephen, don't worry. Not signing now is the right thing to do. It is all going to work out, we will sign a big record deal; it's

---

* At the time, CBS was still probably best known for its Barbra Streisand recordings, but their artists also included such heavyweights as Bruce Springsteen, Bob Dylan, The Bangles, Willie Nelson, The Clash, Billy Joel, Elvis Costello, Earth, Wind & Fire, and continued sales from the most successful double-album of all time, Pink Floyd's *The Wall*.

going to happen." The tables had turned, and it was the artist who was giving her lawyer some business reassurance! The clear implication was that Patsy had everything very well in hand.

Well, as it turned out, Patsy *did* have everything very well in hand.*

There may have been many people from CBS in attendance at the Bottom Line showcase, but there was also a scout from Warner Music. He immediately phoned his London, England, office to get in touch with Seymour Stein, the head of Sire Records, a label Warner had bought seven years previously. He thought Seymour would be very interested in k.d.

To this day Seymour Stein remains one of the true "old school" record people in the industry, whose passion is making great music rather than making hits.** But making hits he has. In 1976 he discovered The Ramones, and co-founded Sire Records to sign them and other acts such as The Climax Blues Band. As the years progressed, he discovered and signed other unique talents, including Talking Heads, The Pretenders, The Cure, The Smiths, and Echo and the Bunnymen.

Seymour's most commercially successful signing occurred in 1984: Madonna. Her first singles and an early album on Sire had some success, then in 1984 — less than a year prior to k.d.'s showcase set at the Bottom Line — Madonna had achieved global recognition when her second studio album, *Like a Virgin*, topped the charts in several countries and became her first #1 album on the *Billboard* 200.***

---

* Two years later k.d. realized a different connection with Patsy Cline when Patsy's long-time producer Owen Bradley came out of retirement to produce k.d.'s *Shadowland* album.

** It's a real inspiration to see somebody like that, in an industry that we think of as being so corporate. I see him at industry events such as the MIDEM Conference, held annually in France. He is driven to be in and around places where music is happening and where talent can be discovered.

*** Madonna has since added seven more #1 albums, to go along with thirty-eight Top 10 singles on the *Billboard* Hot 100.

So Seymour was on a long-term hot streak when he got the phone call from the Warner scout about k.d.'s performance at the Bottom Line. When he discovered that k.d. was appearing at a Klondike Days celebration the following week at the Westin Hotel in Edmonton, Alberta, Seymour got on a plane to Edmonton, arriving jet-lagged halfway through her performance.

At the close of the performance he introduced himself to k.d. and immediately announced he loved her and her music and wanted to sign her.

She was thrilled. Here was the perfect company and the perfect person: a record company that had achieved flagship status with the success of Madonna, together with a head of the company who had a reputation for fostering individuality and creativity. It was a match made in heaven.

Patsy would have agreed completely.

The only practical difficulty was doing the deal. I was put in touch with Seymour's right-hand guy, a lawyer named Rick Streicher. I'd never met Rick before, but we hit it off immediately, and I quickly came to understand why he and Seymour worked so well together. They were both extremely attentive to the small details of their work — Seymour on the creative side, and Rick on the business side — but both were predominantly focused on creating an environment where their artists could flourish creatively.

I was trying to get as much money in upfront advances and the highest royalty terms that I could for k.d., but recording contracts are long and tediously detailed: almost all the definitions and clauses are designed to slowly chip away at the royalties the artist could receive. Royalties at the time were often expressed as percentages of "SRLP," the suggested retail list price,* but were then reduced dramatically by deductions for

---

* Today they are almost always expressed as a percentage of "PPD," the published price to dealers, essentially the wholesale price.

breakage,* packaging costs,** potential returns, so-called "free goods" (essentially promotional costs), discounts for sales at lower than full price, discounts for sales outside the United States, discounts for sales in "new formats" (such as CDs!) and more. The granddaddy of all the deductions was the treatment of recording costs and at least a portion of the video costs as a direct deduction from the artist's royalties; in other words, the artist had to pay for the costs of making their records and usually at least half the costs of making their videos out of their own royalties before they would be entitled to receive a penny.

In fairness to record companies, the majority of releases are unsuccessful. An A&R director who had only one successful artist out of every ten signed would be considered a genius. So the costs of unsuccessful records needed to be recouped out of the revenues from the successful ones. Regardless, the negotiation of each and every clause could easily take months, with the lawyers arguing over hundreds of potential changes to the so-called "standard" agreements.

We didn't have months to negotiate the agreement. In fact, we had only six days — k.d. was leaving for Japan to appear for a month at a World Science Fair (of all things) as part of Expo 85, followed by more travelling and performing in Japan and other parts of Asia. Everyone wanted to have a signed deal before she left.

Rick and I had a conversation. The actual advances and basic royalty terms — including escalations based on success — were relatively easy to work out, as both sides were motivated to reach agreement. The difficulty was the hundreds of technical points in the contract. I then said something to Rick that I've never said to any other lawyer since. "We don't really know each other, we've just met, but we seem to have similar sensibilities. I'm a Canadian, and maybe we do things a little bit differently here, but

---

* A holdover from the 1950s and earlier when 78 rpm records actually did sometimes break when they were shipped to stores.

** A misnomer, since they bore no relationship at all to the actual costs of packaging, the deductions being about ten times higher than the real costs.

the idea of spending months going back and forth negotiating all the technical points will drive up the time involved and the legal bill, and maybe make everybody feel important in the process ... but perhaps there's a way to get it all done by Friday. If you promise to give me absolutely the best technical terms you can conceive of giving, the ones that in the past you have given to true superstar artists after months of negotiations, I in turn promise not to come back with any requests to better the terms."

Rick kept his promise, and I kept mine. He came up with a beautiful agreement. It was wonderful for me as a young lawyer because I got to see a changed contract from a standard opening offer to what was truly a major superstar contract. Seeing what was really possible to negotiate was eye-opening. (It was a source of some pride that fifteen years later, when k.d. switched managers, I got a call from the heavyweight entertainment lawyer who was taking over in Los Angeles, asking how I had managed to secure some of the clauses in that original Sire agreement. "I've been trying to get some of those terms for major clients and haven't succeeded. How did you ever do it?")

Friday of that week arrived, and we all met in a boardroom at the Bayshore Hotel in Vancouver. The idea was to sign the agreement in the afternoon and then celebrate that evening onboard a boat travelling around the Vancouver harbour where k.d. and her band were performing — their last performance in Canada for a while before heading to Tokyo the next day.

There were some technical mistakes in the contract that had to be corrected, and in those pre-computer days making even such small changes wasn't easy. We were running out of time, so we thought, why not sign it onboard the boat?

> **Larry:** There was a local promoter in Vancouver by the name of Bud Luxford, who had a series of shows that he called "Boatin' with Bud," and he booked k.d. to play one. Seymour came to Vancouver, got on the boat with us, and we signed the contract on the boat. My wife

recalls it was her role to keep Seymour from going over the side of the boat ... he wasn't afraid of having a few drinks!

We knew there was a bit of an issue because there would be some press on the boat, and we did not want anybody to know that this signing was taking place. Seymour wanted to have a proper press release at a proper time. So we agreed to keep the signing on the down low. At some point during the night we'd simply go off into a secluded corner and sign away. We hadn't really thought about where the secluded corner might be, and when we got on the boat, we realized there wasn't one.

The only private location onboard was the pilot's cabin, so we sought and received permission to go there after k.d. had played her first set. At the appointed time, we knocked on the door and entered, but it was completely dark inside. "Where is the light switch?" we asked. "Oh, it's

As described in chapter 19, years later k.d. came to our rescue when Neil Young became seriously ill just before the 2005 *Juno Awards*. She galvanized the crowd with a powerful rendition of his song "Helpless."

against regulations to turn on the lights," the pilot said, "It would blind us to what's ahead in the dark!"

Further, there wasn't a table, or even any seats in the pilot's cabin. It was simply a small cramped space with the pilot standing at the controls at the front. After some discussion, we did the only thing we could. We all got down on our hands and knees — on the not-very-comfortable corrugated floor — with Rick Streicher holding a flashlight pointed at the four copies of the sixty-page contract lying open on the floor. One by one we each initialled every page and signed the final page, k.d. on her own behalf, Seymour on Sire's behalf, and Larry and I as witnesses.

It was an extraordinary experience. You had to be there. I still like to think of us all on our hands and knees, as if kneeling at some imaginary altar. For years I would joke with Rick that we could get out of the contract at any time "because at the moment of signing we were outside the territorial waters of Canada and under international maritime law."*

When the night was over, I looked back toward the boat after saying goodbyes and saw k.d. on the deck of the boat, the light from the top of the mast creating a halo around her head. She was as radiant as an angel. A brand new chapter of her life and career was beginning.

I couldn't help but wonder if Patsy might be watching k.d. also — from above — watching and smiling.

---

* In fact, we weren't and, as we both knew, it wouldn't have made any difference even if we had been.

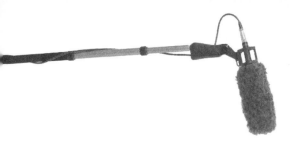

13
COWBOY JUNKIES

In most cases, artists have a very firm sense of their own direction. They are who they are, and if you try to change their artistic direction you're not being a true counsellor. But that doesn't mean they don't need to talk things through, and where the career advice doesn't conflict with their artistic sensibilities, they can be very grateful for a nudge or two along the road. This was true for k.d., and it was perhaps even more true for another big act that came my way.

It must have been starting into winter. Certainly it was dark outside, on a late afternoon in 1987 when my friend and law colleague Graham Henderson came into my office with a cassette tape in his hand. We had only recently started working together at the large downtown law firm of McCarthy Tétrault. Graham had originally thought he wanted to be a litigator, but after six months in the litigation department he had asked to start working with me and learn about entertainment law.

"Would you please listen to this and tell me what you think," he said, and then politely left my office, knowing that the last thing I would want is to listen to a demo tape in the same room as someone who was trying to gauge my reactions to the songs.

The tape was enchanting and hypnotic. The songs were languid and yet arresting, reminding me of k.d. lang in that it wasn't pop music — it simply was, and what it was, was beautiful. The singer's voice was extraordinary, at once angelic and accessible, not deep and powerfully melodious like k.d. lang's, but rather floating like an angel on top of it all. In both cases the singers and their songs defied the pop charts of the time.

I couldn't stop myself from listening again to the tape before heading next door to Graham's office to find out the story behind it all.

Graham described seeing the band at Clinton's, a neighbourhood club, how they were called Cowboy Junkies and consisted of three siblings — Michael, Peter, and Margo Timmins — together with Michael's long-time friend Alan Anton, and how they had already released a self-pressed EP with the improbable (and satirical) title *Whites Off Earth Now!!* The demo tape I had been listening to had been recently recorded, live, on one microphone, during a single twelve-hour session, in an odd location: the Church of the Holy Trinity in Toronto.* But Graham left out one important detail.

Graham neglected to mention that he had already seen the band numerous times, not just because he loved their music, but also because he had become particularly enamoured of Margo.**

In any event, I said to Graham, "Why don't you bring them in for a meeting? Playing this kind of music, they're probably starving musicians. The least we can do is give them some coffee and cookies and have a chat."

> **Graham:** It was the twenty-eighth of November in 1987, right after Trinity Session had been recorded, and I had just started working with Stephen. I had a girl-friend at that point in time, who was maybe the biggest Cowboy Junkies fan in the world. She heard they were doing a show at the Rivoli, so we went. It was nearly empty and she walked me up to the front and said, "You

---

* Michael later recounted that in order to get permission to record at the church, they temporarily renamed themselves the Timmins Family Singers.

** Margo is incredibly bright and forthright. In the early 1990s she was named "one of the fifty most beautiful people in the world" by *People* magazine.

can stand here, but I can't watch this show with you. I have to watch the band by myself."

It was almost a religious experience. So I stood there. Out on the stage walked Marg, and suddenly it's "Good God, I think I'm in love," and I sort of forgot my girl-friend in the back corner.

I remember going in to Stephen and saying there's this great band and I don't really know what to do about it. He said, "You should maybe try to talk to them." And I thought, *I'm not really going to do that.*

But then a few days later Reid Diamond from Shadowy Men on a Shadowy Planet, came bustling out of Vortex Records, and he said, "Our favourite band is about to get signed by a Canadian indie label," and he was horrified at this prospect. He said they deserved better; they should have an international deal. I asked, "How do you know this?" He said, "I was sitting at the Queen Mother restaurant, and who was sitting beside me: Margo and her mom."

I think it's one of maybe half a dozen times I've called an artist. I got Michael on the phone, and they came in for a meeting in one of the boardrooms, with Stephen there as a mentor to guide me through this process.

Margo: We arrived at the office way up in one of the big black TD Bank towers. Before being a singer in the Junkies, I had been a legal secretary. I had not been a very good legal secretary, and lawyers weren't exactly my favourite thing, mostly because they always yelled at me. And now that I'm older, I realize why.

I was very reluctant to have this meeting. I thought, *What does this lawyer want with us? We have no money.* But anyway, we went up the big tower and we were all excited because they took us into the boardroom, and they gave us free cookies and we were really excited. Look! Food! And I asked for some more. And in walked Stephen and Graham. And Stephen started first by explaining — and I think he does this with all the artists — about the realistic prospects in the music industry. Basically, it was, "You're not going to make any money for a long time and probably not then either, and even if you do have some success and start to sell records, you're still not going to make very much money." And it was okay 'cause being musicians we never expected to make any money, 'cause that's what happens.

I can remember thinking ... Stephen was very gentle, soft-spoken, but very precise, and you knew he knew what he was talking about. He wasn't sitting there saying you guys are going to be rock stars; he was sitting there being very honest about the industry, and I immediately liked him. As I say, he was gentle, so I liked that part of him, which wasn't my experience with lawyers....

The Cowboy Junkies were charming and very intelligent. We talked about what they wanted to do, and they immediately made one point crystal clear: they would never sign a major label recording deal. They had zero desire to have anything to do with any record company, anywhere at any time, because they felt it would pollute their music. A small independent label that simply wanted to distribute their music was a possibility, but a major label was not.* They recognized that their music

---

* At the time, the six major labels were CBS (now Sony), MCA (now called Universal Music), Capitol-EMI (now part of Universal), Polygram (which merged with MCA and is now part of Universal), RCA (which was acquired by BMG and is now part of Sony), and Warner Elektra Atlantic (WEA for short, now called Warner Music).

was not Top 40 material, and they didn't want to be influenced to change their music or style in any way.

> **Margo:** Our worry in the early days was that we would lose control. We never really got into music to make money; it would be nice to make money, but we never expected to, and [what we wanted] was to make the music we wanted to make. We were young, but we weren't that young; we weren't in our teens — we were in our late twenties — so we appreciated that a record company's mission is to sell their product, and in order to do that they had a specific plan, and that goes along with singles and all that kind of stuff. We were scared that they would take away what we loved by trying to mould us into a success ... 'cause that's their job. They're not going to sign you so you can sit in your basement and write whatever you want to write. That was our fear, and *The Trinity Session* was to us something really unique, and we really didn't want it to be tampered with ... and we were afraid that by signing contracts that they're bigger than us, and we wouldn't be able to control it, and we would end up losing something valuable, which was basically us, that we wouldn't be able to maintain ourselves as a band. It would destroy us.

At the end of that first meeting I found myself giving them a challenge. The challenge was one I had placed on myself in my teens, and that I have continued placing on myself throughout my life: write down exactly what it is you want.

It seems like it's a supremely easy thing to do, because in short order you could say, "I'd like to have a billion dollars. I'd like to be married to a Hollywood star or starlet." Good, whatever, just write it all down.

Then, once you've written it down, go back and ask yourself *why* it is you want each thing, and whether that's what you really want. Are there other things that you are missing? Slowly you discover that maybe everything you wrote down the first time isn't at all what you want. As you go deeper you start to realize, "I'm not sure I want a billion dollars because it could mean that people engage with me for the wrong reasons, and I might always be questioning where they are coming from. If I had kids, would I be worried that they were going to be kidnapped? And actually, I'm not sure I want to live in Hollywood, starlet or not; maybe I really just want someone who loves me for who I am!"

The more you think about it, the money, the fame, and the lifestyle aren't all that much of a driver. You start to realize health is important. And the love and respect of friends, family, colleagues, and even people that you don't really know all that well are all tremendously important. Each individual will answer the question in different ways; some might want to make more of a personal impact; others might be more outwardly focused. Regardless, if you go through the exercise in depth, it can take a long time to answer the questions: What would I like to be in six months' time? In two years' time? In five years' time? What would my world be like if I could do and be everything that I wanted?

I find it an overwhelmingly powerful exercise because if you can actually get through all the layers of self-deceit and rationalization and wish fulfillment, and actually get down to the core of it all — then fix the core goals in abundant detail in your mind — something amazing can happen. Your mind now clearly knows what it is you are focusing on, what you are really reaching toward. And all aspects of your conscious and subconscious mind can work together to move you toward your goals.

There's one important subtlety to this exercise, and it is perhaps what had triggered me to challenge Cowboy Junkies to respond to it: when you dig down to the real goals, they are inevitably positive. A superficial goal may be negative — to lose weight, or give up smoking — but the real deep-down goal is positive — to be healthy and energized. The problem with negative goals is that they involve focusing on things you don't want, which confuses what the real goal is and probably sabotages it.

Cowboy Junkies knew what they didn't want — a record deal — but the real question was, what *did* they want? They were receptive to the challenge, and we all agreed to meet again.

> **Margo:** I remember him asking us the questions of what do you want, what do you want to get out of this. You have to be honest with yourself before you step into the big pond. He made us feel, even though we were in the dark towers way up above Toronto, that it was safe, and that we were in good hands, and that he knew what those waters held. His whole thing was to be clear: "Who are you guys and what do you want to do?" And that was something we knew — we weren't children — we knew what we wanted to preserve. And Stephen was the right lawyer for us because he could understand and appreciate that. With a lot of people, it's all about, "Don't you want to become a star and don't you want to make a lot of money?" That wasn't our goal, and that part of the business has always scared us, and Stephen got that.

When we regrouped a week or so later, they had clearly done a lot of thinking. They decided their primary goal as a group was to perform music, to share with others the joy they felt in making their music. They hoped that over the years they could perform for lots of people. But they also recognized that in some years their music might be more popular than in other years, and whether they were playing for a small number of people who appreciated them, or a large number of people because their music happened to be in vogue that year, they just wanted to always be playing their music for others.

That was an excellent, positive, and achievable goal. So I asked them if they were open to a suggestion to help them perform to larger crowds.

Of course, they replied yes, and then I asked, "Supposing there was a large record company that allowed you to do exactly what you wanted to do, that contractually would permit you to record exactly the music you wanted, in exactly the way that you wanted, and then would release your music to reach a larger audience — would that be a good thing?"

They agreed, subject to a major caveat, namely that they didn't think that would ever be possible.

"There are at least two major U.S. record executives Graham and I know from past experience who might be open to working with you in that way. And there may be others," I said. "We can't know that unless we try." We went on to discuss the two particular executives, Howard Thompson at Elektra and Bob Buziak at RCA.

Howard was the head of the A&R department at the storied Elektra Records label in New York. From the early days of Judy Collins, Tom Rush, the Paul Butterfield Blues Band, and the Doors, to the then more recent Tracy Chapman, The Cars, and 10,000 Maniacs, Elektra was known as a label that respected artistic vision. And Howard himself was a true music devotee, having worked his way up from being, in his words, "the tea-boy" at Trident Studios, London, to being assistant engineer, editor/copyist, and then disk-cutting engineer, before figuring out that what he really wanted to be was an A&R person, someone who discovers, nurtures, develops, and signs new artists to a record company.

I had come to know Bob Buziak as he had been the manager of my friend and client Tom Cochrane (whose "Boy Inside the Man" single from the *Tom Cochrane and Red Rider* album was in the midst of receiving some well-deserved international attention). But Bob was no longer a manager. He had been hired as president of RCA Records in New York, a label that was undergoing a major transformation under his new leadership. RCA had been largely resting on its laurels as the distributor of Elvis Presley recordings, but under Bob the company was looking to aggressively reshape its repertoire for a younger audience.*

---

* One of Bob's first signings at RCA was Bruce Hornsby.

The band was intrigued and decided to set their goal on Elektra or RCA. So Graham and I asked for, and received, the necessary authority to seek out possible recording deals. Top of the list would be Howard and Bob, but we would also send out tapes to a broad array of other major labels and larger independent record companies in Canada, the U.S., and the U.K. We were all clear, though, that no agreement that gave the band anything less than full artistic control would be entered into. We had to find a record company that really got the music and didn't want to change it.

After the band left, Graham and I talked about how to move forward. In the course of our discussion Graham said something about what *Marg* had said. "Marg?" I asked, ears perking up. Graham stammered slightly, "Sorry, I mean Margo." I raised my eyebrows. And then Graham confessed, "I sort of like her."

I smiled and said, "Graham, you are going to lead this project. I'll give you all the help I can and will be there whenever you need me, but the band and the outside world is going to know that you are the key driver."

Graham: Stephen's style is to make sure you understand what your client wants. A lot of people make the mistake that they know best. Creative control was what mattered most the Junkies. They thought that meant they shouldn't sign with a major record company. Stephen listened to what they really wanted.

What I came to understand about recording contracts is that creative control is one of the shortest discussions you will have in any negotiation with a record company, from that era anyway, because the answer was, "No." I now understand it ... Why? Because basically, the record company thinks, "I don't know who you are. Okay so I've heard a demo; I don't know what your work ethic is; I don't know if you've got a drug problem; I don't know if you stole the song; I don't know anything at all about you. I'm the one that's writing the cheques. I'm the one that's taking the chance. I'm the one that's going to call the shots. All creative decisions will be mine, with your input."

What the Junkies wanted was not about money, so Stephen and I thought maybe there were some labels out there who would give you creative control. Will you at least let us try to find one?

We made a list of all the record companies we wanted to approach, nearly a hundred in total, and Graham took on the task of contacting each of them and sending the tapes out.

Shopping for a record deal is a heartbreaking process. Inevitably, almost all the reactions are negative. You send out the tapes, and the record companies don't listen. You call them up, and they still don't listen. Then the comments start coming back — "It's beautiful, but it's too edgy," or "It's beautiful but it's not edgy enough," and "It's not Top 40, and I don't hear a single." It is hard for an artist not to feel bruised by the process.

And indeed, rejection after rejection came in to Graham, all polite and upbeat, but rejections nonetheless. In the face of it all, the Junkies decided to release *The Trinity Session* themselves, self-pressing some copies to sell at their performances.

In March 1988 things suddenly turned.

In the space of a week two record companies expressed strong interest in signing the band. And astonishingly it was not just any two record companies — which would be heady enough — it was none other than Elektra and RCA, the very two that our original goal-setting exercise had focused on so many months before.

The first in the door was Howard Thompson. He and Graham spoke at length, and he was willing to spend a lot of Elektra's money on a great studio album, and he already had a producer in mind (Lennie Petze, producer of Cyndi Lauper's smash hit album *True Colors*). He also had conversations directly with the band and impressed them with his obviously genuine love and respect for their music. Howard felt the authenticity of Cowboy Junkies was right in line with Elektra's direction.

As the conversation progressed over several days, however, Howard confessed to Graham he was worried about one thing. He felt the band needed to change its name. While Howard's reaction to the name may have been overly sensitive, it was understandable. All record companies were still smarting over the formation three years earlier of a committee of powerhouse Washington housewives, led by Tipper Gore (wife of then-Senator Al Gore). The committee, called Parents Music Resource Center (PMRC), was formed to find ways to increase parental control over children's access to music deemed to be violent, glorify drug use, or be sexual in nature.

The committee's actions led to a Senate hearing and ultimately a labelling system (called colloquially "Tipper stickers") warning of explicit songs or videos. In reaction, many record stores, including large chains, refused to sell albums with the label, and many radio stations refused to play songs from labelled albums. As an example, Frank Zappa's Grammy Award–winning album *Jazz from Hell* was required to be labelled because of the use of the word "Hell," so it was entirely possible that a group whose name included the word "Junkies" would require the label.

Howard was concerned by the name, and as the band learned of his concern, they took it as something they had feared from the beginning — a record company trying to interfere with their artistic vision.

Meanwhile, later that week I got a telephone call from Bob Buziak. We chatted for a bit, and then he got straight to the point. "That tape you sent me is beautiful. I want to put it out." At first, I was a bit confused by what he meant. Then it dawned on me that he was talking about releasing the demo tape as an album. "But Bob," I said, "It's just a demo. We need to make it into a proper album!"

Bob didn't hesitate. "You've listened to it, right? Is it not one of the most beautiful things you've ever heard?" I agreed wholeheartedly. He continued, "Well, I want to put it out exactly as is, and we're going to sell a million copies."

I could hardly believe what I was hearing, but managed to reply, "Okay, so we want a really high royalty rate because you won't have any recording costs!" He laughed and agreed.

> **Margo:** And then RCA and Bob Buziak came along and said, "Whatever you want," and gave us complete artistic freedom. Stephen and Graham were both going, "This is unusual. I've never seen this one in a contract." They were really excited about the whole RCA thing, and that's when we had to sit down as a band — are we going to take this or aren't we? I remember the many meetings when we would try to figure out what to do. At the one that we decided "Let's do it," we were sitting on the porch and we decided — people would kill for this opportunity — and here we were saying, "Oh, maybe we won't do it." We thought, "We're stronger than them. We'll be able to handle this as long as we stick together. We all know what we want." This might have stemmed from the fact that Stephen said, "Figure out who you are and what you want." We were four people very tightly on the same page. None of us wanted to be on the cover of *Rolling Stone*. We just want to make our music. (We were later on the cover in small pictures, never the big one!)

By the end of the week Graham and I were sitting in a boardroom discussing it all with a very happy band. We were surprised and delighted. The choice was never really in doubt from my point of view, but the band had needed to work it all through, choosing in the end, of course, the full artistic freedom offered by RCA.

Graham: Bob was rebuilding RCA and he didn't have many acts. He had Bruce Hornsby, Graham Parker, and Treat Her Right.

Marg and Mike dubbed him Buddha Bob because he had this Zen-like presence, totally relaxed, totally cool. He said, "We want you to be able to develop as a band. It's not about the first record, not about the second, not about the third. If we do something with this record, it'll be a bonus. The first one will lay the base, the second one will build, the third one we'll hit the home run ... or maybe the fourth."

True to Bob's word, the "demo tape" of *The Trinity Session* was released in the fall of 1988 exactly as it was originally recorded. It was not mixed, overdubbed, or edited in any way. And the name of the band remained Cowboy Junkies.

Bob did have one thing wrong, though. The album didn't just sell a million copies: it sold over three million copies worldwide.

There's another nice postscript to this story. Graham and Marg got married that fall and remain happily together to this day. It seems all that time we were helping set goals for the Junkies, Graham was doing a little goal setting of his own!

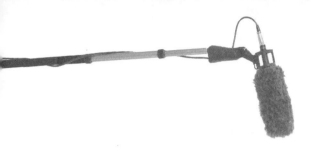

14
BLACK VELVET

Back in the 1980s and 1990s, entertainment lawyers and artist managers were pivotal to securing record deals. This was mostly because A&R directors at major labels were receiving thousands of tapes monthly from aspiring recording artists and had only so many hours in the day to listen to them all. While all the tapes would eventually be listened to, they were generally divided into "A" and "B" piles. Those in the A piles arrived from trusted sources, such as entertainment lawyers and artist managers. Even within the A piles there was a hierarchy, with the ones listened to first being those sent from lawyers or managers who had a track record of sending "quality" tapes, and whose clients were routinely getting signed by one label or another.

When an artist got signed, and had a hit, it was traditional for their entertainment lawyer to receive a commemorative gold record as a thank you. I have dozens of gold records hanging in my law offices from back in the day, and I treasure all of them.

I've since selected three of those gold records to be grouped together on a wall of our media room at home. They represent a coming together of three strikingly different female voices, similar only in their ability to utterly captivate the listener. One is the first American gold record received by k.d. lang for her first Sire album, *Absolute Torch and Twang*. The second is the first Cowboy Junkies American gold record — for *The*

Trinity Session. And the third is a rare diamond record commemorating the sale of over one million albums in Canada alone, for the eponymously titled album *Alannah Myles*. This triumvirate brings together k.d. lang's powerful voice, seemingly emanating from the depths of the universe; the crystal pure and angelic voice of Margo Timmins, and the quintessential female rocker voice of Alannah Myles.

There will never be a lang, Timmins & Myles supergroup in real life, but there is one in our media room at home!

It was Christopher who first introduced me to Alannah in 1979.

> **Christopher:** I was excited to tell Stephen about my new girlfriend, Alannah, and that she had an amazing singing voice! I might have added that she was beautiful and that on our first date she'd invited me in to hear some songs she'd written. We became both songwriting collaborators and a couple, and soon the pursuit of success for Alannah was a driving element in my life. And Stephen was there from the start. We hung out together, and I dragged him to many forgettable gigs

My imaginary lang, Timmins & Myles supergroup.

with various pickup bands. He listened to all the songs and offered trusted insights.

This was no overnight success story. For many years Christopher and Alannah created tapes of new songs and we kept shopping them to record labels, all to no avail.*

> **Christopher:** Of course, I didn't know that it would take us seven years to realize the goal of getting her a record deal and launching a career that brought worldwide success. So many guitar players, so many demos, so many "no thanks" responses from the labels in Canada. They were always polite — I had a high-profile gig on MuchMusic at the time and knew most of the executives well — but the responses were always variations on "I don't hear a hit," "It's not what we're looking for," and "We've already got a female artist." (Yes, that was the attitude at the time, as if there was a quota system.) The gist of it was that I continually had to tell Alannah that yet another label had turned us down.
>
> **Alannah:** They each sent rejection letters based on my music "not being right for their rosters" or things like that.

Alannah, herself, never had any doubts though. She had a very clear picture of herself being a worldwide superstar rocker. It was almost as if she willed herself to be a superstar, and willed Christopher and me along with her. As for me, I had total confidence not only in Alannah, but also in Christopher and his songwriting. We just kept plugging away, year after year.

---

* During this time Alannah also played the role of an aspiring singer in an episode of *The Kids of Degrassi Street*.

Christopher: She was defiant and unwavering in her faith in what we were doing, and that sustained me. And as friends and family allowed doubt to seep into their questions about our progress, Stephen was rock solid. I think he believed in me as much as the music.

Christopher and Alannah kept at it until, in 1986, they began working with a brilliant pianist, composer, and producing talent, Dave Tyson. The threesome collaborated to create three master recordings, which they played for me in early 1987, and I was blown away. They wanted my help in shopping these masters, but rather than proceed immediately I made a suggestion — a suggestion that will seem totally mundane today, but was pretty much unheard of at the time. "U.S. record labels

Alannah Myles and I celebrate her achieving a six-times platinum award at the 1990 post-*Junos* party, the same evening she won three Juno Awards. She would later go on to receive a diamond record award for selling over one million copies of her debut album in Canada alone.

will want to see Alannah perform, but she doesn't have a band, or even a lot of experience performing," I said. "So why don't we pre-empt this. Christopher, you work at MuchMusic and have access to video equipment. Why don't you create a demo video to go along with the masters, showing Alannah performing live in front of an adoring audience."

Alannah: It was Stephen who recommended we include a visual representation of our work by recording a video single for one of our three completed masters. We presented a three-song package to all of the majors in Canada, with "Just One Kiss" as our video, directed by my friend and renowned Canadian photographer Deborah Samuel.

Christopher: We shot a performance video for the song "Just One Kiss" at Toronto's Diamond Club. Alannah's friend, fashion photographer Deborah Samuel, agreed to direct it, and worked closely with Alannah on how the video would be shot.* There wasn't very much of a crowd, but we'd brought in some students as extras, and we kept moving them around the club so that from each camera angle it looked like a large, happy throng gyrating to the music!

We sent the three recordings along with the "Just One Kiss" demo video out to record companies. At first it looked like there were still no takers. But Bob Roper at Warner Music Canada liked it a lot and offered to send the package to his counterpart at Atlantic Records in New York, reasoning that it would take a bigger budget to record than he had access to.

---

* Deb went on to direct music videos for dozens of artists and record companies, as well as working for magazines such as *Rolling Stone, Entertainment Weekly, GQ, Spin,* and *Esquire.*

Christopher: While on a MuchMusic road trip in the fall of 1987, I got the call that changed it all from Tunc Erim, head of A&R at Atlantic. He said, "She is a star. I want her on my label. Who is your lawyer?"

"Stephen Stohn," I replied.

As we started negotiations for Alannah's deal with Atlantic, I met with Tunc (pronounced *Tunj*) on a number of occasions. We all became immediately fond of him — it was almost impossible not to. He was born in Turkey but, in 1966, had come to America by ship. During the trans-Atlantic crossing he had met the mother of two other Turks: the legendary Ahmet Ertegun, co-founder of Atlantic Records, and his brother and fellow Atlantic executive Nesuhi. Tunc had subsequently been offered a job at Atlantic as a tape librarian, and over the years he had worked his way up to become a key part of the Atlantic executive team.

One of Tunc's most endearing features arose from his imperfect English. It was sometimes hard to understand exactly what he was saying, particularly since he was fond of using short aphorisms that were missing something in the translation — ending up sounding something like a cross between Yogi Berra and Yoda. He would say things like "I'm happy as pig!" or "Stephen, I'm not going to go behind the back burner on this one," or "Tell me truth. Stop running 'round the bushes," all the while peppering his conversation with the vague and mysterious phrase "and this and that."*

In any event, the partnership with Atlantic was a delight. Graham Henderson worked closely with me at the time, and often he took the lead in the series of other agreements that followed.

Christopher: By this time Stephen and Graham had lots of experience in dealing with U.S. labels and the

---

* Christopher patterned the character Rudy in his book *Mac in the City of Light* after Tunc, an affectionate tribute.

negotiations began with Atlantic soon after. A management agreement with Danny Goldberg followed. Danny looked after the careers of Belinda Carlisle, Bonnie Raitt, and others; a music publishing deal for Alannah with MCA; and a lucrative merchandising agreement. Alannah was ecstatic and felt vindicated in never giving up on her big dream. And at least partially because it was achieved after so much struggle, I think Stephen took special pleasure and pride in what we'd accomplished.

While we were negotiating all these agreements for Alannah, Christopher asked us about helping to secure a publishing agreement for himself. He had written most of the songs on the album, and a music publisher would undoubtedly be interested in signing him to help administer the songs on the album and to help promote his songwriting career.

I was cautious, though, and put it to him this way: "How much do you believe in yourself?" What I meant was this. It would have been quite straightforward to secure a deal for him, but the terms — including the upfront advance, the effective level of the "commission" charged by the music publisher, and our ability to put an end date on the agreement so that all rights would revert back to Christopher after a set number of years — would all be only minimally favourable since the music publisher would have to forge the deal predicated on the reality that only a small percentage of albums are hits. Until the album was released and had achieved some measure of success, our negotiating leverage would be low.

If Christopher believed (as I did) that the album could be hugely successful, then we would be much better off waiting until later to sign a publishing deal. There were essentially three possible outcomes: (1) the album would be a huge hit, in which case we would look like geniuses by waiting to make a deal; (2) the album would be a minor success, in which case it would be roughly the same whether we did a deal immediately or not, since the upfront advance from doing a deal would be roughly equal to the royalties that would flow to Christopher over time, even without a publisher; or (3) the album would be a complete flop, in which case we would be much better off to make a deal at once, take the relatively small upfront advance, and run!

From the adventures and dreams that Christopher and I had shared in our travels about Europe in 1970, you will know the answer that Christopher gave. His only question was, "How long do you think we should wait until we make a deal?" I answered with a laugh, "Well, the time when we have the most negotiating leverage is fifteen minutes after one of your songs becomes #1 with a bullet on the *Billboard* charts."

It's not that we didn't entertain offers from publishers. Once word was out that Alannah had signed with Atlantic, the publishers were calling us. It's just that we moved very slowly and didn't rush to accept anything.

> **Christopher:** There was considerable interest in my publishing, given that I'd written the lion's share of the songs on the first album. Stephen set me up to meet a number of publishers, big and small, in Los Angeles and New York, and we would compare notes after each meeting. The offers were generous, more than I ever expected to make writing songs, but there wasn't an ideal fit. I was worried that my hot moment would pass and that if the record came out and didn't break through, I would have missed my chance. Stephen was phlegmatic about all of this, saying, in essence, "Trust the Force, Christopher."

Meanwhile Alannah, Dave, and Christopher were hard at work, writing and producing new songs to complete the first album. One of the songs was written by Christopher after he visited Elvis Presley's Graceland mansion in Memphis on August 16, 1987 — ten years to the day after Elvis's death — and witnessed the hordes of fans paying tribute. He saw in the adulation of the Elvis fans "a new religion that will bring you to your knees" and brought that sentiment into a song he wrote, called "Black Velvet."*

Over the ensuing year more songs were created, and the album was honed until, on March 28, 1989, the *Alannah Myles* debut album was ready for release.

There was an issue, though. Tunc and his team in New York weren't sure what the first single should be.

The question was resolved by deciding to use Canada as a test market. "Love Is" was released as the first single, in Canada only, and garnered a good level of success, selling very well and reaching #16 in the charts, but it was not quite enough to convince Atlantic in the U.S. to release it as a single there.

In late July "Black Velvet" was released as the second single, again in Canada only.

This made Christopher understandably nervous about his potential publishing arrangements. The album itself was achieving some sales success in Canada but was not turning out to be a huge hit, at least not yet. One thing I was able to reassure him on: the success in Canada meant that there would be royalties flowing to him regardless. They wouldn't come in a lump sum, as an upfront advance would from a publishing deal, but they would come.

Slowly but inexorably, week after week, the album continued steady sales in Canada, and "Black Velvet" rose in the charts, ultimately reaching #10 in the Canadian charts — not #1, but high enough to convince Atlantic to release it as a single in the U.S.

Late in December 1989, five months after "Black Velvet" had been released in Canada, it was released as Alannah's first single in the United States.

---

* As they prepared the song for recording, it was completed with the help of Dave Tyson, who added the melody for the middle eight (the section of the song with the lyrics "Every word of every song that he sang was for you. In a flash he was gone, it happened so soon. What could you do?")

Christopher: And then a magical thing happened — Alannah's album, which had been a success in Canada, slowly started to make inroads in the U.S., thanks to the cross-border play of "Black Velvet." This put us in a great position in terms of negotiating strength, and I asked Stephen repeatedly and nervously when we should sign a deal. His reply was always, "The time when we have the most negotiating leverage is fifteen minutes after your song becomes #1 on the *Billboard* charts."

The ongoing reference to waiting until fifteen minutes after the song topped the *Billboard* charts was really no more than a standing joke between Christopher and me. I never meant it literally, just as a reminder of the virtue of patience, to wait for the right deal at the right time.

The right time had arrived. A week after its U.S. release, on January 6, 1990, "Black Velvet" entered the *Billboard* Hot 100 chart at #86 with a bullet.

We decided to conclude a publishing deal with an indie upstart called Zomba Music Group, run by the South African–born British record executive (and soon-to-be billionaire) Clive Calder. The record side of the group, under the Jive Records label, had achieved massive success with hip hop in the 1980s and was on the verge of even more success in the pop world, with artists such as Backstreet Boys, NSYNC, and Britney Spears.

Zomba was looking to build up its music publishing side, and Christopher and I were impressed by the company's dynamism. Christopher really liked Neil Portnow, the man who ran the Los Angeles office. Neil is currently the head of the organization that produces the Grammy Awards (you see Neil on every Grammy show).* And Graham and I really connected with Richard Blackstone, who had a unique dual role as

---

* Formerly known as the National Academy of Recording Arts and Sciences or NARAS, the organization behind the Grammys is now known simply as the Recording Academy. Neil has been the president since 2002.

both head of creative and head of business affairs at Zomba. We remain friends to this day.

I think one of the reasons Richard and I got along so well is that combination of creative and business sides. He had been a roadie for the band Squeeze and had produced music scores for documentaries and films. He has gone on to a stellar career, including becoming the CEO of Zomba Music Publishing, the co-president of BMG Rights Management, and the CEO of the huge Warner/Chappell music publishing company.

For his part, Richard was impressed that I shared with him the detailed Lotus 1-2-3 spreadsheets I had created to project potential low, medium, and high income streams for Christopher's songs. They were divided into the various territories of the world, the various types of revenue, and they adjusted for the delays and administrative costs in collecting the revenues.* While to me it seemed a natural thing to create, he had never come across a lawyer or manager who had prepared an analysis like that. In turn, he shared with me the costs that he faced as a publisher, and the types of profit margins he needed to generate to make the deal work. Unlike many negotiations that relied simply on differences in negotiating leverage, we were crafting an agreement to maximize our individual interests while recognizing each other's needs.

It took a couple of months to trade different versions of the agreement back and forth until Richard suggested he come to Toronto to meet with us on Wednesday, March 21, to hammer out the final details and get it all signed up.

Around 6:00 p.m. we were at last ready to sign the agreement. Christopher and Richard were both in my office, pens in hand, when we heard the fax machine running behind me. As we turned to the machine, we saw the first lines of the fax emerge. It was an advance copy of next week's *Billboard* chart.

"Black Velvet" was at the very top — #1 with a bullet.

---

* Lotus 1-2-3 no longer exists. It was IBM's predecessor to the now ubiquitous Excel spreadsheets from Microsoft.

We laughed and hugged each other and agreed to wait fifteen minutes. Then we signed the deal.

As it turned out, the Alannah Myles album went on to surpass even the "high" projections on my Lotus 1-2-3 spreadsheet, selling millions of records internationally (over a million in Canada alone) and winning Alannah a hugely deserved Grammy and three Juno Awards* in the process, plus a Juno Award for Christopher and Dave as Songwriters of the Year.

"Black Velvet" remains to this day a classic radio hit, still generating worldwide royalties over twenty-five years later. Zomba's rights in the songs have long since lapsed, with full ownership resting now with Christopher: the deal Richard and I made turned out to be a great one for both sides.

---

* She won the 1990 Grammy Award for Best Female Rock Vocal Performance, along with Juno Awards that year, for Single of the Year, Album of the Year, and Most Promising Female Vocalist of the Year.

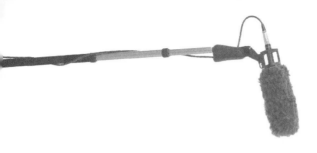

15
WHEN I'M WITH YOU

Sometimes you get lucky, and sometimes you help luck along — or maybe that's not quite the right way to put it. Maybe it's just that if you have a clear vision of your end goal, you can let the universe conspire with you to help you reach it.

Arnold Lanni is an incredibly talented songwriter, performer, and music producer. He's produced dozens of massively successful albums for acts such as Finger Eleven, Simple Plan, and the first four Our Lady Peace albums (including the multimillion-selling *Clumsy* album.)

When he entered my office in early 1986, most of his career was still ahead of him. At that time he was simply a former member of the somewhat successful Canadian rock group Sheriff, which had since disbanded, and he was interested in forming another group, called Frozen Ghost. A tall, almost gangly musician, Arnold was immediately likeable, someone you instinctively wanted to help, someone who was driven by his pure love for music and his good feelings toward the world around him.

He said he was hoping for my help with two things. First, would I help him negotiate a recording deal with WEA Canada (I, of course, said yes). Second, would I help him buy back the rights to a song he'd written years earlier. It was a song he thought he might like to re-record with his new group, and it was a song to which he had a strong emotional attachment: he had written it for his girlfriend, who later became his wife. The story of how he wrote the song is totally charming.

> **Arnold:** Not to overuse a cliché, but songs are like our children. You raise them up to be the best they can be, then you let them out the door and they go find their lives. I wrote this particular song on Valentine's Day, for my girlfriend at the time, who is now my wife. I wanted to get her something nice but had no money; I was living at home with my mom.
>
> I figured I could write her a song, so I went downstairs, where my dad kept his piano, and I sang it into a cassette. That night when she was finished work, we went to the donut shop, where we'd put a couple of quarters into the Galaxy jukebox and buy a couple of French crullers. Part of my plan was, before we go in to the donut shop I'll play her this song in the van and with any luck she'll cry 'cause she'll think that was the sweetest thing I could do. I never thought beyond that. I never once wanted to record it. It wasn't until months, maybe a year later, one of the guys in the band said, "There's that other song." I said, "No, no, that's just a dumb love song that I wrote for Valerie for Valentine's." If it wasn't for the band and the producer insisting that I play it, it would never have happened. The producer said, "Oh yeah, we have to record that."
>
> We made a deal, and looking back I realize how naive I was. I said, "Okay, if you promise me that this could never ever be a single, then we'll record it." Of course he promised, and of course it was a lie!
>
> In that song, all I was trying to say to my girlfriend was, "My life is what it is, but when you're with me, I

feel like everything else doesn't matter," and I tried to say it in the purest, most simple way that I could. That song took maybe six minutes to write. When something isn't meant for a big audience, you're not as precious with it … I called it "When I'm with You."

Arnold explained how several years earlier Sheriff had signed a recording and music publishing agreement with a production company that worked with the group to record a single album called, simply, *Sheriff*. The production company had in turn licenced rights in the recorded album to Capitol Records in Canada, but had retained ownership of the songs themselves, almost all of which had been written by Arnold.*

I told Arnold that I could certainly help him negotiate a buyback but added, "I don't think it's wise to single out that particular song. If the production company knows you have interest in that song, they'll demand a very high price for it, as they'll suspect you have particular plans for it, which in a way you do." Instead I suggested, "Let's offer to buy back the rights for *all* the songs you wrote. They will understand a musician wanting to own his own songs, and I'll bet we'll pay far less for all the songs than we would have to pay for that single song."

> **Arnold:** I remember Stephen saying if we're going to do this, get everything, so it looks like there isn't one song specifically that you're interested in 'cause otherwise they're going to hold one against the other. Just go in and say, "Hey look this guy's got another career going, he wants to package everything together, he wants to clear up loose ends." It was that kind of an approach.

---

* Of the ten songs on the album, eight were written solely by Arnold and two were co-written by Arnold with Sheriff guitarist Steve DeMarchi.

Sure enough, after several months of negotiation (we didn't want to appear too interested), Arnold was able to buy back all of his songs for a total of only six thousand dollars. I say "only six thousand dollars," but to Arnold, that was still a lot of money.

> **Arnold:** I remember calling my accountant … and he said, "Arnold, if you buy it at this price, you're basically overpaying." I said, "I understand that, but this is for me. This is so I can sleep at night." I thought, even if I'm overpaying for it, at least at the end of the day, I can turn around and say to my children, this is what your old man did with his life.

In the meantime, Arnold moved forward with former Sheriff bassist Wolf Hassel, recording an album under their new group name, Frozen Ghost. Things moved forward in a generally positive and somewhat routine manner for the talented duo. By 1987 an anti-censorship song from their first album, reached #69 on *Billboard*'s Hot 100 singles chart in the United States.* A few months later, something extraordinary happened.

An all-night DJ in Minneapolis started playing a track from the original Sheriff album, the song "When I'm with You." The audience liked the song, so he kept playing it, and soon another radio station followed suit.

Arnold mentioned this to me and talked about how exciting it was that a song by a group that no longer existed, that was not being promoted by a record company, and that had no accompanying video was being enjoyed by a new audience. Furthermore, it was a song he now owned, and a song that had special emotional resonance for him and his wife.

It didn't stop there. More and more radio stations started playing "When I'm with You," and in the summer of 1988 Capitol Records decided to re-release it as a single in the United States.

---

* The song was called "Should I See" and the album was called *Frozen Ghost*.

Week after week the song gathered more and more momentum, entering the Billboard Hot 100 Singles chart. Then twenty-eight weeks later, on February 4, 1989, "When I'm with You" achieved the stunning success of being #1 with a bullet.

Six weeks after that it was certified "Gold" by the Recording Industry Association of America.

Frozen Ghost ended up releasing three original albums, and Arnold has carried on as one of Canada's top record producers. In terms of pure, near-miraculous success, though, it's hard to top having a #1 single with no video, no touring act, and little to no promotion. Oh, and a song he'd happened to buy back years earlier!

In Arnold's case it can truly be said, "it couldn't have happened to a nicer guy." He did it all for the right authentic reasons. And if the universe conspired to help him along, well, sometimes you get lucky, and sometimes you help luck along. As our experience with "When I'm with You" shows, sometimes both happen at the same time.

There's another interesting side story to all of this. When Arnold first met with me and we were working on the Frozen Ghost agreements, his brother Rob Lanni was with him. Arnold needed a manager, and he wanted Rob to be that manager. Rob wasn't entirely sure.

> **Rob:** I'd spent most of my life at school and didn't have that much experience. Arnold had gone through a few managers over the years and wanted someone he felt had his interests at heart. He wasn't as concerned about my not having experience — he said, "You'll learn it as you go. Don't worry about it."

I encouraged Rob and told him what I'd said to Larry Wanagas when Larry had first become k.d. lang's manager, namely that that I think there are three essential qualities in a manager: (1) honesty, (2) business sense, and (3) complete conviction that the artist is one of the best talents ever to arrive on Earth. Larry had qualified on all three counts. So did Rob.

Arnold: Rob knew nothing about management. He had two degrees from university, but I can still hear our mother saying, "Don't ruin his life!" During the day he set up a phone line in my mother's basement, and when that phone rang, we knew it had to be somebody to do with music because no one else had the number. When Frozen Ghost got signed, he was still working as a pizza delivery guy. I still have his orange Pizza Pizza jacket.

Today Rob is known one of the top music managers in the world. His current roster includes Our Lady Peace, Simple Plan, Finger Eleven, Justin Nozuka, and a number of others. In 1990 he co-founded Coalition Music, which has become an important music incubator. Housed in a former convent, Coalition Music encompasses education programs as well as the management company, recordings studios, and the Coalition Records company.

But he started out humbly … with great future goals, but humbly.

Rob: In those days, we didn't have cellphones or email so from nine to five I had to be near a land line to make it look like this guy's reachable during the day — he's a manager. The only option was to work nights, and the only job I could find that was flexible enough was being a Pizza Pizza delivery guy. Here's a guy with a couple of university degrees, managing a hit band, and schlepping pizzas around! Nobody knew.

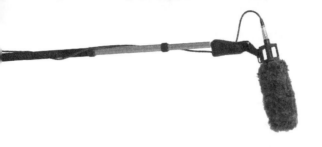

16
DEGRASSI: THE NEXT GENERATION IS BORN

On Christmas Eve in 1996 Linda Schuyler and I were wandering in the dark, just the two of us, flashlights in hand, inspecting the warehouse we had just bought. The rooms were empty — it was pretty much just one hundred thousand square feet of nothingness. Nothingness, except for the large metal barrels that caught the melting snow coming through the leaky roof.

It had been quite a month.

I had just left my position as a partner at McCarthy Tétrault and would now have two jobs. One was working with my friend Graham Henderson in the newly minted entertainment law partnership, Stohn Henderson LLP. The other was working side by side with Linda as the owners and developers of this deserted building — a building we would transform into Epitome Studios — while producing our new *Riverdale* series, the first of what we hoped would be many different series to be produced in the studios.*

The rear parking lot, which we would turn into the backlot exterior sets for *Riverdale* (and later, though we didn't know it at the time, for

---

* Our *Riverdale* should not be confused with the current Netflix series, also called *Riverdale*. The Netflix series is based on the *Archie* comic book series. Coincidentally, however, one of the key writers on the Netflix *Riverdale* is Michael Grassi, a stalwart for many years in our *Degrassi* writing department.

Degrassi, Instant Star, The L.A. Complex, Open Heart, and other shows), was empty except for a huge pile of old tires. Who knew it was a thing to dump old tires into the parking lots of deserted buildings?

Until then we had always shot on location. All the *Degrassi Junior High* and *Degrassi High* episodes had been shot first at Vincent Massey Public School in a western suburb of Toronto, and then at Centennial College, just a ten-minute drive from where we were then standing. This would be our first foray into studio-based production.

Everything was completely silent as we wandered about. Silent except for our voices. We talked about what the future would bring, what it would be like to work together.

We knew it wouldn't always be easy to be husband and wife and business partners at the same time. We agreed to just talk things through whenever it became difficult. If we disagreed, we would just disagree openly and compassionately, and we would make a decision and move on.

We felt it was a saving grace that our interests were different. Linda was mostly driven by storytelling. There were stories that she wanted to tell — not just her own stories, but stories that came from scriptwriters she would work with day-to-day, stories that she could help weave into television shows that made a difference.

I wasn't driven so much by the storytelling. I loved different aspects of production, like diving deep into the music and sound departments, figuring out how this new thing called the World Wide Web might fit in, and, of course, cobbling together and negotiating all the various business arrangements.

We overlapped — Linda liked being involved in the business side, and I enjoyed being brought into the creative side when I could help — but our basic drives were different, and that seemed good.

Our conversation subsided as we walked slowly back toward our car, our footsteps leaving a trail in the snow. We were both lost in thought about what lay ahead. It was all thrilling; it was also a bit frightening.

The next day would start a week of Christmas celebrations, and then, on January 1, 1997, our new futures would begin....

I actually appeared in the background of the five hundredth episode of *Degrassi* (Season 2, Episode 5, of *Degrassi: Next Class*) in the background playing an "Aging Rock Star." This is Linda and me on-set during a break in production of that episode in 2016.

○   ○   ○

We almost hadn't bought that particular building. We'd been close to putting in an offer on a building across town called the Belarus Tractor Factory. We'd been very impressed with the high ceilings at the Belarus building, excellent for building sets, and had gone back several times. Our eyebrows were raised when we didn't see any tractors, other than the occasional pin-up of a pretty girl riding high atop one. Of course, they were selling the building, so we told ourselves they'd probably already moved the tractors to their new location. It wasn't until our final visit that we'd been shown the *coup de grâce*, a beautiful interior boardroom complete with sauna, overlooking an enclosed garden.

But what was in the garden raised a lot of suspicion: one of the largest satellite dishes I'd ever seen. I'd called one of my oldest pals, Geoffrey O'Brian, who at the time was chief of counter intelligence at

CSIS, Canada's version of the CIA. After explaining about the building, I'd asked if he knew anything about the Belarus Tractor Factory. He'd replied very succinctly, "Stephen, we are on an open telephone line. Let me just say that we know our friends at the Belarus Tractor Factory very well indeed!"

So that was that. Rather than get involved in negotiations with the KGB or some similar organization, we decided to go with the building with the lower ceilings and the leaky roof.

We knew nothing about owning and operating a building, but we promptly got a crash course in things like how much a new industrial roof costs, and how many little things can go wrong.* Mostly though, we were focused on prepping the building to shoot the *Riverdale* series we'd created for CBC, aiming to be Canada's first prime time soap opera.

There were no windows in the building at that time and no interior walls; it was just a big empty warehouse. And a large part of our funding for *Riverdale* was coming from a special Canadian government program that required principal photography to commence before March 31, so we had a little over three months to transform the warehouse into a series of working studios, and to turn the rear parking lot into an outdoor street set.

It was a large task, and a team of nearly a hundred craftspersons worked day and night for those three months to get the building ready in time. The carpenters worked during the day and the electricians at night. As they got to know each other better, when the crossover time came they would play a game of indoor ball hockey against each other in what became known as the famous "Carps vs. Sparks" tournament in Studio D.

We had a grand vision for *Riverdale*, more than just wanting to produce a great television series. We had a mission statement. The show should positively impact a generation of Canadians and spread Canadian

---

* The answer, in both cases, is an awful lot.

stories and values around the world through the medium of Canada's first prime time soap opera. At the same time it would serve as a training ground for Canadian actors, writers, directors, technicians, and other creative personnel. It was a heady and overblown mission, perhaps, but we believed in it.

In addition, our business model was unique, for English Canada anyway. Every other territory in the world — including the U.S., but particularly outside the U.S. — had their key prime time soap operas: *Coronation Street* and *EastEnders* from Britain, *Neighbours* from Australia, *Winter Sonata* from South Korea, *Snail House* from China, *Noor* from Turkey (which became a hit throughout the Arab world when it was dubbed into Arabic), and *Because a Mother-In-Law Was Also Once a Daughter-In-Law* from India, along with hundreds of others around the globe.

But in English Canada we were a first.

Setting up a soap opera is initially expensive (you need to build a raft of interior and exterior sets that can be used over and over), but once that initial cost has been amortized, the ongoing per-episode cost is low: the mantra is low cost, high volume. Over three seasons, from 1997 to 1999 combined, we produced ninety-four episodes and had slowly built an engaged audience — averaging nearly four hundred thousand viewers in our Sunday morning time slot. By the end of the third season we had amortized our initial costs and set ourselves up in a position to produce more episodes very inexpensively.

On top of that we had a motivated advertiser, Procter & Gamble, who was willing to contribute to the production cost in return for commercials featuring some of our lead characters. (This seemed very karmically correct, given that the term "soap opera" originated with serial radio dramas in the 1930s, sponsored almost entirely by soap manufacturers such as Procter & Gamble, Colgate-Palmolive, and Lever Brothers.)

For our proposed fourth season of *Riverdale* we'd come up with a very ambitious plan to produce two hundred episodes, enough to broadcast four new episodes per week for fifty weeks in the year, while dropping the per-episode cost to nearly a quarter of other drama programs.

We knew our plan was pushing the envelope, but we thought the worst that might happen would be a fourth season order for a small number of episodes, like twenty-two, which would fly in the face of our "low cost, high volume" mantra, but would at least allow us to continue for another year on a series we had come to love, with actors, writers, and a crew we loved to work with. How wrong we were.

In February 2000, shortly after pitching the new season to CBC, our executive assistant walked into my office with a smile on her face. "Good news!" Carol Anne said. "Slawko just called. He happened to be in the neighbourhood and asked if you and Linda were free to have a quick meet."

Slawko was Slawko Klymkiw, then-head of English-language network programming at CBC.* We had been hoping to hear from him since we were anxiously awaiting news about whether our *Riverdale* series would be ordered for a fourth season.

"No, Carol Anne," I responded with a sigh, "Slawko never 'just happens to be in the neighbourhood.' I think Dr. Death is coming to pay a house call!"

Sure enough, a few minutes later, Slawko let us know that *Riverdale* was being cancelled. I'll give him credit for being classy and coming to deliver the news in person. But being classy didn't make the news any less devastating.

The order was not for two hundred episodes. It was not for twenty-two episodes. It was for zero. There wouldn't even be a two-hour special to wrap up the series for its fans — the final *Riverdale* scene anyone would ever see, the last seconds of Episode 94, had the body of Stephanie Long (played by Diana Reis) floating face down in a pool. Was she dead or alive? No one would ever know.

To this day I think CBC's cancellation of *Riverdale* was a serious mistake. Now, it's natural for producers to think that broadcasters are wrong

---

* Carol Anne DaCosta is now an executive at Canadian Media Producers Association, and Slawko Klymkiw is now the CEO of Canadian Film Centre.

to cancel their shows. Producers almost always feel that their shows are great, that it's improper scheduling by the broadcaster — or the wrong, or not enough, promotion by the broadcaster — that is at fault. We've certainly thought (and said) those things when our productions have been cancelled over the years.

In the case of *Riverdale*, though, we were on a mission to produce something more than a television show. We thought that *Riverdale* would continue for a long time, becoming Canada's *Coronation Street*. In fact, as part of our research for *Riverdale* we visited with executives at Granada Studios in Manchester, England, the home of *Coronation Street*, who were kind enough to share some of their secrets behind producing soap operas, and even lent us one of their long-time directors to help shoot our first season. At the time, *Coronation Street* had been running for thirty-seven years; we didn't see why *Riverdale* couldn't one day be celebrating its own thirty-seventh birthday.*

Three years later, with three seasons behind us, we felt we'd learned a lot about how to shoot and how not to shoot a soap opera, and we were finally hitting our stride.

Linda was particularly wounded by the cancellation. She withdrew from the annual Prime Time in Ottawa producers' conference because she just didn't feel up to facing her peers. Over the next six months she seriously considered leaving the business entirely. She didn't see how she could hold her head high.

> **Linda:** When *Riverdale* was cancelled, I was done. I wasn't producing another thing; I was going to go back to school teaching. I was totally done. I didn't leave the house for about two weeks. I'd put so much heart and soul into it. I'd been to England; I'd been on the set of *EastEnders* and *Coronation Street*, and I really believed this is what Canada needed — its own soap opera. We

---

* *Coronation Street* still continues to this day, now in its fifty-eighth year.

had a business model that was not only about the storytelling we were going to do, but about a behind-the-
scenes learning environment where people could come
through and get trained and go on to other work ... so
it was to be both a production and a training facility ...
we'd made the investment into the building. I couldn't
understand what the CBC was thinking....

It's not that I was stronger; I was just angry. I knew, and still know,
CBC had done the wrong thing. I don't think they understood what they
were doing, cancelling a show that was purely Canadian, telling Canadian
stories appealing to Canadians, and serving as a training ground for talent and an anchor for their prime time schedule — *Riverdale* was and is
everything CBC should have been doing.

You are pardoned if you are thinking to yourself, "This is pretty
much just sour grapes on Stephen's part." It wasn't, though. And isn't.
Here's the proof: the cancellation of *Riverdale* turned out to be the most
positive thing that ever happened in Linda's and my professional careers.

You see, during the previous year we'd thought, why not use the
investment we've made in creating the sets and other infrastructure for
Riverdale as the base for developing yet another soap opera, this time
aimed at teenagers. We'd called the show *Ready, Willing and Wired* —
so-called as the internet and cellphones were starting to become a part of
everyday teenage life.

A key contributor to the development was Yan Moore. A long-
time friend of Linda's and mine, Yan has a great mind and a thoughtful,
self-effacing personality. He was one of our writers on *Riverdale*, but he'd
also written most of the episodes of the original *Degrassi Junior High* and
Degrassi High. When *Riverdale* was cancelled, we moved development of
Ready, Willing and Wired into high gear by hiring more writers to work
with Yan and devoting much more attention to their output.

At the same time, we scrambled to rent out our studio to a third party
so that at least our out-of-pocket costs of property taxes, heat, hydro, and

insurance would be covered for the year. Luckily an ideal renter emerged: Disney came into the studio to shoot the first (and only) season of *In a Heartbeat*, a drama based on the real-life story of high school students who volunteer as part-time emergency responders (while still maintaining their lives as normal teenagers).*

Amid all this frenzy of activity, Yan quietly came into Linda's office one day and said, "It just occurred to me, remember Emma on *Degrassi Junior High*?" Of course Linda remembered. Emma was the baby born to Christine "Spike" Nelson in one of *Degrassi's* most iconic story arcs: Spike becomes pregnant while still in seventh grade and chooses to keep her baby.

Yan went on. "I've just done the calculations. Emma was born in the final episode of Season 2 of *Degrassi Junior High*, which first aired March 28, 1988. That would make her a bit more than eleven years old now, but by the time we produce a show and get it to air, she'd be thirteen and going to junior high herself. Why don't we keep the stories we've been working on for *Ready, Willing and Wired*, but make the lead character Emma. She and her friends are going to school. Why don't we make that school Degrassi!"

We all got very excited. I yelled out, "It's *Degrassi: The Next Generation!*" triggered by my love for the similarly named *Star Trek* series rebirth.** That day began our plunge forward into the development of our new *Degrassi*, which for the next ten seasons became *Degrassi: The Next Generation*.

In forthcoming chapters, I'll talk a lot more about this new *Degrassi*, but for the moment let me leap forward and say that we've now produced

---

* One of the stars of *In a Heartbeat* was Lauren Collins, whom we subsequently cast to play what turned out to be one of *Degrassi's* all-time favourite characters, Paige Michalchuk.

** The original *Star Trek* television series lasted seventy-nine episodes over three seasons and was reborn as *Star Trek: The Next Generation*, lasting 178 episodes over seven seasons. It has since spawned four spinoffs.

425 episodes of it (525 when combined with all the episodes of what we now refer to as "*Degrassi Classic*").* And we've recently celebrated the thirty-seventh year since the first of *Kids of Degrassi Street* was broadcast.

Remember how I'd wondered if *Riverdale* might one day celebrate its thirty-seventh birthday, just as *Coronation Street* had done? Well, *Riverdale* never did, of course, but *Degrassi* has.

Remember, too, that mission statement that went down the tubes when *Riverdale* was cancelled? Well, it turns out it didn't go down the tubes after all. That's the funny thing about mission statements and other clearly visualized goals: sometimes you reach them, but not at all in the way you thought you would.

You'll recall we wanted to "positively impact a generation of Canadians [let's give Degrassi a check mark for that] and spread Canadian stories and values around the world [at last count, new episodes of the series are being broadcast in seventeen different languages in over 237 different territories around the world, so another check mark] through the medium of Canada's first prime time soap opera … [Degrassi isn't technically a soap opera, but it's often called that, and it does have ongoing story arcs, so let's give that a check mark, too] serving as a training ground for Canadian actors, writers, directors, technicians, and other creative personnel" [that's the final check mark, for a four-out-of-four score].

In some ways the new iteration of *Degrassi* even went beyond the mission we'd set for *Riverdale*. To us it's been a way to reassure teens that whatever issues they might be facing, they are not alone, and that they do have power — the power to make choices — but that every choice has a consequence. The issues we have covered include bullying,

---

* Its first one hundred half-hours, which we now refer collectively to as *Degrassi Classic*, consisted of the three televisions series airing from 1980 to 1990, *The Kids of Degrassi Street, Degrassi Junior High*, and *Degrassi High*, followed in 1991 by the two-hour movie-of-the-week *School's Out*.

school violence, coming out, random death, transgender issues, and the most difficult of all, suicide. One of our mottos has been, "If they are talking about it in the halls of the schools, we should be talking about it on *Degrassi*."

All this means that, while it took years for Linda and I to realize it, the cheery "Good news!" that Carol Anne had greeted me with minutes before *Riverdale* was cancelled really was good news after all: if *Riverdale* had not been cancelled, I don't think we ever would have brought *Degrassi* back.

So, thank you, CBC, for cancelling *Riverdale*. That ending turned into an incredibly positive turning point in our careers. But for the record, I still think it was a wrong decision for CBC and an incredible missed opportunity.*

---

* If CBC's head of English services Heather Conway or anyone on the Board of CBC is reading this, I'm open for a meeting: I still think CBC should have its own prime time soap opera, I still think it should be a continuation of *Riverdale*, and I still think Linda and I should produce it at the DHX Epitome Studios!

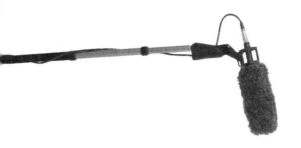

17
THE EARLY *JUNOS*

Trust is important. It's important in interpersonal relationships. It's important in business relationships. And it's important in awards shows. The fans, and the potential nominees and their teams, need to know that the best artists, or musicians, or TV shows, or films, or stage plays, or whatever are being selected in a trustworthy manner.

I first joined the Board of "the Academy" — the Canadian Academy of Recording Arts and Sciences — in 1992. The Academy is responsible for handing out the Juno Awards annually to celebrate the success of Canadian music artists (in the same way that the Grammys celebrate the success of mostly American artists).*

At the time, the record industry was riding high. CDs were the rage, just on the verge of outpacing sales of pre-recorded cassettes. The internet had been invented, but it would be almost a decade before Napster was formed, spawning the digital uprising that would ultimately decimate physical record sales.

---

* The Juno name is a homage to Pierre Juneau, who, as chair of the CRTC, was the champion of the CRTC's Canadian content regulations introduced in 1971 to require a certain percentage of radio and television time to be devoted to programming (or music, in the case of radio) produced in Canada.

Notwithstanding the solid economics of the industry as a whole, the Academy was facing some growing pains. There was some internal dissention, as well as public criticism, about *The Juno Awards* broadcast on two main fronts. First, the *Junos* were seen as behind the times, with nominees who often didn't reflect the artists currently riding high on the charts. Second, there were intimations that the major record labels had too much sway, and fears they might be using their considerable influence to manipulate the selection of nominees and winners.

As to the second criticism, I never found any evidence of such manipulation. In fact, if anything, the industry executives I worked with were bending over backwards to be fair. But that didn't matter in the end: the perception of undue influence needed to be immediately dealt with.

As a new member of the Board, I was promptly appointed to head the Nominating & Voting Committee, an appointment that, as I soon came to realize, was not one to aspire to. The Nominating & Voting Committee is responsible for all the rules governing the process of selecting nominees and winners, and as I later said, "If we do our job exceptionally well, no one will ever notice. That is really the best we can hope for. If we slip up, even in small ways, there will be criticism and outcries." In other words, it is a largely thankless task!

Nevertheless, I took to the role with great enthusiasm. The Committee consisted of some twenty artists and industry executives, representing many different genres of music and many different roles in the industry. They were an extremely knowledgeable and committed group. While I take great pride in the many changes that we together instituted in the *Junos* selection process over the next few years, I am most proud of the way we arrived at those changes: every decision of the Committee was made with unanimous consensus.

We made a series of changes, the first of which was to move toward an objective system of selecting the nominees for the ten major categories, such as Best Album, Best Group, and Best New Artist.* The nominees for these categories would now be based entirely on sales data (or in some cases sales and radio airplay data). Previously the nominees had been selected by voting within the Academy; now, the top-five selling albums in each category would become the nominees.

There could be no collusion, no manipulation; an independent accounting firm would make the determination. It was not a perfect system, and arguments could be made that worthier candidates might be excluded from nomination, but it was open and transparent.

We did still need to address the "block voting" issue. Voting for the winner in each category would still be by members of the Academy — any one of the five nominees could win, regardless of their sales or airplay levels. Because the major labels had so many employees who were voting members, there was fear that they could use their voting clout to secretly collude with the other major labels to coordinate the winners.

The issue had come to a head with a controversy in 1992, a year in which Bryan Adams had been very publicly critical of the Canadian content regulations when his album *Waking Up the Neighbours* — including the huge hit single "(Everything I Do) I Do It for You" — was disqualified as Canadian for radio airplay purposes.** Under the Juno Awards rules, however, Bryan was still clearly Canadian, and had been nominated for seven Junos, largely competing against my friend and client, Tom Cochrane.

I was particularly proud of Tom's success that year. His monster single "Life Is a Highway" from his *Mad Mad World* album garnered a Grammy nomination along with an ASCAP Award for being one of the most-played

---

* Years later, most award names were changed to remove "Best" and add "of the Year," so that they are now Album of the Year, Group of the Year, and so on.

** As the album was recorded outside Canada, and was largely co-written and co-produced with British/South African Mutt Lange, the album wasn't considered Canadian content by the CRTC. As a result of the controversy, the CRTC later changed the Canadian content rules to recognize recordings as Canadian content provided the Canadian contribution was at least 50 percent.

songs of the year. And *Mad Mad World* itself has sold nearly two million copies to date in Canada alone.

So the contest between Tom and Bryan was a particularly even and intriguing one. But when Tom won the most Junos that year, including Single of the Year (for "Life Is a Highway"), Male Vocalist of the Year, Album of the Year, and Songwriter of the Year, Bryan was convinced that the industry was colluding against him, particularly since Bryan did win the Juno for Canadian Entertainer of the Year, the one award which was voted on by the fans, not by the industry members of the Academy. It was seventeen years before Bryan agreed to appear on the show again.

Tom was a totally deserving winner, and I was never aware of, nor did I find any evidence of, any collusion. But we needed to address even the slightest perception that there could have been any wrong-doing, so we placed a cap on the number of employees at each major record label who would be entitled to vote. We also instituted some smaller — more nuanced — changes, such as requiring that all communications with Academy members had to be at their home addresses (to make it less likely that voting would be even subconsciously affected by the office atmosphere). To broaden the voting base beyond the record labels, all artist nominees were offered free membership in the Academy.

These changes seem to have worked; though, it took years before the mistrust in the system gradually waned.

Finally, there was a non-rules–based problem to deal with — some embarrassing situations in which worthy candidates had failed to be nominated simply because they (or their record company) had neglected to submit the nomination forms. As an example, the Best Selling International Album in 1993 was the soundtrack to *The Bodyguard*, featuring Whitney Houston, including her monster hit single "I Will Always Love You," produced by David Foster, and for which he won a Grammy Award. Due to an apparent confusion at the record company over who was responsible for submitting the nomination papers, that year David was never even nominated for a Juno for Producer of the Year.

To address situations like that, an express onus was put on all Board and Committee members to "beat the drums" and ensure that all worthy candidates submitted all necessary paperwork, properly completed and on time. Since that practice was instituted, the problem has not materialized again.

The impact of these changes was not felt overnight. Rebuilding trust takes time. As the years unfolded, though, the Academy garnered more confidence in its process, and more artists and industry executives in all different musical genres became more actively involved, in turn improving every aspect of the show.

One of the big questions the Academy still grappled with was how to increase fan engagement. For years, there had been a Canadian Entertainer of the Year category, voted on by fans, but were there other ways to involve the fans so that *The Juno Awards* would be perceived more as an event for all Canadians, rather than primarily a music industry celebration?

Part of the answer came in an unlikely way, a way that has never been made public until now.

Since 1987 the *Junos* had mostly taken place in Toronto at what is now called the Sony Centre for the Performing Arts,* a venue that worked well for the music industry: the sound was good, it met the broadcast requirements, and with roughly three thousand seats, it could comfortably accommodate the music industry executives and still have room left over for some fans to sit in the balcony.**

The Sony Centre is what is called a "union house," meaning that among other things the stage workers had to be members of Local 58 of the International Alliance of Theatrical Stage Employees (IATSE), headed at the time, and indeed for thirty-eight years, by James "Jimmy" Fuller. I never met Fuller, but he was known as a feisty character who was not afraid to be a thorn in the CBC's side, by pushing strongly for additional benefits for his Local to ensure a smooth and timely *Junos*

---

* At the time, it was called the O'Keefe Centre.

** The exception was 1991, when the *Junos* took place at the Queen Elizabeth Theatre in Vancouver.

broadcast. The Academy itself was not directly involved in dealings with the Local, but the exasperation Fuller generated in CBC executives sparked a thought: might there be a different venue that would help the CBC with its "thorn"?

This in turn sparked other thoughts: Did the venue have to be a theatre? Did it have to be in Toronto? What if the show expanded into a much larger space, an arena? What if the show became a concert event, with the fans front and centre, and the industry executives more on the sidelines?

Excitement at the Academy grew as more and more ideas were floated, and as different possibilities were explored. One of the possibilities rose to the fore: move the show to Copps Coliseum in Hamilton, about a half-hour drive from Toronto. Copps was still a "union house," but being outside Toronto its stage workers were from a different IATSE Local. They, along with everyone in Hamilton, from the city council to the management at Copps Coliseum, turned out to be excellent partners, so much so that five *Junos* took place there over the next years.

There was also some symbolism in the move to Hamilton — many felt it was the birthplace of rock and roll in Canada since it was the first city Ronnie Hawkins had played when he moved to Canada from Arkansas in 1958.

Most importantly, we were all swept away by the energy and enthusiasm that erupted on Sunday, March 26, 1995, as Rick Mercer and the entire cast of *This Hour Has 22 Minutes* leaped onto the stage to host *The Juno Awards* live from the Copps Coliseum in Hamilton. The fans were front and centre, with a mosh pit close to the stage. Live performances by Moist, Barenaked Ladies, Ashley MacIsaac, Sarah McLachlan, and others kept the crowd on its feet, and thunderous applause greeted the awards announcements, including The Tragically Hip's win for Entertainer of the Year, and Buffy Sainte-Marie's induction into the Canadian Music Hall of Fame.

The *Junos* had become a concert attraction with awards given out, rather than an awards show with performances. With ten thousand screaming fans, the modern *Juno Awards* were born, focused on the fan experience: North America's first prominent awards show in an arena.

The Academy has received well-deserved plaudits for its move to a fan-centred concert experience. While these plaudits are absolutely deserved, I think a silent thank-you needs to be sent to the "thorn" for igniting the thought process. It might never have happened were it not for him.

It wasn't all unicorns and roses, though. A few years later, a different labour issue arose in Hamilton. In the end, it, too, led to some new thinking.

Until 1999 producing *The Juno Awards* broadcast had always been the sole responsibility of CBC. While the Academy was responsible for mounting the show itself, including providing all the performers and presenters, CBC hired all the technical and production staff and produced the actual television show. But CBC was in danger of a strike.

It may not sound like the Communications, Energy and Paperworkers Union of Canada (CEP) has too much to do with television, but it does.* A few years earlier, Canadian members of the National Association of Broadcast Employees and Technicians (NABET) joined CEP and, as a result, CEP represented some eighteen hundred camera operators and technical staff at CBC.

Everyone had been aware for some time that there was a possibility that CEP would strike CBC, as the two had been without a contract since the summer of 1998. The president of the Academy at the time was Daisy Falle. Daisy had been involved with the Academy since its formation decades earlier to manage and develop what had originally been the Gold Leaf Awards (and previous to that, the RPM Awards), founded by Walt Grealis with the help of Stan Klees, and voted on by readers of their weekly music trade publication *RPM* Magazine.**

---

* Or rather it did, and its successor does. It has since merged with the Canadian Auto Workers, and the combined entity, known as Unifor, represents over three hundred thousand workers.

** *RPM* was a play on words, referring both to "revolutions per minute," such as the standard 45 rpm singles and 33-1/3 rpm vinyl albums, and also to "Records, Promotion, Music."

> **Daisy:** I was with the organization right from the start in 1974, and I did everything. I sold tickets, I did the membership right from scratch, and all the dealings, including acquiring the rights from Walt and Stan. The first time we had a press conference to announce the nominees in 1976, nobody showed up, not even my directors. People were so uninterested. And to see it go from that to where it is now is amazing.

In preparation for the possibility of a strike, Daisy and I, along with some other senior members of the Academy administration, met with CBC and secured their agreement that the Academy itself would mount the production of the *Junos* in 1999. In effect, the Academy would produce the show and then license the broadcast rights to CBC. In this way, production of the *Junos* would be one-step removed from the CBC, and hopefully one-step removed from being shut down by a strike.

A new company, CARAS Productions Inc., was formed. With Daisy and me as signing officers, this new company proceeded to directly hire all the necessary technicians and production staff for the *Junos*, including Lynn Harvey as the show's producer.

It was good that we had taken this precaution, even though at first it appeared that it was for naught. On Wednesday, February 17, 1999, CEP workers walked off the job, and amid the havoc this created with the CBC's normal broadcast operations, CEP made it clear they were preparing to picket CBC's broadcast of *The Juno Awards*, scheduled for less than three weeks later, on March 7.

Since we were now an independent production company, a picket would not directly affect us; although, it raised the spectre of confrontation, possibly escalating to violence. More to the point, though, was the likelihood that other union members (including our friends at IATSE) would refuse to cross the picket line, and this could seriously impact our production.

We remained hopeful that the strike would be short-lived, but as the broadcast date approached, our hopes were dimming. On the Tuesday five days before the broadcast, Daisy and I met to discuss enhanced security with Hamilton police, the RCMP, and management of Copps Coliseum. At first the meeting was exciting, sort of like Spy vs. Spy, as we discussed setting up secret methods of getting the broadcast signal out of Copps Coliseum to the CBC broadcast centre. (The main method would be the highly visible satellite dishes, but we would also have separate microwave and telephone-wire links.)

The meeting became more sobering when the discussion turned to the advisability of hiring additional security personnel, including bodyguards for Daisy and me. That brought home the reality of the situation we were in; it seemed very over the top, but as we looked around, we realized everyone in the room was serious.

> **Daisy:** There were all kinds of threats and a bomb scare — we had RCMP and police, and suddenly it was very frightening.

Daisy and I regrouped that afternoon, decided enough was enough, and requested a meeting directly with CEP.

It's amazing what a little truth-telling, empathy, and common sense can accomplish. Yes, the union was involved in a high-stakes dispute with CBC, and they could not afford to display any weakness. But despite how unions are often portrayed in the media, they are not monoliths. They are made up of human beings. And as we discussed the problem human to human, it turned out the Academy and CEP had something in common: we both had issues with CBC.

In CEP's case, the issues related to job security and working conditions; in ours, they related to the creative direction of *The Juno Awards* themselves. CBC wanted the broadcast to appeal to older viewers and were always pressing for artists like Anne Murray to be featured on the show. We loved Anne Murray and knew she would increase ratings on the broadcast, but we also wanted artists who were currently riding high on the charts, as well as rising stars who would appeal to a much younger audience.*

The CEP held no grudge against us, and indeed their leaders were genuine music fans. They didn't really want to do something that would hurt Canadian musicians, but they felt their hands were tied — the *Junos* broadcast was very useful leverage in their struggle with CBC.

Daisy and I left the meeting, and on our way back to our hotel we brainstormed back and forth until we came up with a plan. We presented it to the Board of the Academy in a hastily arranged conference call.

The plan was based on the common interests we and CEP had, recognizing CEP's genuine issues, and giving them a public relations win — if CEP agreed not to picket, in return we would assist CEP in constructing and providing signage for a series of information booths outside Copps Coliseum to let everyone attending the show know of the grudges CEP felt they legitimately held against CBC. Further, we would issue a press release in which the Academy thanked CEP, expressed understanding of their issues, and credited their refraining from picketing as a goodwill gift to the musicians of Canada.

The Board gave their approval, and we sent the plan to CEP along with a proposed press release. It took CEP only a few hours before they called back with a simple answer, "Yes. And thank you."

The crisis was averted. The information booths were set up, and there were no disruptions to the broadcast.** The 1999 awards went off without a further hitch.

---

* The issue came to a head two years later, when the Academy was intent on asking Nelly Furtado to perform. CBC was very resistant since her first album *Whoa, Nelly!* had only just been released, and CBC gave little credence to our pleas that she was destined for superstardom. CBC relented in the end, but not until after some very bitter discussions. Not only did Nelly perform on the show, but she also won three Junos that year. The album was also nominated for four Grammys and won for Best Female Pop Vocal.

** The CEP strike against CBC continued though, lasting another four weeks.

Well, actually, that's not true. There was a hitch that we never told anyone about: Céline Dion was very ill.

> **Daisy:** At the same time Céline Dion, the headliner, was not well, and there was a distinct possibility she might not be able to make it. We were having a fit. She was terribly ill; her face was chalk-white at the rehearsals.

But like the trooper she is she did the show. In the end, she had to lip-sync. She did it perfectly. Nobody knew.

In fact, the show went off well enough that Lynn Harvey and I were nominated for a Gemini Award (now called the Canadian Screen Awards) for Best Music, Variety or Comedy Program or Series. We didn't win — we lost to *This Hour Has 22 Minutes* — but both Natalie McMaster and Jesse Cook won Best Performance Geminis for their performances on the show.

Importantly, Daisy and I and the entire Board of the Academy now had a taste of what it was like to mount our own production of *The Juno Awards*, independent of CBC, and we all liked it. Our appetite was whetted.

Our current agreement with CBC gave them broadcast rights until 2001, another two *Junos*. We looked forward to substantial renegotiation when the agreement came to an end.

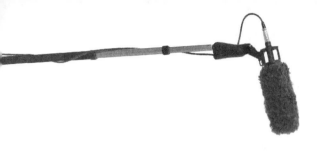

18
KISSING THE COD

The headquarters for the English-language division of CBC is a colourful twelve-storey building in downtown Toronto, with a breathtaking central atrium extending almost to the roof. CBC's executive offices are located on the upper floors, overlooking the atrium on the inner side, and downtown Toronto on the outside.

In late November 2001, I found myself in a corner office in those upper floors, preparing to open negotiations on a new three-year agreement for *The Juno Awards*. The instructions to me from the Board of Academy were clear: the Academy wanted to have much more control over production of the show.

While I was prepared to meet resistance, I wasn't prepared for the CBC's opening salvo. Before I could start making my pitch, the CBC executives stated an opening condition to moving forward. They loved *The Juno Awards* and said it was a key pillar to their annual programming, but ... and it was a big "but" ... CBC intended to cut their licence fee to the Academy by two-thirds.

What they were seeking was impossible. The CBC licence fee covered the majority of the production budget. The *Junos* have always been meant to showcase Canadian talent as being world-class; slashing the production budget would create a death spiral, where the top talent would refuse to appear in a show that lacked the glitz and production value their status deserved.

I remonstrated immediately and forcefully, but it was clear the CBC position was no mere starting point, it was a firm line. (Ironically, CBC's decision meant they were indeed open to ceding a lot of control to the Academy, which was the silver lining in an otherwise doomsday cloud.)

A telephone meeting of the Board was quickly arranged for the next day. The Board was incensed and could hardly believe what they were hearing. Different Board members immediately expressed their eagerness to explore other broadcast opportunities until I outlined the legal impediment to doing so.

The existing agreement with CBC contained what is colloquially called a "right of first refusal." The wording was not precise, but it was clear that at the very least the Academy would have to negotiate exclusively and in good faith with CBC before moving elsewhere. CBC might also have had the right to match any offer that came from another broadcaster. So I was dispatched to continue negotiations with CBC over the next while; the Board would bide its time over the Christmas holiday period, and we would see what the new year would bring.

We made limited progress. After many meetings during the ensuing weeks, including some behind-the-scenes entreaties from individual Board members to their contacts at CBC, we were able to coax the CBC into raising their offer somewhat, but it was still significantly below what we needed.

The time had come to move on. "We need to start talking to other potential broadcasters," I said to CBC. "Fine," they said, "You'll never find anyone else willing to pay as much as we are offering."

"Not necessarily true," I countered, and asked, "You are aware of course that Bell Canada has recently bought the CTV Television Network. Have you focused on the fact that, as part of their enticement to win CRTC regulatory approval for the purchase, they have committed to create something called *The Great Big Canadian Show*? With a budget of $1.5 million per year, almost exactly the amount we need? Before you send us off, are you sure you don't want to rethink this all?"

Their reply was pithy. "We're quite sure. Go with God."

To this day I don't know whether CTV was thinking of the *Junos* when they made the commitment to creating *The Great Big Canadian Show*. I do know that six years earlier Ivan Fecan, who was the president and CEO of CTV throughout this period, had approached me to say that CTV would be very interested in the *Junos* if the CBC ever ended its agreement with the show. He would certainly have been aware of the cost of mounting the *Junos*, and at the very least would have had that in the back of his mind when CTV made its commitment. A press release at the time referred to *The Great Big Canadian* Show as "a spectacular variety television event," to occur annually for at least seven years, with an average budget of $1.5 million per year, based on "stars, musical genres, Canadian festivals, or events in music or comedy."

It was tailor-made for *The Juno Awards*. Indeed, a supporting document to that press release went on to specifically refer to music stars Alanis Morissette and Céline Dion as routinely appearing on American television. "As for Canadian variety, one of the things that we have noticed is that we can't afford to put our own big Canadian stars on television any longer," then–CTV executive vice-president Trina McQueen was quoted as saying. "With this kind of budget, we may be able to attract Canadians who are now international stars and make a go of that kind of programming."

Academy president Daisy Falle, together with board member Steve Herman, made the first foray into CTV.

> **Daisy:** I went over with Steve Herman — at first, they were reluctant to deal with us because they thought we were using them as a bargaining chip with CBC.

But once CTV realized that the Academy was serious about moving networks, things started to move quickly. CTV confirmed they were very interested in the *Junos*, but more than that they were keen to explore the idea of moving the *Junos* to different locations across Canada.

They were prompted in this by the then–federal Minister of Industry, Brian Tobin, who until a year earlier had been the premier of

Newfoundland. It was during his tenure as premier that Newfoundland undertook an aggressive tourism marketing campaign, including celebrating such milestones as the five hundredth year since John Cabot's voyage of discovery, and the thousandth year since the Vikings had landed on the province's shores. Enticing *The Great Big Canadian Show* to Newfoundland would have even more marketing potential in Tobin's view, and he couldn't contain his excitement at the thought that *The Great Big Canadian Show* might actually be *The Juno Awards*.

This was all well and good, and music to ears of the Board of the Academy, but there was a stark reality to be faced: moving the show outside Toronto would significantly increase the production costs. Lighting,

Linda and me celebrating with Ivan Fecan at *The Juno Awards* in Vancouver.

sound, and camera equipment would need to be transported. The artists, the record company personnel, most of the technical and production crew, and the Academy staff would need to be flown in and lodged. Furthermore, the only possible venue in St. John's, Newfoundland — Mile One Stadium — was tiny compared to Copps Coliseum in Hamilton.* Not only would this drastically reduce ticket sales revenue, the limited space meant the set designs and the logistics of set changes would require complex planning.

To get a sense of what might be in store, I met with John Brunton, the head of Insight Productions. A gregarious visionary known for his trademark moustache and cowboy hat, John had acted as the producer for some earlier *Juno Awards* and was well-regarded by CTV, for whom he was currently producing a late-night music/talk show called *Open Mike with Mike Bullard.*

> **John:** Oh my God, Stephen and I have gone through all kinds of crazy experiences on the *Junos.* When we decided we were going to take the show out to St. John's, when it switched over to CTV, that was a white-knuckle ride. We were going from a major market situation into … the unknown. We didn't know what we were going to deal with.

After several meetings and some preliminary research, the one thing John and I were quite sure of was that producing the *Junos* in St. John's would cost almost twice what we were used to in Toronto.

But necessity is the mother of invention. Members of the Board of the Academy, including Steve Herman along with then–board chair Ross

---

* Stretching for 7,699 kilometres (4,784 miles) from St. John's in Newfoundland to Victoria in British Columbia, the Trans-Canada Highway is the longest national highway in the world. While there has been debate over which city is the starting point, St. John's has effectively usurped this mantle by naming its sports arena Mile One Stadium, and its associated convention complex Mile One Centre.

Reynolds, met with various prominent Newfoundlanders and found that Tobin's enthusiasm had spread to all levels of government as well as to local Newfoundland agencies and businesses. Altogether, a group of regional and federal entities agreed to provide over a million dollars of additional funding to the Academy for *The Juno Awards* to be held in St. John's. (In the end, it all proved to be a wise investment for Newfoundland: later studies showed that over ten million dollars in direct revenues to Newfoundland arose from their hosting of *The Juno Awards*.)

John: Stephen and I felt that the opportunity to move the show across the country could be a source of revenue for the show. We started thinking about the *Junos* travelling a little like the Grey Cup. Could it become like the Grey Cup weekend, and could we invite musicians from across the land to play in all the bars in that town, and could we create almost a whole festival around the *Junos* and literally take the music to the people?

In America the *Grammys* used to be spiked in either New York or L.A., and that's still been the case all these years — to kind of ignore what I would call the "flyover states." We really felt very passionately that we should take almost the opposite approach. We should take the show to towns that would really appreciate it and it would be the biggest show that had ever shown up in that city. That was certainly the case in St. John's; they'd never seen a show like that before and the fans blew the roof off the place. The show took on a life of its own and it's something we'll always be very proud about. It started something, and Brian Tobin recognized the cultural value of that as well as the great fan experience. I don't think the CBC figured that tourism boards would bid for the *Junos* to come to their towns like they've done very aggressively since that first show in St. John's.

But we are getting ahead of ourselves. The Academy still had to conclude an agreement with CTV and the move away from CBC.

Nailing down the agreement with CTV was relatively straightforward as the major part of their commitment was already laid out in their CRTC filing for *The Great Big Canadian Show*. The Academy wanted what they felt they had lacked at CBC, namely control over the selection of artists and major creative decisions for the show. CTV wanted approval rights but also assurance that the production would be first-class (which of course the Academy wanted as well). All the various interests were resolved by entering into a three-way agreement that gave both CTV and the Academy the input and rights they needed, while entrusting the actual production of the show to John Brunton and Insight Productions. I would continue as executive producer alongside John.

I remained concerned, though, that despite CBC's insistence that they would never offer such a high licence fee, they might try to hijack the show by offering to match the CTV offer. On a pure dollar basis, that would have satisfied the needs of the Academy; but CTV had something much more to offer than simple dollars, something CBC could never match. CTV's acquisition by Bell Canada meant it was now associated with an array of very popular specialty TV channels and radio stations (including MuchMusic, Discovery, and TSN), as well as new sister companies such as the internet portal Sympatico and Canada's national newspaper, the *Globe and Mail*. So I asked for, and received, a written commitment to over five million dollars' worth annually of promotion and publicity through all these associated entities. Ed Robinson, then CTV's head of comedy and variety, stated at the time, "We offered a few things I take it the CBC was not able to match, a lot of that being promotions and our specialty channels." *

It was good that we had received this commitment. It was surprising, but not shocking, when CBC's response came. After months of refusing

---

* Nine years later Ed became the board chair of CARAS after my tenure as chair ended.

to restore the licence fee to its previous levels, suddenly they said they would match the CTV offer.

I dutifully relayed the CBC position to the Board of the Academy, but the Board was in no mood to entertain any further discussions. They felt disrespected by CBC, and they were looking forward to a new era with a new network and a new sense of purpose: a cross-Canada show that would bring the Juno celebration into many different regions of Canada, and would not only showcase Canadian music but also help bring Canadians together in a unified viewing experience.

CBC fought back at first, insisting they had the right to match CTV's offer, but of course they could never actually match the written commitments that CTV had given for publicity and promotion. After a while CBC grudgingly withdrew, and we were off to St. John's.*

The events leading up to the first CTV broadcast of the *Junos* on April 14, 2002, at Mile One Stadium, remain vividly in my memory.

The people in St. John's were overwhelmingly welcoming to all the visitors and were so proud of hosting the *Junos*. The provincial legislature even passed a regulation that in the event of a widespread power failure (not that uncommon during the cold, foggy nights of April), power would be diverted first to the local prison, and next to Mile One Stadium, to ensure that the broadcast would not be interrupted. (I presumed, but never asked as I wasn't sure I wanted to hear the answer, that hospitals were further down the priority list only because they had sufficient backup generators to withstand a relatively short outage.)

They saw the broadcast as a wonderful chance to showcase for the rest of Canada how special their city and province were, but it was more than that; hospitality and openness simply ran in their blood. For centuries strangers had been welcomed into Newfoundland homes as a matter of course. Indeed, just half-a-year earlier Newfoundlanders had welcomed into their homes some seventeen thousand mostly

---

* Sixteen years later the *Junos* have returned to CBC, with the first broadcast scheduled for March 2018 in Vancouver.

American airline passengers stranded for over a week by the 9/11 terrorist attacks.*

For the visiting artists, it was amazing because they became part of the community. They played in local clubs but then got invited back into people's kitchens to continue jam sessions until the early morning. And the bigger stars felt especially secure: there were no mob scenes or need for entourages, just typical Canadian politeness, respect, and inclusivity. I recall seeing Shaggy, who was on top of the international charts at the time, waiting for a taxi outside the Hotel Newfoundland.** (All the local limousines had been booked months earlier for the high school proms.) The taxi didn't come and didn't come. Remaining unfazed Shaggy simply turned around, went back into the hotel, and crashed a local prom in the ballroom of the hotel, dancing with the teenagers, causing a sensation, and having a great time.

The Kissing the Cod ceremony was emblematic of the warmth with which St. John's treated us. During the week prior to the broadcast, many artists and music industry executives were invested into the Royal Order of Newfoundland Screechers. My investiture actually occurred earlier, during a scouting trip, but followed the long-established protocol, a protocol that remains somewhat foggy in my mind since it involved drinking a local version of rum called "screech," followed by me passionately kissing a (thankfully dead) cod fish on the lips. I was then required to respond to the question, "Is ye a Screecher?" with the exact proper words, "Deed I is, me old cock, and long may your big jib draw!" *** Failure to use the exact words required more drinking of screech until, ultimately secured the coveted certificate from the Royal Order.

---

* The kindness and compassion shown to the stranded travellers has now been enshrined in the hit Broadway play *Come from Away*.

** He was nominated that year (and won) for Best Selling International Album for *Hot Shot*, featuring the single "It Wasn't Me."

*** Roughly translated as, "Yes indeed, my old friend, and may there always be wind in your sails!"

All in all, the St. John's *Juno Awards* proved to be the kick-off of a brand new national music event. Over the next few years the *Junos* moved across the nation, touching down in Ottawa, Edmonton, Winnipeg, Halifax, Saskatoon, Calgary, and Vancouver, before returning once again to St. John's and then back to Toronto.

By then it had become way more than just an awards show and concert. Starting in St. John's, the Juno week expanded to include fan zones, receptions, concerts, club performances, industry gala dinners, and songwriters' circles. Two years later Jim Cuddy of Blue Rodeo instituted another annual rite, the Juno Cup hockey game, which matches National Hockey League alumni ("NHL Greats") against musicians and entertainers ("the Rockers") with proceeds going to the MusiCounts charity.*

It was everything CTV and the Board of the Academy had hoped for. The modern *Junos* had been born.

---

* In the Juno Cup's fourteen years to date, the NHL Greats have contrived to win every time, always in dramatic fashion and normally by a one-goal margin, with the single exception being 2009 when the Rockers eked out a 12–11 victory in an overtime shootout.

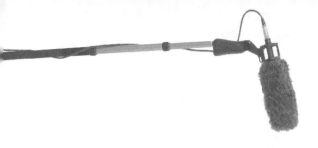

19
JUNO MOMENTS

DRESS REHEARSAL

Tickets to the St. John's *Juno Awards* sold out in under five minutes, months before the show, partly so fast because of the intense local demand, and partly because Mile One Stadium was so small that there just weren't that many tickets available for sale to the general public. On the night before the broadcast, though, somehow a rumour started that a large block of tickets would open up for sale.

I didn't pay too much attention to the rumour even when the local radio station picked it up. We all knew it wasn't true. Well, actually, it held a tiny sliver of truth: we always held back some seats around camera locations until the day of the show, just in case the cameras needed to be moved a bit. So there were, in fact, about twenty partially obstructed tickets that would become available when the stadium box office opened at 10:00 a.m.

When I woke up at 5:30 a.m. and looked out my window toward the stadium, hundreds of young fans were lined up in the freezing cold of that dark April pre-dawn, snaking toward the ticket window. They had clearly been there all night. My heart went out to them; all but a handful were going to be bitterly disappointed. On top of worrying about their disappointment, I knew it was a potential public relations nightmare.

I quickly dressed and headed over to the stadium, an idea percolating in my head.

Nothing could be promised to the young fans, but we could let them know that we would try to get them something to reward their cold overnight vigil, maybe some swag, maybe something more. We handed out wristbands to everyone in line and told them to go home, get warm, and come back around noon.

Meanwhile I got on the phone to the then–chair of the Academy, Ross Reynolds, and we started reaching out to record companies and artist managers with a potential plan: would they permit these young fans to attend the dress rehearsal, which would take place starting at noon in what would otherwise be an almost empty stadium?

The dress rehearsal is one of my favourite few hours in the entire *Juno* production. It runs during the day of the show — prior to the evening broadcast — and enables the artists, the director, the lighting director, and all of the other members of the crew to discover potential issues with nuances of performance, moving of equipment, camera angles, microphone levels, scripted comments, and anything else related to the production. The entire show is rehearsed in order. Often an introduction, a skit, or a performance is interrupted and started again if a problem arises.

The initial reaction to our plan was one of skepticism; artists strive to be seen in their best light, not in a rehearsal when things are much looser, and they are working out potential kinks in their performance. But once everyone understood what the young fans had been through, all the artists agreed — and sure enough, that afternoon those young fans were treated to the show of a lifetime, up close and personal, seeing it all in the making, a dress rehearsal featuring Barenaked Ladies, Nelly Furtado, Sum 41, Sarah Harmer, Alanis Morissette, Daniel Lanois, and Nickelback.

The actual broadcast show went live at 8:30 p.m. local time (7:00 p.m. Eastern). The show went off exceptionally well, and cheers from the crowd were thunderous. But the performance I remember most fondly was that afternoon dress rehearsal, with those young fans having an experience they would never forget.

HIGHS AND LOWS

People often ask about my favourite Juno moments. There are so many highs from my time with *The Juno Awards*, dozens and dozens of them, that I'll have to restrict myself to a few.

The thing is, almost all the lows were really highs as well. Live television is like that, which is why it is so energizing: the adrenalin builds inexorably as the clock counts down to the start time. No matter what had gone wrong, or was about to go wrong, at 7:00 p.m. the red light would go on, and we would be on the air from coast to coast (and in later years, throughout the world via the internet).

Some of my favourite moments from over the years are probably yours as well. My first few, though, are more personal.

Christopher Ward was nominated in 1978 as Most Promising Male Vocalist of the Year. It was his talent as a singer that got him nominated, but the songs he was known for singing were ones we had written together. He didn't win (the honours went to David Bradstreet), but as they say, it was truly a thrill to be nominated.

In 1983 an off-air teachable moment occurred when the organizers decided to host a stand-up lobster-and-champagne reception for everyone prior to the show (which was held that year at what was then called the Harbour Castle Hilton Hotel in Toronto). It seemed like a good idea on paper, but when you think about it, no one can eat lobster standing up, particularly with a glass of champagne in one hand. So no one ate — they just drank. By the time then–governor general Ed Schreyer was onstage inducting Glenn Gould into the Hall of Fame, people in the back of the room were so drunk they were throwing buns. You had to be there.

One of the all-time killer *Juno* performances occurred in 1989, with Rita MacNeil singing "Working Man," backed by the full Men of the Deeps male choir; there was hardly a dry eye in the house. That same year was a banner one for Graham Henderson's and my law practice, with our clients such as Blue Rodeo, Glass Tiger, Honeymoon Suite, and Tom Cochrane & Red Rider nominated for Group of the Year (Blue Rodeo won the category and also won for "Try" as Single of the Year, and Glass Tiger won for Canadian Entertainer of the Year). In the rising star class, our clients 54-40, Blair Packham and the Jitters, The Northern Pikes, and The Pursuit of Happiness were all nominated for Most Promising Group of the Year.* Meanwhile, k.d. lang was in the middle of a three-year run as winner of the Country Female Vocalist of the Year category.

In 1991, *The Juno Awards* took place in Vancouver, the first time they had been outside Toronto. I was there as Dave Tyson's "date" as we were both there solo. Dave won two awards, for Producer of the Year and Songwriter of the Year, but there were two additional highlights for me.

First was Leonard Cohen's thank-you speech for being inducted into the Hall of Fame — it consisted almost entirely of the lyrics to his powerful "Tower of Song." It was one of those moments that still reverberates. (Two years later, back in Toronto in 1993, Leonard won Male Vocalist of the Year — even though he mostly spoke his lyrics — he quipped, "It's only in a country like this that I could get the Male Vocalist of the Year Award!")

Second was a young Céline Dion singing her first English-language hit, "Where Does My Heart Beat Now," which was a thrilling performance that led to a raucous standing ovation.**

A final moment for now — it's not an obvious duet at all, but when it happened in 1992 it was pure magic, as classical cellist Ofra Harnoy joined Celtic-style harpist (and long-time client of Graham's and mine) Loreena McKennitt in a heart-stopping performance. As an added bonus, on that night Loreena won her first Juno Award, for Best Roots & Traditional Album.

---

* They lost to Barney Bentall and the Legendary Hearts.

** And Céline went on to win two Junos that year for Female Vocalist of the Year and Album of the Year.

CHOOSING THE SONGS

Once the performers have been chosen for a *Junos* broadcast, the next task is choosing the songs they will perform. That is harder than you might imagine. From our point of view as producers of the show, except in special circumstances we want each artist to perform one of their hit songs — ideally the one they've been nominated for that year.

Often, though, the artists are tired of performing their hit songs. They perform them almost every night when they are on tour. And they feel that their diehard fans will be delighted to hear a song they haven't heard before, or maybe a new single that has just been, or is about to be, released.

However, the audience for *The Juno Awards* broadcast does not just consist of diehard fans for each artist. Most artists have become experts at understanding what works best in live concert performances; some confuse that with being experts on knowing what works best on television. That can lead to serious challenges.

When, for example, we requested that Our Lady Peace perform their monster anthem "Innocent" at the 2004 *Juno Awards* in Edmonton, we thought it would be one of the top moments on the show. At first, they said they did not want to perform "Innocent," but after a long debate with them and their managers, they relented. Or so we thought.

As producer and fellow executive producer of most of *The Juno Awards* broadcasts since 1996, and as head of Insight Productions, which has produced every *Junos* broadcast since 2002, John Brunton was at the epicentre of the debate.

> **John:** Our Lady Peace had a big anthem and a huge radio hit, and everybody seemed to love it. We rehearsed the song, we set up our camera movements and lighting cues based on the song, our audio

department worked painstakingly to mix the sound exactly to the band's specifications, and we went through the dress rehearsal to make final adjustments to all the elements of the performance.

Within seconds of Our Lady Peace starting their performance during the actual broadcast, we all realized it was not "Innocent" they were playing, it was a song we had not heard before or prepared for. There was nothing we could do.

> **John:** All the lighting cues and our camera angles were wrong, and the sound mix was way off.

The audience in the Rexall Place was not aware that anything was wrong; they didn't know it was not the song we'd planned for. For them the band was there and performing well, even if the sound was weird. It was the home audience, who saw the awkward camera shots and cuts, who bore the brunt of the song switch.

> **John:** It was as if you could hear the clicks of television sets turning off across the country.

About two weeks after each broadcast, we are given the so-called "minute-by-minute" ratings report. As its name suggests, it breaks down the audience for each minute of the show. When we received the "minute by minute" report for those *Junos*, we saw the ratings had dropped all the way through the Our Lady Peace segment until they reached the low point for the entire show.

There's a lesson here: kids, don't do this at home.

MORE MOMENTS

One of the greatest Juno moments occurred in Ottawa, in 2003, when Shania Twain hosted the awards. Shania lit up the stage every time she appeared. When she first came out, in a sleeveless dress with hockey's Ottawa Senators logo across the chest, the crowd went wild. During the course of the show she changed into six different custom-designed outfits inspired by Canada's NHL franchises. (In honour of their hockey rivalry, the crowd mock-booed her glittering Toronto Maple Leafs turtleneck with baggy white pants.)

It was a comeback year for Shania; her hugely successful album *Come On Over* had been released five years earlier, followed by extensive concert tours, but she had taken the most recent two years off for the birth of her son. Her album *Up!* had been released a few months earlier, and the single "Up!" was already a huge hit. Her next single, "Forever and for Always," was timed to be released simultaneously with *The Juno Awards* broadcast.

My eyes still get moist when I recall her singing "Up!" dressed in a glitzy red Montreal Canadiens ensemble, sporting a prominent number 9 on her thigh in honour of arguably the greatest hockey player of all time, Maurice "Rocket" Richard. During the course of her performance, she went stage left to unleash a large red banner, then stage right to unleash another large red banner. As the song drew to a close, she unfurled from the middle of the stage a huge white banner with a large red maple leaf in the centre, turning her backdrop into an enormous Canadian flag. It was a very emotional, very dramatic, and very Canadian moment.

Shania was featured in another one of the truly great *Juno Awards* shows — she was inducted into the Hall of Fame during the fortieth-anniversary show, held in Toronto in 2011 and hosted by Drake. Dressed in a tuxedo, Drake was a consummate professional, and a perfect host. Linda and I were beaming.

There were, though, two drawbacks to that *Juno Awards*. First was the major disappointment that Drake did not win any Junos that night, despite having been nominated for six of them. It was a surprising let-down, though he didn't allow it to affect his hosting duties (highlights of which included quizzing senior citizens on their hip hop knowledge and sparring with Justin Bieber over Skype).

Second was that Linda and I were seated behind the then-mayor of Toronto, Rob Ford, who was clearly extremely bored and not enjoying himself. We were relieved when, about twenty minutes into the show, during a massive tribute to the Yorkville music scene in Toronto, he abruptly got up and left, never to return.

Not all Juno moments are as big as those Ottawa and Toronto shows. Some are just little moments. There was the time Nelly Furtado arrived at the beginning of the 2007 *Junos* in Saskatoon, on a high wire, flying "like a bird" in an homage to her hit song. Part of the script was that the high wire wasn't going to work and it was going to be very awkward — it was a delightfully self-deprecating moment (and John Brunton and I and the lawyers at CTV worked for days to assuage the insurance company that having Nelly Furtado on a high wire was going to work out okay).*

There was another moment that I didn't even know had happened until after the show: the set exploded in flames during a pyrotechnics explosion. To the audience it was just pyro as usual — and our crew dealt with it quickly, safely, and effectively — but in fact there was major damage.

It happened at the 2006 *Junos* in Halifax when Nickelback were performing. Now, I'm not a big fan of pyrotechnics — or at least, not on television. Pyro is great in a concert setting as the loud bangs and flashes really electrify the audience. On television, though, it just doesn't come across, a few moments when the screen pixels out, and it's over. And it's

---

* Nelly later quipped, "I'm Like a Nerd."

expensive. But pyro was a major staple of Nickelback's performances, and when a group like Nickelback wants pyro, they get pyro.

> **John:** When those flames started to pop up we were thinking, God help us. So much pyro that they fried our projectors. Our projectors were the biggest part of our set, and they were never to be seen again by the Canadian public after that.

But undoubtedly John's and my favourite little moment is the first appearance by Feist on the *Junos* in Edmonton in 2004. It was just Feist and her guitar in the centre of the huge arena, in a beautiful circle of light.

> **John:** It should have been so simple. Of all the complicated technology we had on that show, somehow it was this performance when something went wrong. Her guitar wasn't plugged in properly at the beginning of her performance. She was cool as a cucumber, and one of our guys ran out on stage and managed to sort it out. She'd stopped singing the song. And then she started up again, and it was so graceful and beautiful the way she did it … she sang so emotionally, so poignantly. I think Stephen and I just about had a heart attack that night when the simplest of setups that you could possibly conceive of was, somehow, messed up. But as it turned out I think it galvanized people coast to coast, and we all fell in love with her in that moment.

Between *The Juno Awards*, *Degrassi*, *Instant Star*, and the "Jay and Silent Bob Do *Degrassi*" special, a lot was happening in 2005, and this is me leaning back in the boardroom taking it all in.

BAD THINGS COME IN THREES

The Juno Awards of 2005 were held on Sunday, April 3, at the MTS Centre in Winnipeg, Manitoba, hosted by comedian Brent Butt of *Corner Gas* fame.

Even before we arrived for the week of the show, we had been dealing with a strike at the MTS Centre. The strike would not affect us directly, but we worried about the possibility of one individual or another becoming overzealous, perhaps interrupting the broadcast in some way or inadvertently threatening the safety of the fans or the performers.

We had flown my friend and labour lawyer John Barrack out for the week to help us, and between John and the goodwill of the local union officials, over a series of meetings we gradually became satisfied that everything would work out well on the labour front. The strike would continue, but in designated exterior areas only, separated from the fans and the performers.

By late Wednesday, just as we were starting to relax a bit, with worries about the strike subsiding, the news broke that Pope John Paul II was very ill, hovering near death. You might wonder how this would impact *The Juno Awards*, but it became a major topic of conversation between us and the broadcasters — we had to plan what would happen if the Pope died on Sunday evening during our broadcast. We likely would have had to cancel a major portion, or perhaps all, of our broadcast to allow for breaking news coverage on CTV.

You may not realize how horribly jaded and cynical television producers and broadcasters can be: during the discussions we even seriously floated the theory that the Pope may have already died. News video showed the Pope from behind, seemingly propped up, and there was no way to tell if he was dead or alive. Under that theory, the Vatican would choose the most impactful time to announce his death, namely during Saturday evening prime time in Italy, so that the churches would swell for Sunday morning Mass.

For the record, Pope John Paul II did die on that Saturday evening, during prime time, at 9:37 p.m. Central European Time to be precise, in the Apostolic Palace, Vatican City. As such, our discussions on that potential issue came to an end; *The Juno Awards* broadcast would continue in full, as planned — or, as it turned out, not quite as planned.

It was Friday when we received news that our star performer, Neil Young, had just been hospitalized in New York and was being treated for a brain aneurysm.

> **John Brunton:** Neil had said the only time he'd ever perform on the *Junos* is if the show ever went to Winnipeg. Of course, we went out of our way to take the show to Winnipeg, in part to get Neil on the show. We already had all Neil's equipment on the stage, and Neil's road manager was with us when we got the news.
>
> It was heartbreaking. Arguably, Neil is the most important artist that's ever come out of the country. I was a massive Neil Young fan since I was a kid. A huge low point for both Stephen and me. We were worried sick for him to pull through. Thank God he did.

With Neil in intensive care, we had a performance slot to fill. It was k.d. lang who stepped into the breach. She was already scheduled to sing Leonard Cohen's "Hallelujah"; she agreed to sing an additional song as well, a tribute to Neil, a song he wrote that was originally recorded by Crosby, Stills, Nash & Young — "Helpless."

> **John:** On the flip side, k.d. — bless her — stepped up and blew the roof off the place singing "Helpless." We went from something that was a terrible moment, an enormous body blow, into k.d. making one of the most memorable performances in the history of *The Juno Awards*.

As the show finished that year, I turned to Linda and said, "Another show down. Piece of cake!" She knew exactly what we'd been through that week; she just rolled her eyes.

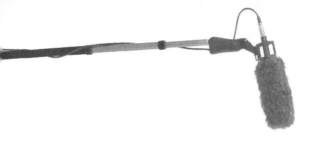

20
TOURING THE STUDIO

Over the years as *The Juno Awards* were evolving, our Epitome studios were also evolving.* Starting in early 1997 we had the fun and challenge of transforming a previously empty warehouse into four interior stages and a backlot set, along with attendant dressing rooms and hair, makeup, wardrobe, editing, and writing spaces, as well as our corporate offices.

While there are some standing sets that have remained pretty much the same since then, most of our sets have been radically transformed in an ongoing manner, first as needed for our *Riverdale* series, then for our *Degrassi* series, and then for any of the many other shows, large and small, that we have been involved with over the years. Over a matter of weeks a hospital triage area may turn into a funeral parlour, a university admissions office, and a police interrogation room.

I love giving tours of the studios, largely because of their ever-changing nature. Walking about, you cannot help but feel the energy of different ideas and dreams becoming manifest.

Since there are no formal tours and you can't pay an admission fee to see the sets, my tours are usually for visiting business colleagues,

---

* Since our acquisition by DHX Media, they're now known as the DHX Epitome Studios. People sometimes ask us why we named the company Epitome. I usually just reply, "Well, Paramount and Universal were already taken."

contest winners, politicians, or just new friends. I like to start by having them imagine what it was like on Christmas Eve back in 1996 when our purchase of the first empty warehouse had been completed, and Linda and I were wandering alone through the completely dark one-hundred-thousand-square-foot building, with flashlights to guide us through the numerous drums catching melted snow as it dripped through the roof.

While the individual sets have changed dramatically over the years, the actual overall set-up is still pretty much what we created during our first few months of owning the building. The floors for the sets are still polished concrete, painted as needed to look like wood or tiles or whatever a scene calls for. The sets themselves are still about 75 to 80 percent of the size of the actual rooms they are portraying; not because we needed the space, but to accommodate the illusion created by a film camera that makes objects appear bigger than they are.* Sets built actual size would look too big on the screen.

Each of the sets has at least one wall that "flies," meaning that it can be quickly removed to allow cameras to shoot from different angles without intruding too much into the space.

As we tour the various sets, being careful to step over cables, we need to stop every few minutes and remain silent until we hear the appropriate buzzer (one buzz means the cameras are rolling, two buzzes means they've stopped). It's always a treat to come to an area where actual shooting is happening and chat with the cast and crew about how the day is progressing. We watch for a bit but then retreat to let them get on with their work. If there are kids on the tour, sometimes the director will let one of them yell "Action!"

We walk through the interior sets where the great food fight took place; where Cam jumped from the balcony; where Eli lived and hoarded; where Drew and Bianca hooked up in the boiler room; and the gym where so many games, assemblies, proms, blood drives, and science fairs have taken

---

* Hence the adage, "The camera adds ten pounds to your figure."

In the gym, a "school photo" picture of the 2012 *Degrassi* cast, with me as the "teacher."

place. We wend our way to the exterior sets, two intersecting streets with huge green screens that allow us to realistically simulate downtown street-scapes, whether in Toronto, New York, Paris, or wherever. There's also the mansion set, with its heated saltwater swimming pool (it had originally been the Lux Motel set for our *The L.A. Complex* series and is now the set for the wealthy Hollingsworth family on *Degrassi*).

I often stop at the spot where one of our most iconic *Degrassi* scenes took place: the school shooting that left the character Jimmy Brooks par-alyzed and in a wheelchair. Jimmy was played by Aubrey Graham, now better known by his middle name "Drake," arguably the top entertainer in the world today. Not that long ago producer Stephanie Cohen joined me on a tour, and when I pointed out the location where Jimmy was shot, Stephanie just laughed. "That's not the spot; it's over here in the next corri-dor!" Turned out she was absolutely right. I'd confused the corridor where Rick confronted Emma and Sean, and ultimately died, with the corridor where Jimmy was shot. I was mortified. (And then we laughed about all the people I'd so passionately misled on years and years of tours.)

While we walk through the corridors, I'll often be asked about the hundreds of actors who have been on *Degrassi*. While Drake, after winning Grammys and multiple other awards, is the best-known *Degrassi* alumnus, stars such as Nina Dobrev (*Vampire Diaries*), Shenae Grimes (*90210*), Landon Liboiron (*Hemlock Grove*), Jake Epstein (*Spiderman* and *Beautiful* on Broadway), and Ricardo Hoyos (*Transformers*) also got their start on *Degrassi*. Many others (such as *Green Arrow* star Stephen Amell and *Grey's Anatomy* star Sandra Oh) have appeared on *Degrassi* as day players or extras in the early stages of their career. And numerous other stars have made guest appearances, including Chaz Bono, Colin Mochrie, David Sutcliffe, Billy Ray Cyrus, Shay Mitchell, Natasha Bedingfield, Perez Hilton, Alanis Morissette, Kevin Smith, Jason Mewes, Keke Palmer, Pete Wentz of Fall Out Boy, Ed Robertson of Barenaked Ladies, and Adam Lazarra of Taking Back Sunday.

While touring the sets, I always make a point of showing off our offices since we shoot not just in the sets proper, but also in almost every other square inch of the building. One room I'm particularly fond of is the otherwise nondescript production boardroom. There's nothing remarkable about it; it's just a big room with a screen and sound system, but it is the location for two of our most intriguing parts of the *Degrassi* process — auditions and read-throughs.

Of course, Drake (or Aubrey, as he was then known) was one of the thousands who have auditioned there. Years later on *The Tonight Show with Jimmy Fallon* he would recount his first audition:

> **Aubrey:** It was a real pivotal day in my life because it was the first audition I went on, so that's already a monumental thing. It was also the day that I got accepted by these really cool Jewish kids at school, and they were finally like, "Yo, come over!" I had this really tug-of-war moment where I actually did something that I probably shouldn't have done that starts with a "w" and ends with "eed." That was my first time

[smoking], and we did it out of a starts with a "b" ends with a "ong."

It was crazy because I started really getting paranoid. I thought I'd just completely ruined my life. I started splashing water on my face constantly — it was like a Clearasil commercial! I showed up to the

Me with Nina Dobrev ("Mia"), backstage at the *25th Annual Gemini Awards* in 2010, where *Degrassi* was honoured with a moving tribute that Nina helped present.

audition and got just a little less paranoid, went in and did what I could, was just devastated, I couldn't tell my mom.

I must say, we had no idea he was high. All we knew was that he was incredibly charismatic, and he managed to convey the single attribute that we look for most in a young actor: vulnerability. So he got the part. But as he went on to say to Jimmy Fallon, "Kids, don't do this at home!"

Aubrey: I don't understand people that can actually go out onstage under the influence of anything really. I have to be straight and clear-minded.

The production boardroom has seen its own share of drama in the audition processes, but it is also where we hold read-throughs, when the actors, writers, directors, and Linda and I gather a few weeks before principal photography takes place to listen to the actors read through the script.

For most shows the actors are sent the scripts in advance and have a chance to study them and bring their own interpretation to their characters as the read-through progresses. Our *Degrassi* read-throughs are different; the actors have never seen the scripts before. They simply read aloud the lines for their respective characters as the lines come up. They've had no time to prepare for how their character "ought" to be saying the lines, or what emotions they should be portraying.

This allows us to gauge their reactions to the script in real time. And following the read-through we have detailed discussions with the actors about their thoughts on the scripts, what they felt worked, what didn't, and whether they had personally gone through anything like that themselves. We then make adjustments to the scripts based on this extraordinarily valuable feedback. It's like having our own super focus group.

This process is particularly effective because *Degrassi* cast members are age-appropriate: the actors in real life are about the same age as the

At the 2013 *Emmy Awards*, Linda and I are joined by *Degrassi* writers and producers, as well as cast members Cristine Prosperi ("Imogen"), Luke Bilyk ("Drew"), Munro Chambers ("Eli"), and Stefan Brogren ("Mr. Simpson").

Me with Eric Osborne ("Miles"), Sara Waisglass ("Frankie"), and Ricardo Hoyos ("Zig") inside the Microsoft Theater in Los Angeles, attending the 2015 *Emmy Awards*.

characters they portray. As a result, unlike most other teen shows, the cast changes organically. Each year new younger characters are introduced while older characters graduate and leave the series (other than for occasional guest reappearances). We feel that the ongoing changes in the cast result in more authentic portrayals of the teen experience, that a teenage actor can portray the naïveté and vulnerability of a teen in a way that a world-wise older actor cannot, even if the older actor is otherwise youthful-looking.

The ever-changing nature of the cast also means that issues and stories can be revisited over the years through the eyes of different characters who have different points of view, keeping the storytelling fresh. This may be one reason why the franchise has lasted as long as it has.

We usually start or end the tour outside my office. Now, the office itself is not particularly intriguing, although it's a cool place for me to work. I have a picture of The Beatles on the wall, a *Star Wars* lightsaber, and other memorabilia. The room has a long, rounded desk that allows me to spread my work out, and I keep it fairly dark. Outside my office is an area where a number of the awards are kept.

On a tour we'll take some pictures of me pretending to present an award to one of the visitors; usually they'll pick the Emmy because it looks so beautiful. To be clear, the two we have are technically Emmys, but they are International Emmys, so the competition is largely foreign and not coming from the U.S. One of my dreams has been to win a Primetime Emmy, where the competition for a show like ours tends to be from large studios like HBO, Disney, and Nickelodeon, but as I write this chapter, we haven't yet won a Primetime Emmy (though we have been nominated four times).

We then say our goodbyes, and I go back into my office to sign some cheques or make some calls. In a week or so there'll be a new tour, and it truly will be new. Some new sets will have been built; we'll stop off to witness new scenes being shot; there'll be new cuts in the editing suites to take a look at; and we'll have a chance to chat with different crew members and actors along the way. In a sense, the tours never really end, and maybe that's one reason I love giving them so much.

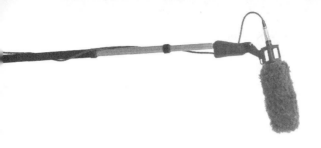

21
TIME STANDS STILL

You know from the Cowboy Junkies chapter that in everyday life I'm a big fan of writing down your goals, refining them to ensure they are authentic, and then allowing your subconscious mind to conspire with the universe to manifest those goals into reality. In some ways producing a television episode is a lot like that.

The *Degrassi* writing process starts in the writers' room, a big square room with a large round table in the middle. The key difference between this and any other production room is that three of the walls are covered with large whiteboards containing handwritten and colour-coded story points that the writers are contemplating for each episode of the season. Because of this we keep the room confidential and off limits.

Here in the writers' room the storylines are debated and honed, not just for each specific episode, but also for story arcs that cover many episodes and in some cases entire seasons. It was here that the idea for the iconic episode "Time Stands Still" first arose.* The year was 2004 and

---

* For many years *Degrassi*'s protocol was to name individual episodes in homage to great 1980s songs. This one was named after the Rush song "Time Stand Still" ("Stand" without a final *s*), but an editing error somewhere along the way led to the additional *s* being added.

brainstorming was taking place for potential storylines for Season 4 of *Degrassi*. Aaron Martin was the head writer.

> **Aaron:** When I was in a small-town high school back in the eighties, there was a shooting at a party, and it always stuck with me because one really good friend of mine and another guy I knew both ended up dying. That's something, obviously, that you never forget. The other writers and I were talking about how different it was — that back in the eighties when something like this happened, it was violence on yourself or your close people versus the broader type of school shootings that started happening. The culture had become more violent, with more peer pressure and bullying, and we started seeing that in the schools.
>
> So we really wanted to explore what would happen with a kid in school who is pushed to the edge, to the point where he sees the only way out as being extreme violence.

One of the rules we try to follow in *Degrassi* is to have the big events happen to main ongoing characters. We don't bring in a new character for a few episodes to become pregnant or commit suicide or become addicted to cocaine; if these events are going to happen, they are going to happen to one of our leads.

But for a story about a school shooting, it would not be believable to have one of our leads suddenly jump out of character and become a shooter. We would have to make an exception to the rule. Therefore, the first problem Aaron faced was deciding who would be the shooter.

He immediately thought of the character Rick Murray, who in the previous season had been in a jealous, abusive relationship with his girlfriend Terri MacGregor, a relationship that ended with Rick in a rage, pushing Terri to the ground, where she accidentally hit her head on a cinder block. Rick had been immediately expelled from Degrassi and had not returned. Aaron mused, what if he did return in Season 4 after serving the term of his expulsion? He might well be someone who could get pushed to, and over, the edge.

Before proceeding further Aaron approached Linda and me with his idea. We were immediately supportive. It was a vitally important issue to address, and an extremely difficult story to tell well and responsibly, but in many ways it was the ultimate story about the devastating impact that bullying can have.

We proceeded to find out if Ephraim Ellis, who played Rick Murray, would be available for Season 4. He was.

> **Ephraim:** In the previous season I was brought in as an abusive boyfriend character — like a stealth-abusive boyfriend, 'cause he's the guy you'd least expect, kind of a shy dork. That storyline ended after three episodes when I ran off. I thought that was the end of my entire character on the show, and then eight or nine months later I got a call saying they wanted me to do some more episodes the next season, and I said to myself, "Well, sure, but my story is over; I don't really see what else I could be doing." And then they pitched the "Time Stands Still" arc, which had me coming back to the school and trying to reintegrate myself into society but everybody hating me, and it becoming this cycle of violence. I kind of knew immediately as they were pitching it where it was going.
>
> Linda said they'd wanted to do a school-shooting episode for a while because those kinds of events are such big important events in the news and in history, but they hadn't really figured out an organic, character-driven way to do it before. That year when they'd been pitching stories around the writers' room,

they remembered my character and they thought maybe that could work.

Aaron worked with the entire team of writers to come up with a general story arc. It would start in the first episode of Season 4 with Rick's return to school and end eight episodes later with the shooting. Brendon Yorke was tapped to write the two-part episode that culminated with the shooting, and veteran Stefan Scaini set to direct the episode. It was not yet decided whether the shooting would result in any deaths; at this point the writers were mostly focused on making Rick's descent into despair not just believable, but also, if possible, somewhat sympathetic.

> **Aaron:** We weren't trying to sensationalize it; we were trying to tell the story in a realistic and humane way so that the shooter wasn't evil. He was just a kid who was so pushed to the edge that he mistakenly thought that his only way out was to unleash violence on people.

> **Brendon:** Rick was brought on as a villain, but what *Degrassi* does so well is that you get those scenes like him trying on his Dad's suit to [help the viewer] understand where this kid is coming from even though he's doing bad things. It's not like people are bad or good — we tried to show that everyone can be both, and it's the choices you make that really define you.

We were very concerned that a story so emotional still be authentic at its core, and that all the surrounding events be grounded in real-life experience, not just the imaginations of our writers. We brought in an outside expert, Barbara Coloroso, an internationally recognized speaker and consultant on bullying, grieving, nonviolent conflict resolution, and restorative justice. Barbara lived in Littleton, Colorado, where the

Columbine school shooting tragedy had unfolded, and her book *The Bully, the Bullied, and the Bystander* had been published just two years after that tragedy.

> **Stefan:** When we set out to do this episode, Stephen was very instrumental in insisting we bring in a consultant, so we flew in Barbara Coloroso, and she acted as a guide and a mentor and someone to help us focus on what the facts were and what we need to say as responsible filmmakers and storytellers in presenting a story like this. Barbara was very helpful for me, as the director, to understand what was going through these peoples' hearts and souls leading up to the shooting, at the shooting itself, and in the days and weeks and months following it.

> **Aaron:** She did a bullying seminar with us so that we could do the school-shooting episode in a way that was responsible. She told us about the wide range of factors that go into this kind of bullying, not just the bully and the victim, but the whole circle surrounding both sides that fosters a sick relationship that ends in an explosion of violence. Over two days we talked through all the different aspects of bullying and victims and people who stand by and encourage it, people who stand by and don't say anything. We tried to make sure that we had characters representing each one of those subsets within the show.

The writers were now in a position to shape the entire story arc. Season 4 would begin with Rick's return to *Degrassi*, and a protest against his return led by Emma and Paige. This would lead to Rick being beaten up by Jay. Emma would witness the beating and realize that the protest against Rick had gone too far; the bully had become the bullied.

In this way the writers set up a dynamic in which, over the course of the eight episodes, almost all the main characters could interact with Rick, and their attitudes toward him could shift, with some of them becoming sympathetic to Rick's plight. This would also allow the audience to become at least partially sympathetic.

Rick would misinterpret Emma's new support for him, and he would develop an unrequited crush on her. Another character, Jimmy, would also discover that Rick was doing his best to fit in and would become supportive. Ironically, these two would become Rick's intended victims when he reached the breaking point.

The stage would then be set for the "Time Stands Still" two-part episode itself. In that episode Rick would be part of the *Degrassi* team in a "Whack-Your-Brain" competition. Rick would correctly answer the tie-breaking question, winning it all for *Degrassi* and seemingly integrating him back into the school's favour. But at that moment a prank by Spinner and Jay would cover Rick in yellow paint and feathers in front of everyone — his moment of triumph would become a moment of utter humiliation.

Against this backdrop Principal Raditch would emblemize the do-nothing bystander — a school administrator who chose to disregard the caustic atmosphere that was slowly but surely enveloping Degrassi.

Further, Spinner would have a fight with his best friend Jimmy over the treatment of Rick and, in a moment of spite, would make Rick falsely believe that Jimmy had been the mastermind behind the entire yellow sliming.

Aaron: There was Emma, who played a role; Jimmy, who was actually supportive of Rick, but who ended up, because of Spinner's stupid prank, being Rick's victim. In those episodes Spinner is just as much of a

While the character Rick (played by Ephraim Ellis) was a bully, he also became the bullied, and it was this sliming of him that led to the fatal showdown between him and Jimmy.

bad guy as Rick is because his actions actually lead to Jimmy being shot.

Brendon: Another thing that's interesting about this episode, and the arc in general, is that Linda was okay with our heroes — a couple of the leads, Jimmy and Spinner, and Sean to an extent — being, in effect, bullies themselves against this abusive boyfriend. There were several episodes that led up to the school shooting where Rick was increasingly isolated, ultimately becoming pranked by being covered with yellow slime just as he was triumphing at a quiz show. There was a lot of buildup and preparation. Everybody was in a place you could understand emotionally, and it wasn't just sensational. We understood why Rick was doing it even though it was a terrible thing to do, and we understood why the other kids around him were feeling the way they did about him.

Up until the day of the read-through for "Time Stands Still," there was still debate going on about the actual outcome. We knew that Rick would confront Jimmy and shoot him, but how serious would the injury be? We knew he would also confront Emma, leading to a struggle for the gun between Sean and Rick, but would either of them die?

We agonized over these decisions. I think in our hearts we always knew there would have to be tragic consequences; we had to be authentic to what happens in real life. Still, we had many conversations internally, and with our broadcasters, until the decision was finally made: Rick would die in the struggle. And Jimmy would end up paralyzed and in a wheelchair for life, his dreams of being a basketball star forever shattered.

As we approached the read-through, none of the actors knew in advance what they would be reading, with two exceptions — Ephraim and Aubrey.

Aaron: That read-through was weird. It was our darkest episode. We prepped our two main actors. I remember pulling in Aubrey and saying "Good news. Bad news. The good news is we've got an amazing storyline. The bad news is we're going to end up making your character paralyzed." And he was totally up for it and excited by it.

Stefan: Linda and Stephen were always great about keeping the storylines from the cast so they didn't know what was coming. Linda used to conduct it almost like an exam. The scripts were always face down on the table in front of each actor. The cast, cleverly, always tried to look through the back page to see who had the last line because whoever gets the last line will usually tend to be the "A" plot of the episode.*

When they turned the "Time Stands Still" script over to start the read-through, none of them other than Aubrey and Ephraim had any idea what was coming. By the end of it the cast was devastated. They were in tears. In the process of the read-through they had lived the story. I was moved — during the read-throughs I watch the actors. I don't look at the page. I want to see how they are interpreting the lines, and which direction they're taking, in case I have to make adjustments. As they were reading the lines, you could see the tears welling in their eyes, but they continued. They were brave, they were

---

* This had been rectified by the time of this particular read-through. Earlier in the year, once we had realized what the cast was doing, the writers played a prank by creating a false last page in which every character died in a tragic, catastrophic crash. The looks of confusion on the actors' faces at the start of that read-through were priceless, particularly since they couldn't admit they were cheating by reading through the last page. Since then, we've used thicker paper!

fearless, and they didn't stop ... they kept reading with commitment. I think it was the strongest read-through I'd ever attended. A lot of times you get to the end of a read-through, and everybody's been fooling around and there's a certain levity, but for this one, everyone was riveted — they were focused. Their performance level was as if the cameras were rolling. At the end of the read-through I remember looking over at Linda and thinking, "Oh my God, this is going to be quite the ride."

A few weeks later we filmed the episode (yes, in those days we still shot on film). There's always a lot of preparation for any episode, but as you would expect, this one required much more.

Stefan: From a visual standpoint, I did not want to make it sensational. I did not want to turn it into action/adventure. I wanted to tell it from a very raw and, at times — I won't say documentary, but in a way that feels a little more experiential, like we were in the moment, rather than observing it from afar, putting ourselves in it. That's something that Stephen and Linda are wonderful about. They said, from day one with *Degrassi*, "We see it through the kids' eyes." Even the angle of the camera has to be from the kids' eyes. We are never observing it as third party; we are witnessing it from their perspective. And this one, more than ever, I wanted to make sure that we got that.

Aaron: The weirdest thing was being on-set when there was a gun on *Degrassi*. That was just creepy. Everyone's emotions were higher, and the director Stefan Scaini was on edge because it just felt ... wrong. Then when we saw it edited, it turned out to be so amazing.

Iconic moment from *Degrassi*'s "Time Stands Still" episode, as Jimmy (played by Aubrey Graham) is shot by a classmate, ending up paralyzed and in a wheelchair.

Stefan: It was something I talked with Aubrey quite a bit about, how he was going to react and how we played it off of Mike Lobel (who played Jay), because a lot of the shooting is witnessed through Jay's eyes. I said to everyone, "We're not doing a heroic death. We're doing a very ugly, awful, awful moment here. There's no heroism here, no glamour." This had to have rawness to it. And the lead-up to it had to be very unexpected.

Aaron: Rick could have been a one-dimensional psychopath, but he wasn't. He was a screwed-up kid, and Ephraim is such a good actor that he pulled it off.

"Time Stands Still" is an iconic episode, not only because of its difficult subject matter, but also because of its embodiment of core *Degrassi* principles, that nothing is black or white, that it is not always clear what is right or wrong, and that we all are empowered to make choices, but every choice has a consequence. And the consequences are not just events that unravel in the short run; they can reverberate throughout a lifetime.

> **Brendon:** The most terrifying thing — and we did it later when JT got killed outside of a party that went bad — is writing the next episode. The aftermath. You don't want it to be a real downer, it has to be entertaining, and at the same time a major thing happened and you can't ignore it.
>
> **Aaron:** We made sure that we followed through with all the characters who were impacted by it. We followed, of course, Jimmy's storyline, which kept going for seasons because he was in a wheelchair no matter what. That took his character, who was the fun-loving jock, and made him into something more than that in the seasons after that....Within that season Jimmy had to physically heal himself, and after that he had to emotionally heal himself. Emma went down a very dark road; she ended up traumatized, with PTSD basically, and it manifested itself by her becoming promiscuous and self-destructive. And Sean, his character ended up leaving the school because he just couldn't deal with it. Spinner had to come to terms with what his actions did to his best friend, who was going to be in a wheelchair for the rest of his life.

There were a host of other impacts woven into scripts for subsequent episodes. One seemingly small one deserves special mention: the removal of Principal Raditch as principal. It arose out of a conviction that Barbara Coloroso had stressed over and over in our meetings with her — that there are no innocent bystanders, and that failing to acknowledge bullying for what it is, or to simply dismiss it, is to be complicit in the bullying. She was particularly critical of the aftermath of the Columbine tragedy, where she felt there should have been an entire change in the school administration, to recognize its role in an environment where bullying was ignored. In the fictional world of *Degrassi*, at least, we made that change.

I don't normally get involved in the editing of an episode; that's Linda's domain. Her favourite parts of producing an episode are working with the writers and editors. To her they are very similar processes. She calls the edit "the final draft of the script."

In the case of "Time Stands Still," though, Linda called me into the editing room because the final scenes weren't having the impact she wanted. The script called for various pieces of dialogue as different characters reacted to the tragedy, but as we sat in the editing suite, the words just weren't cutting through the way they had been intended.

I had a suggestion. By coincidence I had recently heard tracks from a new and as yet unreleased album from Canadian indie artist Melissa McClelland.* There was a very slow and melancholy track on the album called "Rooftops" that musically and lyrically conveyed deep feelings of emptiness and aloneness.

One of the core themes of *Degrassi* is "You are not alone." You may think that whatever you are experiencing or feeling is unique to you, but be reassured that there are others who experience and feel what you do, and there are yet others who can support you. You are not alone.

But Rick Murray felt utterly alone. And in reacting to the shooting tragedy, we as the audience also couldn't help but feel the emptiness of being alone.

---

* Several years later Melissa and her husband Luke Doucet formed Whitehorse, a successful folk-rock duo that won the Juno Award for Adult Alternative Album of the Year in 2016.

I suggested we remove all the dialogue and just feature the faces of the characters reacting to the tragedy while playing the "Rooftops" track.

We tried it, and we were all in tears as the song and the episode ended. And that was how the final scenes remained. It wasn't exactly the ending Aaron and the writers had in mind when they began it all months earlier. Yet everyone had done their jobs perfectly. And the episode had turned out even better than we ever could have hoped:

The roof slips beneath my feet
As the branches back away from me
The softest grass turns to concrete
But I will fly
I will fly
You will see

'Cause I am playing God
I am raising hell
As far as I can tell
I am all alone
Alone in this world
Alone*

---

* Words and music by Melissa McClelland. © 2004 Starcana Music Inc. Thanks to Six Shooter Records. All Rights Reserved. Used By Permission.

22
DEGRASSI MOMENTS

IN-N-OUT

A funny thing happened on our way to the 2005 *Teen Choice Awards*. Stacey Farber ("Ellie"), Aubrey Graham ("Jimmy"), and I were in a white stretch limousine, making our way to the Gibson Amphitheater at Universal Studios in Los Angeles, when we got one of those good-news bad-news phone calls. The good news was that we had won! *Degrassi* would be named Choice Summer TV Show, and we would receive one of the coveted surfboards that all winners receive.*

The bad news was that we were an "off-air" winner. Our category would only be briefly mentioned on camera. Further, our limousine would not be allowed to enter the red-carpet limo zone, which was reserved only for celebrities who would be appearing "on-air."

It was a bit demeaning, but we could only laugh. The winners had been decided by online voting, and our small but fanatic *Degrassi* fan base had swamped the system, creating a slight embarrassment for the Fox Network, which hosted the *Teen Choice Awards*. *Degrassi* had

---

* It's an actual custom-made surfboard, with a different painted design each year. The surfboard was apparently chosen to symbolize the freedom of summer vacation for teens.

beaten major network shows that drew huge audiences: *Big Brother*, *Dancing with the Stars*, *Hell's Kitchen*, *American Dad!*, and *The Princes of Malibu*.

Our limousine was diverted to the Curious George Parking Garage, leaving us about a fifteen-minute walk to the Amphitheater via the outskirts of the Universal Studios Theme Park. Even though we arrived at the Amphitheater on foot, Stacey and Aubrey are so attractive that nobody questioned that we would be walking the red carpet. In fact, journalists and photographers descended upon the pair, and it took us almost half an hour to make our way through the throngs. It was August, and sweltering, and we were glad to finally get to our air-conditioned seats, where we enjoyed the show, hosted by Hilary Duff and featuring some great performances by artists such as Gwen Stefani, Black Eyed Peas, The Pussycat Dolls, and Simple Plan.

Pictured here with me are Stacey Farber ("Ellie"), B.D. Freeman ("Mr. Ellis") and Aubrey Graham ("Jimmy") following our winning the Teen Choice Award for Best Summer Series in 2005.

After the show we made our way out back to where several tents had been set up for celebration parties. Of course, we headed to the "Winners Tent" — only to find that, once again, since we were not "on-air winners," we weren't allowed in.

This was too much. We'd flown down from Canada, we'd won, and we were being disrespected. (Today with Aubrey being who he is, they would have been begging us to join their feeble little party!) But we had the last laugh, and it was Stacey who made it happen. We were very hungry by this point, and Stacey became a young woman on a mission. "Stephen, have you ever had an In-N-Out Burger?"

What's that?" I said, to which both Aubrey and Stacey yelled almost at the same time, "Oh my God, we are going to In-N-Out."

And so it was that, as evening drew nigh and a hot summer breeze swept across the hills of Los Angeles, an air-conditioned white stretch limousine pulled into the drive-thru lane at the In-N-Out Burger on Lankershim Boulevard in North Hollywood. The driver rolled down the window at the drive-thru booth, like the Rolls Royce in the Grey Poupon ads, and soon all the occupants of our limousine (including the driver) were inhaling multiple In-N-Out burgers (Animal Style, of course: extra Thousand Island spread, mustard grilled patties, and extra pickles).

I have been fortunate in my life to have eaten in some of the finest restaurants in the world, but I have to say, that evening meal, with Stacey and Aubrey in the limousine parked at the In-N-Out Burger after a long and exciting — yes, disrespected, but winning — day was one of the finest of them all.

There is a postscript to this story. My friend Jim Jackman and I, together with fellow In-N-Out aficionado Kevin Smith, worked for a while to try to bring In-N-Out to Canada. When it turned out the owners of In-N-Out weren't keen to franchise into Canada, we even trademarked our own burger name "Straight Up" (Our slogan was "How do you like your burger? Straight Up!") and worked with some fast-food executives with the aim of starting a burger chain in Canada that might come close to the holy grail of In-N-Out's made-fresh-to-order burgers and fries. In the end, the volume of our television work overcame us, Jim relocated to Los Angeles, and the Straight-Up Burger remains but a dream.

NINA

I have a favourite story about Nina Dobrev — such a favourite that I always remind her of it when we see each other, to the point that she must be quite sick of me telling it!

She may be better known today for playing the lead on *Vampire Diaries* for many years, but we will always know her as "Mia Jones" on *Degrassi*. To me, the most striking thing about Nina is how incredibly hard-working and dedicated she is. Yes, she is a beautiful and talented actor, but what really shines through is her commitment to being absolutely the best she can be at whatever she is doing.

Nina was part of the first cohort of Degrassians to take part in a Free the Children volunteer trip, on this occasion to build a school in the Maasai Mara (a ten-hour bus ride outside Nairobi) in Kenya. In the ensuing years our *Degrassi* cast members have volunteered to take part in a number of such trips, paying their own ways to locations such as India, Ghana, Ecuador, Haiti, the Amazon, and Nicaragua to work in local community projects.

But this was the first such trip. Nina was joined not only by fellow Degrassians Ray Ablack ("Sav"), Dalmar Abuzeid ("Danny"), Charlotte Arnold ("Holly J."), Marc Donato ("Derek"), Jake Epstein ("Craig"), and Jamie Johnston ("Peter"), but also by Craig Kielburger, the co-founder — along with his brother Marc — of Free the Children (and the affiliated organization Me to We). So not only did they work with local Kenyan children to build the school, but they also spent time with Craig partaking in local community activities, and learning about the importance of being ambassadors for change.

Jake Epstein ("Craig") and Nina Dobrev ("Mia") in conversation with local Kenyan children during their time in the Maasai Mara in 2007, helping to build a school.

Nina Dobrev ("Mia"), Charlotte Arnold ("Holly J."), Jake Epstein ("Craig"), and Linda surrounded by Craig Kielburger and other *Degrassi* cast members and crew, and local helpers, as they build a school in the Maasai Mara, Kenya.

The trip took place in 2007 after shooting *Degrassi* Season 7. On Labour Day Monday, Nina and the other Degrassians were covered in mud as they worked through torrential rains to complete the school they were building in Kenya. The next day they made the long trek back to Toronto, where on Thursday of that same week, Nina walked the red carpet at Toronto International Film Festival in a stunning red dress as a film she starred in (Jeremy Podeswa's *Fugitive Pieces*) was the opening film at the festival. To cap it off, the next morning the entire front page of the *Toronto Sun* newspaper was a picture of Nina, resplendent on the red carpet.

To me it's a wonderful conjunction, truly from the sublime to the sublime — from being covered in mud in Kenya, successfully completing a hugely worthwhile community project, to seventy-two hours later, dazzling on the red carpet, celebrating a wonderful but completely different kind of success.

SHENAE

All of our cast and crew are professional, but if there was a prize for professionalism, I think Shenae Grimes would claim top honours.

We were filming the twelfth episode in Season 7, and Shenae's character "Darcy" was in a very emotional scene. Earlier that season Darcy had tried to cope with being a rape victim, but she suppressed her emotions and was later paying the price, going down a destructive path of lies and promiscuous behaviour. In one particular scene she begins to make advances toward Mr. Simpson, trying to hug and kiss him. When he insists she stop, she threatens to hurt herself with a pair scissors.

We had already filmed the wide shot but were shooting the close-up on Darcy's face as she cut a chunk from her hair and threw the scissors down. She carried on with the scene, and at first no one realized anything was wrong — but when the director yelled "Cut!" Shenae crumpled to the ground. Turns out, as she had thrown the scissors down, they had

During the filming of this scene Shenae Grimes ("Darcy") seriously gashed her thigh but kept acting. No one realized what had happened until the director yelled "Cut!"

gashed her thigh, and suddenly there was a lot of blood. We rushed her to the hospital, where she received over a dozen stitches. A few hours later she was back on-set, insisting on completing her scenes for the day.

Other TV producers became very aware of how talented Shenae was. After we had finished shooting that season, we got word that Shenae would be moving on to star, for five years, in the drama *90210* on The CW.* Professional that she is, she graciously agreed to act in the first few episodes of Season 8 of *Degrassi* so that we could write her character out.

OnSet

There is no question I am what they call "an early adopter." Every September I line up to be the first to acquire the latest iPhone. I wear an Apple Watch, drive a Tesla, and apply updates to all of the above instantly when available. Almost everything in our home is controllable digitally.

You might think this would make me an expert in predicting where technology is going, but no, I am rife with failure at such predictions. When Google first arrived, I never made the connection that a search engine could lead to huge advertising dollars. To me it just seemed like a glorified telephone book, quite uninteresting, and completely outside the mainstream. When Twitter was first launched, it seemed to offer only a tiny fraction of what Facebook was already offering, in effect just excerpting the subject line of a Facebook post — and clearly doomed. Similarly with Instagram and Pinterest, I believed they offered just a part of what Facebook offered, not worthy of too much attention.

---

* *90210* was the fourth of five series which shared an ongoing timeline and characters: *Beverly Hills, 90210*; *Melrose Place*; *Models Inc.*; *90210*; and the reboot of *Melrose Place*.

Having said that, back in the early 1990s, in a published paper for the Canadian Association of Broadcasters, I did correctly predict the advent of streaming services which would mould their offerings by learning what you did and did not like. I called it the "one-channel universe" to distinguish it from what cable was then offering, namely the "500-channel universe." I didn't have any sense that this would be accomplished via the World Wide Web — and had absolutely no knowledge or foretelling of the ubiquitous internet — rather I assumed it would occur via some two-way interactivity over traditional radio and television signals. In a way I guess it is over-the-air that we mostly receive the internet to our various devices, so on balance let's call that prediction a quite successful one.

Whether or not I am good at making predictions, I am certainly good at working closely with people who are brighter than me and smarter about technology — a prime example being Raja Khanna.* We worked together for over a decade, in a partnership that laid the groundwork for *Degrassi* becoming what the *Washington Post* has called "the most digitally savvy show on (and off) TV."

In early 1997 I was asked by a student committee from Osgoode Hall Law School at York University to give a talk on legal aspects of the media. As the head of the student committee, Raja reached out to me after the talk to say how interested he was in what I'd had to say, and to ask if he could come and have a coffee with me.

> **Raja:** Stephen talked about the idea of personalization. He talked about how curation would no longer be done by humans. The book he later got me to read was Ray Kurzweil's *The Age of Spiritual Machines*. He's always been ahead of the curve on that very leading edge of

---

* Most recently Raja has been the CEO, Television & Digital, for Blue Ant Media Inc., overseeing the company's nine television networks, its international distribution group, and its production division along with various internet properties.

what back then was probably considered "nerd-dom." Now of course, the nerds run the world.... I remember leaving there going "I want to be just like that guy."

Over coffee, it became apparent how extraordinarily bright and perceptive and forward-thinking Raja was. He explained that even though he was in law school, he had decided he didn't want to become a lawyer. In fact, thanks to a five-thousand-dollar loan from his father, he had already set up his own web design and interactive business, called at the time Snap Interactive.

Then he made a proposal: he would like to design and create the website for the new Stohn Henderson law firm that Graham Henderson and I had formed — and he wanted to do so for free. He explained that it was his way of promoting Snap Interactive since I would likely then recommend Snap to my clients. But he also hoped that I would consider mentoring him.

Raja: This was on the advice of my older sister Roma who had articled at McCarthys with Stephen. I basically told her, "I don't know if I want to be a lawyer, but if I want to be a lawyer, the only lawyer I could possibly imagine being like is Stephen Stohn, but there's only him and maybe a couple of others in a similar place in Canada. So what do I do?"

She said, "Why don't you offer to do his website for free?"

I called Stephen to do their corporate website in exchange for mentoring credits. And that's how it started. We did Stohn Henderson's site for free, and I got to know him a bit better, and when he started thinking about *Riverdale* he called me and said. "What do you think?"

That turned into my first large paying gig.

I accepted his offer, and he did create the Stohn Henderson website, and I did, indeed, recommend Snap to many of my clients. While Raja may have thought I was mentoring him, it was better than that: we were mentoring each other.

It turned out that projects I was directly involved in became the major source of business for Snap in its early years — Raja and I worked together on some fascinating interactive projects. When Linda and I were producing the first season of the *Riverdale* soap opera, we turned to Raja and Snap Interactive to create the website for the series.

The website was primitive by today's standards. It had the features you might have expected, giving information on the cast and characters, and providing updates on *Riverdale* news. But it also included a feature that was way ahead of its time: one of the very earliest examples of what would now be called a webisode series. Called *OnSet*, it was a video soap opera, based on the lives and loves of people ostensibly working behind the scenes on the *Riverdale* production crew. We created short scripts and sent a video crew to shoot scenes on and behind our *Riverdale* sets.

Raja: I convinced Stephen that not only should we make a website for *Riverdale* but we should make this crazy interactive soap opera that happens behind the scenes of the actual soap opera, and we're going to do it all in streaming video, which no one had ever heard of before. That was the year that the RealPlayer came out, the first app on which you could stream video.... We were right at the leading edge of that whole thing.

Here's what I'll say that's not good about Stephen Stohn — as the first business guy that I met when I was a student in law school, he basically said "yes" to everything, which meant he set me up for interesting expectations for the rest of my career! Instead of saying, "You're insane," like any other reasonable businessperson would, he said, "I love it, let's do it," and then wrote me a big cheque.

While *OnSet* had a few fanatical viewers, the technology was still in the early stages. Each episode was roughly a minute long and was viewable through what was then called the RealAudio plugin embedded in the website. But on the dial-up modem that most people used to access the internet back then, it could take fifteen minutes to download the one-minute episode. Further, the picture was tiny, appearing on the computer screen in a window only a couple of inches wide. So almost nobody watched it.

> **Raja:** We did *Riverdale* and won every web-design award there was to win around the world at the time. But no normal person, no fan of *Riverdale* ever went to that website, it was so complex and strange. But Stephen and I and everyone else at the company got a little drunk off the adrenalin of this innovation we were doing. Stephen's like a kid in a candy store with this type of stuff, and so was I. We just had so much fun that we wanted to do it again, and do it smarter, and we built on what we'd learned when *Degrassi* came around a couple of years later.

So, was the *Riverdale* website a success or a failure? You'll know by now my answer to that: it was a resounding success. It allowed Raja and me to explore new ways of thinking about what made a website engaging to audiences, and it allowed Snap to expand its presence in the interactive world. This early video soap opera experiment led us to more radical innovation several years later, with the launch of the *Degrassi* website, and then the *Degrassi* webisodes that became so popular.

But that is another story....

AND THE TRUTH SHALL SET YOU FREE

Ken Murphy's bio talks about his history behind the development and growth of many successful digital channels and interactive media projects over the years, and about how he was part of the original management team which launched and grew The Sports Network (TSN). Then it goes on to say, "When he's not spending time with his family, Ken is an art lover, skier, naturalist, and avid collector of rare vinyl records." In other words, Ken Murphy is a really cool guy.

My friend Raja Khanna and I were sitting in Ken's office at CTV, pitching him our plan for a *Degrassi* website. It was early in 2001, and we were in the midst of preparing to shoot Season 1 of *Degrassi: The Next Generation*, which would launch that fall on CTV. Back then the internet was still very young. More to the point, website building was still very expensive.

Largely due to Raja's brilliance, we had come up with a plan for a revolutionary new website to engage viewers of the new iteration of *Degrassi*: viewers who registered at the www.degrassi.tv website would become "virtual students" at Degrassi Community School, and each would have their own "locker page" where they could post pictures, write commentaries (the word "blog" hadn't been invented yet), post surveys, and send "D-mails," which were Degrassi messages to other "students."

These features were cutting edge in and of themselves — remember this was long before the advent of MySpace or Facebook — but added to this was our plan to have the *Degrassi* characters themselves be part of the ecosystem. In this way viewers would be interacting directly with the *Degrassi* characters (who would be activated behind the scenes by our *Degrassi* scriptwriters, to keep their online characters consistent with their television personae).

Raja: The idea was you got a locker page, which now you'd equate to your home page on Facebook: your

The Homeroom Page

Find your way around with the Global Navigation bar

Dynamic chalkboard updates with all the latest news and stories

Important real-world information, education, and other helpful content

Meet other virtual students

Set up your own space on Degrassi

Join the lively discussion on Club Message Boards

Home page of the *Degrassi* Website Walkthrough in 2001, which Raja Khanna and his team at Snap Media prepared.

home screen, your news feed. You could share notes back and forth with other viewers so you became a notional student at Degrassi. You were given assignments that you had to complete; you were given a way to communicate with other students; you were given tools to build clubs and communities. It was really what is now called social media, but back then we called it a community engine.

Some of the students at the school were actually the fictional characters, but instead of being these two-dimensional, flat, fake people, we put real writers behind them. So if you interacted with them on their locker page, they'd write you back. They were your friends or they were in your homeroom with you, and those behind-the-scenes writers were writers that actually worked on the show, and really understood the characters, and could write authentically from each character's world view.

The website would cost $1.2 million to build, since it required inventing features which didn't then exist commercially.* We had asked CTV to contribute part of the cost, arguing that the website would not only serve as promotion, but also foster a deep engagement between *Degrassi: The Next Generation* and its viewers, which in turn could boost ratings and contribute to the longevity of the series.

To their immense credit, the CTV television executives in charge of *Degrassi* were prepared to accept what we were proposing, but they didn't pretend to fully understand what was happening on the internet, so they asked their colleague Ken Murphy to meet with us, as he had experience in interactive ventures.

Ken listened to our pitch. He complimented our vision and understood it was an exciting and far-reaching project, but he came right to the point. "You are asking for an extraordinary amount of money for a project that is completely unproven. How do I know that the website will actually engage viewers in the way that you describe? How can you convince me that you aren't going to fail?"

I am not a practising Christian, in the sense that I don't go to church (or at least certainly not regularly) and do have profound doubts about all religious institutions. But there is a phrase from John 8:32 that I have found to be remarkably powerful: "And the truth shall set you free." It amazes me how often, when facing difficult situations, speaking the plain truth can provide a path forward.

"Ken, I can't promise you we won't fail. In fact, given what we're proposing, you can argue we likely will fail," I responded, looking him in the eye. "But we are going to put everything we have into this website. We are going big. I can promise you this: if we fail, we won't just fail. We will really, really, really fail!"

Ken just looked at us in silence for what seemed like a long time, then said, "This is the first time someone has admitted that to me. I almost

---

* Today it would likely cost less than ten thousand dollars, an indication of just how far digital technology has advanced.

always say no; in fact, as I walked into this meeting, I was expecting to say no today." He paused. "What you're saying is true, all these projects involve very significant risk. But you seem to be clear-eyed; you're not fooling yourselves. It's an exciting project. So, I'm going to recommend to our management team that we partner with you on this, but not quite in the way you were expecting." Raja and I weren't sure what he meant. "I'm going to recommend that we give you the investment you wanted, but that in addition we give you five million dollars' worth of advertising and promotional support for the *Degrassi* website across CTV and our other specialty networks. This way you can have the best possible chance of success."

As we walked out of the meeting, Raja and I turned to each other and said, "Did that just happen?"

> **Raja:** Ken not only gave us promotional time, he gave us access to technical teams, he gave us equipment, he gave us the hosting — we connected through Bell Sympatico. They basically turned on the whole Bell Globemedia machine to support us. We ended up producing that first version of the *Degrassi* web property for a budget that looks like a TV budget.

Ken's and CTV's confidence in us turned out to be well-founded. The website became enormously popular, attracting over twenty-eight million hits per month, and signing up over nine hundred thousand registered users. It became the template for many of the digital and social media initiatives we have since undertaken.

> **Raja:** We built a community engine that was so successful it blew up all our servers. We had nearly a million young viewers on our platform within months. It broke every server we had.

Most importantly, the website did exactly what we had hoped: it fostered a deep engagement between our viewers and our *Degrassi* characters.

> **Raja:** I think what this site did that few other television websites have ever done is that we actually inculcated people into the *Degrassi* brand. They came there to chat and hang out with friends, and they became part of the *Degrassi* world.

SOME OF OUR TEAM REMEMBER AUBREY

Aaron Martin (writer): Aubrey was such a sweet kid. I knew him as a teenager. The last time I saw him before he became Drake, it was in an early episode of the series *Being Erica*, where we hired him and we were burying him alive for a frat hazing. It was 4:00 a.m. in a graveyard in Toronto, and he said, "Yeah, I've got this album coming out and I hope it does well." It was the one that made him a superstar.

Brendon Yorke (writer): We wrote an episode where Jimmy was going to rap for the talent show at school. We'd heard that Aubrey was trying to become a rapper. We didn't know how seriously to take it, but we knew he had some skills. But he was super resistant to doing it on *Degrassi*, and it took us a good two-hour meeting to convince him, and then he said, "Okay, I'll do it as long as I can write the rap." And I said, "Oh, thank God." He came in with the most beautiful thing you've ever heard. It was totally on theme and … it blew us all away.

And that's the moment I knew that he had enough talent to actually pursue this. Of course, no one thought he'd become the biggest rapper since Kanye.

Stefan Scaini (director): I remember when I was rehearsing with Aubrey and he mentioned, "Hey, I've got this CD that I did." And I said, "Oh cool, I didn't know you were a musician!" and he said, "Yeah, I do that, too." What a sweet, wonderful guy, and his commitment to his performing, as an actor, was astounding because he always wanted to do it right. It's not like he would breeze in and do it and have fun. He took it all

Roma Khanna and Raja Khanna join Linda and me in celebrating *Degrassi's* 2002 Gemini Award win for Most Innovative Website.

very seriously, and he was one that loved being directed. He'd say, "Give me something, what do I need, what am I missing, what am I not getting in this moment?" and then we'd sit down and I'd say, "This is probably what Jimmy'd be feeling," and he'd say, "I'm going to run with that." He was like a sponge when it came to direction.

Ephraim Ellis (actor): There are two different types of fan reaction. There's the one that's normal fan sort of stuff where someone will come up on the street and say, "Man, those episodes were really great, powerful work." And that will really brighten my day. And there's the other kind of fan reaction like a random tweet, "Hey, why did you have to shoot Drake?"

Even ten years later there are random people on Twitter asking me why I had to do this thing for pretend on TV. I didn't write it! I often reply to those things on Twitter in public so people can see: "Because it was in the script!" That's the joke, every time I do a play, in the program they have the recent credits, but the last sentence is always, "However he is probably still best known for his role as that guy who shot Drake on *Degrassi*."

MOONLIGHT IN CANNES

It sounds glamorous to spend time at a television or music festival in Cannes, in the sunny warmth of the south of France. In fact, to be honest, it is glamorous, but maybe not quite in the way you think. A lot of the time is spent in back-to-back meetings in tiny booths or crowded hotel bars — but some of the best meetings are those over a lengthy lunch or dinner at one of the excellent restaurants in the region.

I remember fondly one such dinner in 2003. CTV had ordered a first season of *Instant Star*, but hadn't yet ordered Season 4 of *Degrassi: The Next Generation*. Meanwhile, Viacom's teen specialty channel The N (now called TeenNick) in the United States had ordered Season 4 of *Degrassi* but weren't yet keen about *Instant Star*. We needed both broadcasters to sign on to each series to make the financing work.

The MIPCOM television festival in Cannes was being held, as it always is, in October, and I would be in attendance, as would Bill Mustos from CTV and Sarah Lindman and Meeri Park Cunniff from The N. Normally we prefer to keep our broadcasters relatively separated from each other. Different broadcasters have different mandates and different issues. It's easier to deal with them one-on-one and, for example, to nudge CTV to accept a certain storyline or way of proceeding because "The N likes it that way," and vice versa — harder to do if they're always talking to one another.

But in this case I invited them all to a Saturday night dinner at a Michelin-starred restaurant called La Bastide Saint-Antoine, just north of Cannes, hoping that the enthusiasm of each broadcaster for the show they had already ordered would rub off on the other. (The danger of course was that the reverse would happen, but surely the ambience of southern France would keep everything very positive — wouldn't it?)

I arrived an hour early, just to make sure everything would be perfect. Dusk was creeping over the landscaped grounds as I headed up the driveway to the beautiful eighteenth-century mansion that houses the restaurant. It was an ideal setting. (So ideal, that in the 1970s the Rolling Stones had stayed in that same mansion for over a year.)

It was lucky I had arrived early. Everything was not at all as it should have been.

The young woman at the front desk was helpful, but puzzled. There was no reservation for a Monsieur Stohn. Did I have the date correct? In my passable but hesitant French, I encouraged her that we had called twice to confirm the reservation; surely, it must be there — perhaps my name had been misspelled?

No, after triple-checking, there was still no reservation. Furthermore, "*Pardon monsieur, je suis tellement désolé,*" the restaurant was fully booked. There was no possibility of eating there that night.

The others did not have French cellphones; there was nothing I could do but wait for them, smile at the young woman at the front desk, and encourage her to keep checking — perhaps someone would cancel at the last moment.... But as 8:30 p.m. grew closer, and my guests would be arriving shortly, it looked like I would be eating humble pie, nothing more.

As I stared despondently out the window toward the little sculpture garden, it suddenly hit me. Maybe the answer was staring me right in the face. "*Mademoiselle!*" I asked, "*Le jardin ici, c'est possible ...*" then I got a bit flustered. I was trying to ask if they could set up a table in the little garden, even a card table, but the phrase "*table à cartes*" didn't seem to work.

Then she got what I was trying to say and called the manager over. Sure enough, they found a table in the kitchen, draped a cloth over it, brought four chairs out from the foyer, and when Bill, Sarah, and Meeri arrived, they were ushered into our "private dining area" in the sculpture garden. We drank champagne, ate a gorgeous meal, and as dessert was being served, we were blessed by a full moon rising over our sculpture garden, a full moon that seemed ours alone in our personal little sanctuary.

And yes, we left La Bastide Saint-Antoine that night, all happily talking about how both series would be produced. It was a Hollywood ending — perfect after all.

23
A NEW HOPE

"**I** have a very bad feeling about this."

So says Luke Skywalker as the Millennium Falcon approaches the Death Star in the first *Star Wars* movie, *Episode IV: A New Hope.** The phrase recurs in every *Star Wars* movie. Of course, whoever utters the phrase is correct — something very bad is about to happen — but in the end good triumphs over evil, catastrophe is averted, and the Force remains with us.

Life isn't always like a *Star Wars* movie, but sometimes it seems close.

In July 2009 Linda and I were walking toward the Bell Media headquarters at 299 Queen Street West in Toronto. Season 8 of *Degrassi: The Next Generation* was in the course of being broadcast, and we were in the midst of production for Season 9.

We had been called in to meet with the CEO of Bell Media, Ivan Fecan. Before we entered the building, Linda turned to me and said, "I don't have a good feeling about this." I agreed. It was as if we were being called into the principal's office, if not the Death Star.

Sure enough, in the meeting Ivan got quickly to the point. "*Degrassi* has had its day. It's been great, but it's gotten tired. It's time to move on."

It took a moment before it sank in that he was cancelling *Degrassi*.

---

* When we next change the name of the *Degrassi* franchise (it's now called *Degrassi: Next Class*), I'd like it to become *Degrassi: A New Hope*.

We immediately tried all the producer tricks of (a) assuming he meant that the season after next would be the last one (Ivan immediately corrected us — no, this season was it); (b) surely, he would want at least a reduced number of new episodes to celebrate the thirtieth anniversary of the first *Degrassi* going on air? (still no, this was it); and (c) how about a two-hour movie special to wrap up storylines and end the series with a bang? (Still no.)

But then Ivan went on to say. "I loved that movie you just did, the one set in Hollywood. I want to do more like that." Linda and I were remarkably restrained.

> **Linda and Stephen:** You mean *Degrassi Goes Hollywood?*
> **Ivan:** Yes.
> **Linda and Stephen:** The one that really is just the last four episodes of this season, packaged together as a two-hour movie special?
> **Ivan:** Yes.
> **Linda and Stephen:** The same season that you just said was tired, and had had its day, and this was it?
> **Ivan:** Exactly! You've got it.

Only in the convoluted world of network television would something like that make sense.

What Ivan liked was the concept of Canadians going down to L.A. to get their big break. Could we create a spinoff series to follow the lives of some of the characters from *Degrassi Goes Hollywood?* He would give us two hundred thousand dollars in development money for the new series.

We are producers. We said yes.

As Linda and I walked back along Queen Street, we agreed between us that we could tell no one about the cancellation of *Degrassi.* We were still in production. Revealing we had been cancelled would be a morale crusher. We would spin the meeting as having been all about putting us into development on a brand new series.

Manny (played by Cassie Steele) backed by the band Stüdz (played by Dalmar Abuzeid, Raymond Ablack, and Jamie Johnston) with Mia (played by Nina Dobrev) singing "Life Is a Show" to win an audition in the *Degrassi Goes Hollywood* special.

To this day almost no one knows that *Degrassi* was actually cancelled in 2009. There was a long-shot possibility, though, one I might call "a new hope." Our U.S. broadcaster TeenNick had been discussing with me the idea of developing a new series that would have a large number of episodes and run on a nightly basis — in effect a soap opera, but a limited-run one, where the storylines would be wrapped up within a set time period, similar to the Latin American telenovelas. A few months earlier when I'd first mentioned to Linda what TeenNick had been talking about, she was not interested. But given our new circumstances, I wondered if we might reinvigorate *Degrassi* by suggesting that *Degrassi* itself be transformed into that new series.

Over the next week I quietly worked on about a hundred different potential funding models, finally reaching an "aha" moment when all the variables combined together into a perfect storm. By notionally think-ing of the forthcoming season as being two mini-seasons, and creating different funding models for each mini-season, we could fund the new overall season with significantly reduced licence fees required from our

Outside the "Dot" set in the studio backlot in 2010, Linda and I are surrounded by the cast of *Degrassi* jumping for joy during the production of Season 10.

Canadian broadcaster. The outside world would know this as Season 10, but internally it would be Seasons 10A and 10B.

But to make this perfect storm work, some huge assumptions had to be made. We would have to double the number of episodes being produced, triple the per-episode licence fee paid by our U.S. broadcaster, TeenNick, and reduce the cost per episode from $800,000 to $550,000, while still maintaining the same quality.

Making these assumptions come true might seem ludicrous. Almost as ludicrous as destroying the Death Star by using a one-man snub fighter to evade enemy defences, manoeuvre straight down a trench, and fire a proton torpedo into a thermal exhaust port only two metres wide.

But let's look at the assumptions one-by-one.

We knew TeenNick wanted more episodes; our model suggested forty-four episodes, and this worked for them.

Most U.S. broadcasters at the time were used to paying licence fees that covered most of the production costs of a television show. Because of the contributions from Canadian tax credits and funding agencies, TeenNick had for years been able to acquire *Degrassi* at a far lower cost, namely at about a third of what they would have paid for a similar U.S. series. That made much more sense in the early days of *Degrassi: The Next Generation*, but now that *Degrassi* had become their number one original series, they were more than willing to up their licence fee, indeed, to triple it.

Meanwhile, by increasing the number of episodes we produced, some of the large one-time costs (such as set-builds) would be spread out over more episodes. This alone would lower the cost per episode by about 15 percent. We needed to lower the costs further by approaching everyone involved in the production and lowering what they were paid per episode. That sounds harsh — everyone would have to take a pay cut per episode — but because the number of episodes was being doubled, over the year everyone would actually be making much more.

There is an adage that goes, "You can have it faster; you can have it cheaper; you can have it better. Pick any two." I went around to the heads of every department, quoted the adage, and then said, "But no, actually, we have to have all three!"

Everyone rose to the challenge. Everyone. They took it as their personal missions to make sure that the quality of the show actually improved, and that we produced faster, cheaper, and better. And we did. Until then it had taken three and a half days to shoot an episode; we reduced that to two and three-quarters days. Everyone came to work totally prepared every day, working as fast, as efficiently, and as inventively as they could.

I called our friend Corrie Coe, the head of independent production at Bell Media, and said, "I know Ivan thought *Degrassi* was tired. But what if we double the number of episodes, reduce the Bell Media licence fee to about an eighth of what it once was, and propose moving it to the specialty channel MuchMusic instead of CTV itself. Could you walk down the hall and ask him if he would still think it's tired?"

She laughed, and called back about five minutes later. "We're in. He loves the idea. And he thinks it's perfect for MuchMusic. It will give a real boost to the network!"

And so it was that Season 10 — a season that, unknown to the outside world, had been cancelled and therefore would have zero episodes — ended up spanning forty-four episodes, twenty-four of which were broadcast nightly in August in a segment marketed as "Degrassi: The Boiling Point." The ratings were great on both MuchMusic and TeenNick, enough to get us almost immediately ordered for yet another forty-four episodes in Season 11.

And that new series that Ivan had put into development with us? We worked on it over the next two years under the title *Highland Gardens*, eventually changing the name to *The L.A. Complex* when it launched on a combination of CTV and MuchMusic in Canada, and The CW in the United States.

Who knows. Maybe that day, walking down the street toward that fateful meeting with Ivan at Bell Media, the Force was with us after all.

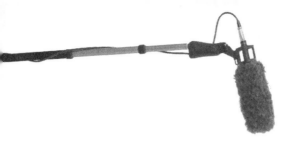

24
DEGRASSI OF THE DEAD

Linda and I love that our studio is a training ground, an environment where members of our cast and crew can grow in their careers, whether it's one of our actors (like Aubrey, Nina, Shenae, Jake, Ricardo, or so many others) developing their craft and going on to become famous elsewhere; or a summer student (like Nick Wong) working his way over the years into becoming an award-winning editor; or a web writer (like Brendon Yorke) working his way into becoming our head writer, and one of the best script writers in Canada; or any of so many other writers and crew members who master their craft while working with us and accelerate their careers forward.

Older fans of *Degrassi* will remember Stefan Brogren from way back in 1987, when he made his first appearance as Archie "Snake" Simpson in *Degrassi Junior High*. At the time he hadn't acted before. He had auditioned for the role of Joey Jeremiah. While Linda and her partner Kit Hood felt he was not right for that role, they were impressed with his fearlessness and intelligence, combined with vulnerability, and were convinced he would be a good actor. So they created the Snake character to include him in the cast. As the years unfolded, their confidence in him proved well placed. He became one of the most loved characters in *Degrassi*.

Thirty years after his first appearance, Snake is still at Degrassi Community School, only now he's the revered principal of the school, Principal Simpson.

Stefan is not just a charismatic and accomplished actor. Over the years he has honed his talents behind the camera as an award-winning director, writer, and producer for the *Degrassi* franchise, and also for some of our other series, such as *Open Heart* and *The L.A. Complex.**

Stefan's career outside of acting really took off during Season 5 of *Degrassi: The Next Generation* when we remembered our first attempt at a webisodes series — the 1997 *OnSet* online soap opera experiment — and decided to revisit the concept of web-based mini-episodes.

> **Stefan:** Stephen pulled me aside. He had never done this before, and I thought, "What did I do?" He said, "I'm coming up with a plan to do some sort of little shorts for the internet or for mobile phones." This was the language we were using at the time. "We don't know what it is yet, but I'd like you to be involved in this thing on the story side. Would you like to be a producer? Or director? Or something?"

The word "webisode" hadn't been invented back then. (We called them "minisodes," and when we released them, it was under the name "Degrassi Minis.") We really had no idea what would work, and what wouldn't. I paired Stefan with our brilliant producer Stephanie Cohen,

---

* Among his many other accomplishments, Stefan was the first Canadian actor to use the word *fuck* on Canadian prime time television, when CBC ran the *Degrassi* movie *School's Out* uncensored on January 5, 1992. In an argument with Joey Jeremiah (played by Pat Mastroianni) about Joey's sexual escapades, Snake yells, "No, you're going to listen to me! Joey Jeremiah spends his summer dating Caitlin … and fucking Tessa … oh, what ethics, what a hero … let's have a great big hand shall we? A great big round of applause!" unaware that Caitlin (played by Stacie Mistysyn) has just walked in and overheard the argument. The second actor to so use the word was Stacie Mistysyn a few seconds later, as her character, Caitlin, blurts out, "Tessa Campinelli? You were fucking Tessa Campinelli?"

figuring that between the two of them we'd find a nice balance between creativity and practicality. We just started trying out different ideas.

We assumed, when we were shooting them, that these shorts would be seen on a computer screen at quite low resolution, so we wouldn't really need to worry about the quality of the camera or the production overall, and we'd use a lot of close-ups.

> **Stefan:** We were coming up with a new language for how we would do a webisode versus how we would do a TV show. I said, "Stephen, maybe if we do phones it has to be just talking heads; it's got to be close-ups the entire time."

> **Stephanie:** In those first days we weren't allowed to do very quick pans, because it would cause the picture to pixilate.

> **Stefan:** We asked ourselves, how long can a kid stare at his phone? We made rules like, "Anything longer than thirty seconds and they're not watching."

> **Stephanie:** And then we had to break the rules when they weren't working. We came to realize it's all about storytelling, more than the particular technology.

While there had been some short-form internet series back then, we were one of the first to use the main characters and main sets of a television show as the basis for a webisode series. In the beginning we didn't have continuing stories; each webisode was stand-alone. We created storylines like "What if Craig Picked Emma" and "What if Emma Was Jay and Jay Was Emma." Two of my favourites were "What if Jimmy Was Never Shot" and "Pirates of the Cafeteribbean" (in which everyone at Degrassi is a pirate).

They became incredibly popular, and a fun way for our fans to engage further with our characters. And for us it was a training ground as well, an opportunity for different crew members to step up. In the same way that Stefan was learning about directing, if you were the assistant camera on the television show, maybe you could become the director of photography on a webisode. We had an actor who wanted to try becoming a boom operator, so we just let him do it. The actors had fun, the crew was trying new things, and everybody loved doing them.

As we got more webisodes under our belt, we started shooting them with close to the same quality as the television show. And Stefan started doing more and more of the writing.

> **Stefan:** We had our plan, and Stephen just let us roll with it. I knew something about directing, but this let me try different crazy things and find out what worked. He let me work with the writers and come up with a plan of attack of what these webisodes should be. By the second year of doing webisodes I just wrote them all myself, with the help of Stephanie.

> **Stephanie:** Stefan would come up with the ideas, and I'd put them in proper dialogue, and because of my production experience I could make them shootable.

In 2007 the broadcasters were asking for something related to Halloween, so Stefan came up with the concept for *Degrassi of the Dead*. In the beginning it was four webisodes, depicting Degrassians escaping others who had become zombies from eating genetically modified food. One of the Degrassians was Jimmy (played by Aubrey Graham). As a zombie, the undead Jimmy got to lose the shackles of his wheelchair, enabling Aubrey to perform a long and wonderfully prophetic robot-dance while Stefan channelled Vincent Price chanting *Thriller*-like lyrics, including lines such as:

Undead Jimmy
A zombie that grooves
Come on rotting homeboy
Bust some funky moves
Do the Robot!
Do the Robot!
D – d – d – d – d – d – d – d
Do the Robot!

The students perished
Their flesh was fed
Your soul won't rest
At Degrassi … of the Dead!

Degrassi of the Dead was so good that we added some interviews with cast and crew and repackaged the four webisodes into a half-hour television special.

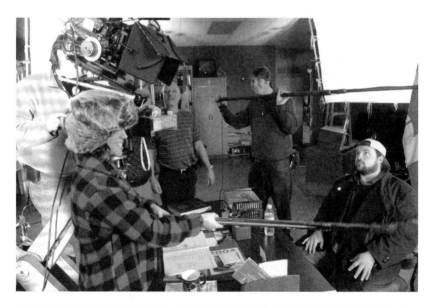

Alanis uses a hockey stick to try to attract Kevin Smith's attention during the filming of the "Jay and Silent Bob Do *Degrassi*" special in 2005.

I am joined by Kelly Carlson and Vivica Fox, along with Lauren Collins ("Paige"), Stacey Farber ("Ellie"), Adamo Ruggiero ("Marco"), and Stefan Brogren ("Mr. Simpson") outside Grauman's Chinese Theatre during the shooting of the *Degrassi Goes Hollywood* movie special in 2009.

It was during that same period that Stefan became friends with Kevin Smith (indeed, we all became close with Kevin and his co-conspirator Jason Mewes; they were heroes to all of us). Kevin and Jason had starred as themselves in a three-episode arc in Season 5, called "Jay and Silent Bob Do Degrassi," in which Kevin and Jason come to Canada to film their next movie, the plot of which involves their alter egos Jay and Silent Bob being forced to go back to high school. And what better high school to shoot in than Degrassi Community School? Shenanigans ensue.*

---

* At the very last moment we added a new character, the principal of this fictitious school. Kevin asked Alanis Morissette to act the part, but she was in Los Angeles, about to head to Vancouver. She was such a trooper though — and such a Canadian — she decided to take the red-eye flight to Toronto that night, act in *Degrassi* the next morning, and then take the afternoon flight to Vancouver. She played the role brilliantly, and was so very funny in the role.

Kevin was impressed with what Stefan and Stephanie were creating with the webisodes, and he was especially intrigued with Stefan's style as a director. So when we asked Kevin if he would direct and star in our *Degrassi Goes Hollywood* movie special, Kevin agreed, but subject to one condition: Stefan would work as a shadow alongside him — Kevin would become Stefan's mentor in the world of directing.

As we moved closer to shooting *Degrassi Goes Hollywood* in the early fall of 2008, Kevin's work schedule kept getting busier and busier. At first he insisted that he could still both star in and direct the movie…. Then a few weeks later he called to say we should write his acting role down, that he couldn't appear in the show as much but could still direct…. Another few weeks after that he called very apologetically to say he couldn't direct the show after all. Stefan would have to be the director, but Kevin would assist him.

We would never have thought of having Stefan make his first television-directing debut on our movie *Degrassi Goes Hollywood*. But the universe seemed to slowly conspire to make it happen. And Kevin had such faith in him.

In the end, Stefan ended up directing *Degrassi Goes Hollywood* entirely on his own. Kevin was so entangled in other work that, while Jason continued as one of the stars of the show, Kevin could only spare a few hours to participate — he appeared in a few (very funny) scenes via Skype.

Stefan proved to be superb as a director. Not only did we love him, but the U.S. production team loved him, too. After one scene I chatted with the head of the Los Angeles crew who, with no prompting, expressed his admiration for Stefan's directing style, comparing him favourably to Clint Eastwood, in that he knew what he wanted, got great camera angles, and most importantly was fearless about moving on quickly to the next scene — not squandering precious time with unnecessary retakes.

The movie was a great success. A few months after it aired, Stefan won his first Gemini Award (now called the Canadian Screen Award) for Best Direction in a Children's or Youth Program or Series.*

It made Linda and me so proud. The environment we had created had helped yet another one of our team to spread his wings and accomplish greatness. And to this day Stefan is one of our top contributors to *Degrassi* and our other series — not just by being a great director, writer, producer, and actor, but also by becoming an inspiration and mentor to the younger members of our team. The circle of mentorship goes on!

---

* Around the same time, I got a call from Ron Haney, then the head of the Directors Guild of Canada, who said, "Stephen, we've got a bit of a problem here. Is it possible that one of your directors is not a member of the Directors Guild?" Turns out that in his excitement, Stefan had forgotten to join. He'd built up some credits in directing the webisodes but had not actually become a member. I fell on my sword, apologizing and prostrating myself to Ron, who kindly took it in good humour and talked his Board into backdating the paperwork accepting Stefan into the Guild.

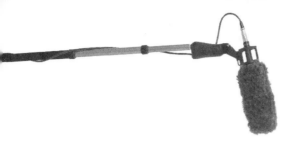

25
HOCKEY NIGHT IN CANADA

While my work with *Degrassi* went on, I also continued to be involved in the music scene, and not just through *The Juno Awards*. The Stohn Henderson LLP law firm that Graham and I had founded in 1997 was growing into what is now Stohn Hay Cafazzo Dembroski Richmond LLP, and I continued to act for music industry clients.

In 2008 we produced Season 8 of *Degrassi: The Next Generation*, and Season 4 of *Instant Star*, while the *Junos* took place at the Saddledome in Calgary, Alberta (hosted by Russell Peters). In that same year a major issue came to a head involving me as a lawyer and an iconic piece of Canadian music.

There is a reason that Canada's second national anthem — the one that starts "Dah dah dah da duh da-uh-aaaaah!" — is not called the "Hockey Night in Canada Theme."

Actually, there are two reasons, a short one and a long one. The short reason is that the CBC, not the composer, Dolores Claman, owns the trademark on the phrase "Hockey Night in Canada." The long reason is a lesson in how important a genuine apology can be.

If you'll permit me to go on a bit of a tangent here, I chanced upon a study that astounded me during my tenure as a partner at McCarthys. It set out the results of a survey of U.S. medical malpractice lawsuits, showing the reasons the claimants had filed the lawsuits. Over a third of the claimants reported they would never have filed the lawsuit if they had simply received an explanation and an apology in the first place. (Among its many fields of expertise, McCarthys is known for acting for the medical profession whenever malpractice suits arise, so the study was of direct interest to the firm.)

In other words, a simple explanation and apology could have prevented a significant number of major lawsuits from ever taking place.

Now we'll return to … let's call it "The Hockey Theme." Dolores Claman had written the song in 1968 at the behest of McLaren Advertising, who had been engaged by CBC to provide a promotional tune for *Hockey Night in Canada*. The song rapidly became ingrained in the Canadian national consciousness and was synonymous with the game of hockey. (Ironically, when she wrote the song, Dolores had never seen a hockey game herself; she had simply imagined the pre-game anticipation, the game itself, the intermissions, and the post-game euphoria, and she wove her imagined experiences into an extraordinary melody.)

Dolores's success with "The Hockey Theme" was no fluke. Over the years, she and her husband, Richard Morris, had written over three thousand commercial jingles, winning dozens of international awards in the process. My eyes still tear up at the memory of one of those songs, "A Place to Stand," which I first heard as part of the groundbreaking film of the same name at Montreal's Expo 67 Ontario pavilion.

In 1993 Dolores assigned worldwide administration rights in the song to Copyright Music & Visuals, headed by my friend and client John Ciccone. John is an expert in all aspects of music, particularly those involving television and film, including rights clearance, song and artist placement, and original music score creation and adaptation.

John became, and remains to this day, a fierce protector of "The Hockey Theme" and of Dolores. I never met Dolores in person, but I spoke with her a number of times on the phone from her home in England. It was always clear to me that she had absolute trust in John, and rightly so: John worked every day to prove that trust was earned.

John: At first all CBC wanted was a jingle for their sponsors at the beginning of the *Hockey Night in Canada* broadcast. After a year or so they decided to bring it back as the theme of the actual broadcast, but they never got a licence to do that. That went on for about twenty-five years. In my first conversation with Dolores she said, "Can you help me out with this copyright stuff?" I said, "Let's have a look at the sync licence," and she said, "What's a sync licence?" *

I felt the blood rush to my feet because this was twenty-five years of unlicenced use. I was like Fred Flintstone with the steam coming out of my ears. This is Canada's second national anthem; you can't be messing with this stuff. Dolores is our Betsy Ross; she sewed our Canadian flag!

After Dolores and John talked it all over, Dolores took responsibility for not having known what her rights were and decided to forgive the twenty-five years of unlicenced use and just look forward. An agreement was negotiated that gave the CBC the necessary rights to use the song as the theme for hockey broadcasts for a number of years, but allowed Dolores to retain international rights, as well as the rights to license the song outside of hockey broadcasts.

For a number of years, the agreement seemed to be working well for both sides. Then John started to receive reports that CBC was using the song outside of Canada — in the United States, Japan, Ireland, and Scotland — contrary to the terms of the agreement.

At first, the issue seemed to be a minor one. John called CBC, asked that they confirm what international uses had occurred, and asked them to suggest in good faith an appropriate payment for them. CBC promised to respond, but several months later it had not done so.

---

* Short for "synchronization licence," a sync licence authorizes the reproduction of a song "in synchronization or timed relation" with audiovisual images.

That was when John called me. For the next two and a half years we had various meetings and telephone calls with CBC to try to resolve the issue. The individuals we negotiated with were pleasant enough, and seemingly concerned and responsive, assuring us that they would find out what the story was, but then months would go by with nothing happening.

John became more and more frustrated. While he wanted fair payment for the extra uses of the song, money was not the real issue — in his heart he simply felt that people should live up to their word, in this case the words of the agreement, and should admit when they'd done something wrong.

> **John:** If they had just said, "Yes, we licensed it to Japan, Ireland, and Scotland," whatever, we would have been on track. They'd still have the song today.... We'd already forgiven twenty-five years, and then we wasted more than two years waiting for them to give us some information on it. And they were non-responsive.

It became worse when John felt his efforts to license the song outside of hockey broadcasts were being stifled by CBC.

> **John:** It seemed like I'd be licensing to someone, for example a phone company, and CBC would come in after me to advise the phone company that they didn't want them using their title without paying them, too. I felt like CBC was trying to own the song without owning it.

This type of "running interference" was a sea change for me. I tried what I could, tried to see things from CBC's point of view, and tried to think of different ways to meet the needs of both sides. John was very appreciative of what I was doing but, truth be told, in the end I had seemingly gotten us nowhere.

John: Stephen was always trying to come up with a fair and reasonable idea for everyone. He was respectful of their needs. He always had a wonderful fresh way of looking at something. When the CBC was interfering with us using the song with others because of their trademark rights in the title, Stephen just said, "Well, let's just change the title of the song. Let's call it "The Hockey Theme."

Simple beauty, like a George Harrison guitar solo.

In the end, though, they pretty much stopped responding. So Stephen said, "Now we've got to take them to court."

I'm not a litigation lawyer (and you'll recall my view of going to court from the earlier "My Lawyer" chapter), so I helped John and Dolores hire an outside lawyer to proceed from there. As a result, over the next four years from 2004 to 2008 I was no longer directly involved but, from time to time, acted as a sounding board for John and Dolores as the case slowly wended its way through the issuance of a statement of claim, various attempts to reach a settlement, and attempts at mediation.

At first we thought that CBC would accept a settlement including an amount to compensate for past transgressions, plus an ongoing licence that would broaden CBC's right to include international rights.

John: I offered them the ability to continue as we had for the last ten to fifteen years ... it worked out to about five hundred bucks a game. You spend more on starch on Don Cherry's collar.* All of our real income

---

* Don "Grapes" Cherry is a commentator for *Hockey Night in Canada*, known for his outspoken manner and flamboyant style of dress.

would come from selective careful licensing outside of the hockey broadcasts.

As the matter progressed, though, it became clear that the only practical solution was for CBC to simply buy the song outright — in this way there would no longer be any need for John and Dolores to interact with the CBC in the future.

Of course, this led to the question: what is the fair market value of "The Hockey Theme"? To our minds this was relatively straightforward. John and I felt that, while arguments could be made for higher or lower values, somewhere in the range of ten to fifteen times the average annual earnings of the song over the past five years would be in line with how major music publishers could value the song.

However, there was another factor that impinged. John and Dolores felt that in the various negotiations CBC was constantly denigrating both the work that Dolores had done in creating the song and the value that the song had as part of the hockey broadcasts.

> **John:** We reached a point where it was a huge disrespect to the song and to Dolores. I remember a CBC lawyer saying, "I can hire a kid in his basement, give him a few grand, and I'll own the copyright in the song." This is the sort of thing that we had to listen to. "We'll just have a contest to find a new theme song, and no one will care that we dropped your song." At another point, someone at CBC said, "No one's going to want this song. TSN's certainly not going to want it. It's too heavily associated with us."

This perceived disrespect gnawed at John and Dolores.

On the first day of June 2008 things were finally coming to a head. John and I had a long conversation as CBC had issued a deadline of 5:00 p.m. the next day for John and Dolores to accept an offer by CBC to purchase "The Hockey Theme" for an amount that John and I felt was less than one-third of its true market value.

The deadline kept being pushed. There was a back and forth between CBC and John, but by Friday evening, when no resolution had been reached, CBC issued a press release:

> TORONTO, June 6 /CNW/ — After more than 13 months of negotiations, CBC is saddened to announce that a deal has not been reached with the rights holders for an extension of "The Hockey Theme" — CBC'S *Hockey Night in Canada* theme song.
>
> "We share with all Canadians the disappointment of this news, as we feel as strongly about the theme as they do," said Scott Moore, executive director of CBC Sports. "We are proud of the association with the former theme song and are saddened that we were unable to reach a deal, especially when we presented an offer which we believe was not substantively different from what the rights holder had proposed to us. We love the song and know this is a huge disappointment for us and for millions of Canadians. As of today, CBC Sports is moving forward with our plan to have the Canadian public compose the new *Hockey Night in Canada* theme song."
>
> CBC, in conjunction with leading music producers Nettwerk Music Group, will conduct a nationwide search, inviting Canadians to write and record an original song for CBC'S *Hockey Night in Canada*. Then, in a debate that is certain to dominate conversations throughout the country, fans and a jury of experts will choose the best new composition. CBC will offer $100,000 for the winning song, which will then become the new "official theme song" of CBC'S *Hockey Night in*

Canada and will be heard in every broadcast. A portion of the new theme song's royalties will be donated to minor hockey in Canada. Details surrounding the contest will be announced next week.

I was in Vancouver at the time (dealing with some issues relating to the use of music in the forthcoming Winter Olympics), and it wasn't until reading the newspaper the next morning that I became aware that the news had become public. I immediately called John. I couldn't get through to him, so I left a long voice mail saying I was sure that CTV and their affiliate The Sports Network (TSN) would want to purchase the song, telling him what great guys the heads of CTV (Ivan Fecan) and of TSN (Rick Brace) were, and mentioning that I would be happy to call them directly.

When John called back, he apologized for having been unavailable but said it was because, when I called, he was already on the phone with executives from CTV and TSN — and they had agreed to a deal! Not just a deal, but a deal exactly in line with what John and I had thought the fair market value of "The Hockey Theme" was. The exact price has never been made public although newspaper reports at the time quoted a CBC executive as saying that the composer had been seeking about $2.5 million.

John: I was getting calls from every media outlet in Canada when CBC dropped the song and said they were going to have a contest. The *New York Times* and the *Observer* in London were calling me — "What the hell's going on there; your country's up in arms. We don't even know what hockey is!" We had two satellite TV broadcast trucks straddling the sidewalk and a camera crew in the bushes.

All these people started calling with offers to save the song. One guy went to his bank manager and said,

HOCKEY NIGHT IN CANADA

"Let's collect a dollar from everyone in Canada that wants to save the song and we'll keep it on the air."

Then CTV called and said, "What's going on over there?" They ended up saying, "We'll take it." They were the knights in shining armour that pulled it out of the fire. Because they broadcast hockey games as well, it meant "The Hockey Theme" would still be alive and associated with hockey. They were so fair, reasonable, and respectful. I got more done in one morning than I did in ten years with CBC.

When John was talking with me, it wasn't the dollars he wanted to dwell on. It was the respect that CTV had shown. He got very emotional as he described the conference call they had conducted with Dolores, in which CTV had thanked her for the "honour" and the "privilege" that they be allowed to become "the caretakers" of this "important and cherished piece of Canadiana."

For John, it was that respect, for the song and for Dolores, that he had really wanted all along.

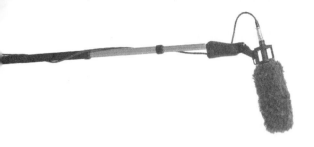

26
JACOB HOGGARD

In 1950, UCLA Bruins football coach Henry Russell "Red" Sanders told his group, "Men, I'll be honest. Winning isn't everything." Following a long pause, he continued, "Men, it's the only thing!" * But sometimes you need to look beyond winning to what you're really striving for. It turns out that, actually, winning isn't everything — or the only thing — after all.

The recent wave of televised singing competitions had their origin in 1999 with the launch of *Popstars* in New Zealand. The success of *Popstars* inspired Simon Fuller to create the British show *Pop Idol* in 2001. The format was then reshaped and moved across the Atlantic as *American Idol*, debuting on the Fox television network on June 11, 2002, and rapidly becoming one of the most successful shows in the history of American television.

In turn, the format spread throughout the world into over fifty different versions as diverse as *Australian Idol*, *Arab Idol*, *Bangladeshi Idol*, *Indonesian Idol*, *Indian Idol*, *Latin American Idol*, *Idol* (Poland), *Idols* (South Africa), *Pakistan Idol*, *Vietnam Idol*, and, on June 9, 2003, *Canadian Idol*.

---

* The quotation is widely, but wrongly, attributed to Green Bay Packers coach Vince Lombardi, who did say it but, undoubtedly, had heard it years earlier from Sanders.

The front-of-camera structure was relatively straightforward. A panel of judges critiqued the competitors' performances, but it was up to the viewers to decide — by telephone and text voting immediately following each episode — which of the competitors would move forward and ultimately win in the competition, and which ones would be eliminated.

Behind the camera the structure was more complex. The winner would be signed to a recording agreement with the company then known as BMG and now known as Sony Music,* as well as a management agreement, a music publishing agreement, and a merchandising agreement, with an initial album to be released very shortly after the season finale episode (the episode in which the prizewinner was voted the overall winner).

But if you think about it, that's almost an impossibility. How could a recording agreement, a management agreement, a music publishing agreement, and a merchandising agreement be negotiated, finalized, and signed within the month following the final episode — much less the recording and release of a full album of material featuring the winner?

The answer, at least in Canada (and I have no reason to doubt a similar procedure would have been followed elsewhere in the world), was twofold. First, the various agreements needed to be negotiated and signed long before the final episode to become effective in the event the competitor won. Second, at least some of the songs for the album that the winner would record needed to be created well in advance, ready for the winner to step into the studio to sing them immediately following the final episode. In fact, in the case of the one song that would be released as the album's first single, each of the top three finalists would go into the studio prior to the final episode to sing their own version of that song. Two of these versions would be discarded, and the winner's version of the song would be released shortly following the final episode.

---

* Bertelsmann Music Group (BMG) acquired RCA Records and associated labels in 1987. In March 2004 Sony BMG Music Entertainment was formed, owned 50/50 by BMG and Sony Music. In 2008 Sony bought out BMG's interest, and the company reverted to Sony Music.

The negotiation of the various agreements needed its own special behind-the-scenes procedure, one that I like to call "Lawyer Idol." It would not have been possible to have every competitor hire their own lawyer to negotiate the agreements; indeed, it would have been unfair to have different competitors negotiate different terms and conditions in their respective agreements. When the competition had been whittled down to about a hundred remaining competitors, these "survivors" were gathered to hear a short talk from each of three veteran entertainment lawyers, followed by a question-and-answer session. The three lawyers were then sent outside the room, and the competitors held a discussion among themselves, culminating in voting two of the lawyers "off the island." The remaining candidate became their single designated lawyer.

For the first and second seasons of *Canadian Idol*, I "remained on the island" and became that single designated lawyer. Before the series even went on the air, I got to know the finalists very well.* We discussed the meaning of the proposed agreements, what changes we would like to see in them, and what the individual finalists' dreams and hopes were if they won. Some of them, like Jacob Hoggard, have remained friends of mine over the years.

Jacob: I met Stephen on the set of *Canadian Idol.* I had previously dropped out of high school and was building houses and was coerced onto the show by my family. My mom — don't tell Stephen this — she actually forged my signature on the application!**

---

* The top eleven finalists in Season 1 were Ryan Malcolm (the ultimate winner), Gary Beals, Billy Klippert, Audrey de Montigny, Jenny Gear, Toya Alexis, Tyler Hamilton, Mikey Bustos, Karen-Lee Batten, Candida Clauseri, and Richie Wilcox. In Season 2, the top ten finalists were Kalan Porter (the ultimate winner), Theresa Sokyrka, Jacob Hoggard, Jason Greeley, Shane Wiebe, Elena Juatco, Kaleb Simmonds, Joshua Seller, Manoah Hartmann, and Brandy Callahan.

** That made me laugh! I never knew about that until I read the transcript of the interview Jake did with Christopher for this book.

I was then introduced to Stephen as my first entertainment lawyer, and he graciously walked me through the process, as far as helping a young musician understand their rights as a creative individual and welcomed me into that entire world of having someone advocate for you. At that point, we got on so well he took me down to the set of *Degrassi*, to the boardroom and the school, the cafeteria for an actual lunch — pretty surreal.

It was so nostalgic in so many ways, *Degrassi* was a show that I grew up watching as a kid after school. Such a defining influence in my life — it was *Degrassi* and *Saved by the Bell*.* We created a relationship that ended up lasting well over a decade so far.

I would then do what I could to negotiate positive changes in the agreements and report back the next week to the competitors on what had been accomplished. Over the course of many weeks, the issues were debated and whittled down until finally there were baseline agreements that could be signed. There was pressure on both sides to reach final agreements because no competitor could proceed to the live broadcasts involving the top ten or eleven finalists without first having signed off on the agreements.

While all this was going on, you will recall that one of the challenges facing the *Idol* producers was how to get the winner's first single, and then an album, released as soon as possible after the final episode. The solution they had come up with was to have a "songwriter boot camp" creating all the songs.

The concept of a songwriter boot camp had been created by Miles Copeland in the early 1990s. He had become the manager of his brother Stewart's band, The Police, and led them to become one of the biggest

---

* In 2012 Jake and his Hedley bandmates appeared in a one-hour special *Degrassi* episode called "Degrassi: Las Vegas."

bands of the 1980s.* He'd leveraged that success to co-found I.R.S. Records through a deal with A&M Records.**

His innovative management style and the success of The Police (and many of the other bands Copeland was affiliated with) enabled him to, among other things, purchase a fourteenth-century castle in the southwest of France, the Château Marouatte.

He decided to use the castle for business, inventing the "songwriter boot camp" in the process. He built three sixteen-track recording studios in the castle and then invited superstars — such as Jeff Beck, Carole King, Ted Nugent, and his brother Stewart — along with artists looking for songs for upcoming albums. Shrewdly, to these he added lesser-known artists and songwriters from his own label and management company.

In total, there were twenty-four invitees. Each boot camp day began at 10:30 a.m. Copeland divided the participants into groups of three, taking care to mix superstar artists and songwriters with emerging talent. And then the magic began; they proceeded to grind out hits, reportedly upward of a hundred hits over the years.***

The *Canadian Idol* producers attempted to replicate the success of the Château Marouatte by inviting notable songwriters to songwriting camps to write songs for the *Idol* winner.

However, the *Canadian Idol* songwriter camps faced some drawbacks. Chief among them for the first season was that the camp took place a week after the finale episode, so there was real pressure to put together a full album of songs almost immediately. The writers had just been introduced to the winner, Ryan Malcolm, and had little time to gauge his range, musical taste, and any particular strengths and weaknesses they should take into account in their writing.

---

* The Police's first album was released on A&M Records in 1978 with the hit single "Roxanne."

** I.R.S. stood for International Record Syndicate.

*** In 2011 the American performing rights society ASCAP began their own annual songwriter retreats at the Château Marouatte with many notable songwriters.

Also, while Miles Copeland had strategically divided his participants into groups of three, the division of the *Canadian Idol* songwriters was, at least initially, much more haphazard. Christopher Ward was one of the songwriters:

> **Christopher:** I had just returned to Toronto after living in Paris for two years, and I got an invitation to attend the first Canadian Idol writing camp. As none of our possessions had arrived, I had to borrow a guitar and rent a car to get to the daily sessions at Phase One studios in Toronto. It turned out to be a chaotic experience with songwriters clustered in isolation booths, behind baffles, and on couches in hallways frenetically trying to compose songs that would make the cut. Unlike future *Idol* camps, this one took place the week after the winner had been chosen, so we had some idea of the style of the artist, and the winning song, performed on the show's finale, had already been written. But it was frantic. The powers that be, a.k.a. the record label, had decided that we would write and record two complete songs a day, changing writing partners for each session. Mismatches abounded. I think it was my first session when I found myself in a room with three lyricists and one lonely piano player!
>
> At some point on day one the winner, Ryan Malcolm, was trotted out in front of forty competing songwriters to say hello and give us some guidance as to his musical direction. He looked more nervous than he had at any time on TV. I seem to recall him saying he wanted to sound like Coldplay. This led to the creation that week of a hundred or so atmospheric pop songs with enigmatic lyrics and Coldplay's downstroke guitar parts. And we all found ourselves trying to second-guess what the label or the show or his management might want us to be writing.

It was a recipe for mediocrity. There were exceptionally talented writers there — people like Rob Wells, Andrea Wasse, Luke McMaster, Simon Wilcox, Fred St-Gelais, and Dave Tyson, who've had incredible songwriting and production careers — but the unrealistic deadline and haphazard pairings derailed most of the creativity that could have emerged.

Ryan was escorted to some of the sessions to briefly join the process and offer input. He was gracious and engaging, but it's a tough spot to be put in, walking cold into rooms of writers in mid-song.

I never wanted to do this again!

The *Canadian Idol* producers recognized the problems, and in the second season of *Idol* they reorganized the camps, moving them to the summer months before the winner had been chosen. That alleviated a lot of the time pressures, but it created a major issue: the winner would have limited input into the songs they were singing (and certainly zero input into the first single). The songs would be almost entirely created and selected by the time the winner had been chosen.

During the final weeks of that second season I got a call from Jacob Hoggard asking if we could meet in secret — as we later put it, "at an undisclosed location somewhere in the free world." We ended up in the back recesses of a Second Cup coffee shop, talking in hushed tones.

He came right to the point, "Should I really try to win? Or not?"

Jacob: As the season came to an end and every week we lost competitors, we would either be ushered back to Stephen's office, or he would come meet us at the set, and we'd talk about these contracts. Eighteen-year-old me at the start of the show thought, "Yeah, give me a pen. I'm in 'cause I'm on TV." As time went on, in my spare time waiting for everyone else to finish, I'd read the contracts and kind of discovered on my own that maybe this wasn't the most favourable outcome if I was to actually win.

From Jacob's perspective, there were two large downsides to winning. First, he was a songwriter, and putting out an album written by other songwriters, and into which he'd have marginal input, was not his dream. Second, he had an existing band named "Hedley," and he was keen to make his first album a band effort, not a solo one. The record deal he was committed to if he won was for him alone, not for his band.

> **Jacob:** I started to understand the pretty critical issues that I had with the contracts and felt that I was bound to something that I wasn't sure of or wasn't agreeing to. And at that point I found myself at a real crossroads. And Stephen was instrumental in giving me the confidence to kind of bow out of it.

Jacob and I had a long and fascinating discussion about the pros and cons. There was a clear upside if he won, of course, since winning would mean some large cash advances and instant notoriety.

In many ways the dilemma was archetypal for an artist (and in an adapted form, archetypal for every human): do you take a path that doesn't reflect your authentic art, but may lay a foundation from which you have a possibly much-improved chance to eventually pursue your authentic art? Or do you choose to be authentic from the start, knowing that choice may preclude you from being as "successful" as you might otherwise be in a popular or commercial sense.

There is no right or wrong for this choice; different artists, different humans, will pursue different paths. It depends on someone's own inner concept of success. In Jacob's case, he had a very clear vision of who he wanted to be, and it didn't involve putting out a solo album of someone else's songs.

Jacob: In short, I didn't want to win because I didn't want to be stuck with that contract, and Stephen empowered me. I'll never forget him saying, maybe flying in the face of everything he was taught, "At the end of the day it's just a piece of paper."

That alone was liberating, and at that point I made the conscious decision to change my mind and not follow through, and maybe bail out and just kind of hope that I didn't win. I got what I wished for and so, thankfully, was able to separate myself from the franchise and build a career on my own and independently of the show — which was crucial.

We may never know and, indeed, despite what he thought, even Jacob may never really know which path he chose. It wasn't as if he alone could arbitrarily choose between winning or not; the public voting mechanism was the ultimate arbiter.

Jacob: I never held myself back or was inhibited … I can't honestly tell you that I half-performed because I don't think I've ever done that. I did certainly reach out to my fans and my family and the people that I could get a hold of and asked and encouraged them, "Please vote for somebody else."

The end result is a matter of public record: Jacob placed third.*

One little-known fact about the *Idol* structure is that while the winner was awarded, among other things, a recording deal with Sony Music,

---

* Kalan Porter was the winner that year. The sixth-place finisher was Elena Juatco. Over a decade later we hired Elena to star in our *Open Heart* TV series as "Scarlet McWhinnie, a doctor at Open Heart whose stunning beauty often leaves her razor-sharp medical skills underestimated by others."

any of the non-winning finalists could end up with the same prize. Sony had the right within thirty days following the final broadcast of the season to sign any of the finalists to exactly the same arrangement as the winner. It was possible that, within that thirty-day period, Sony would exercise its option to sign Jacob to a solo artist recording agreement.

While those thirty days ticked away, something else started stirring: Jacob was tracked down by the then up-and-coming music manager Darren Gilmore.*

> **Darren:** I wasn't involved with Jacob and Hedley until after *Canadian Idol* had wrapped. I wasn't a *Canadian Idol* guy — never watched the show, not once. There was someone that I knew from the studio who said, "There's this young artist, and he's incredible." She showed me some footage of Jake on a breakfast television show performing this song "Trip" that he wrote. I loved the song and started researching, found out about the *Canadian Idol* connection, and chased him down.
>
> Fortunately, we hit it off. But he couldn't enter into any management arrangements because he was in this thirty-day window where he could be signed to Sony and to a bunch of other contracts, including a management contract. So we had to lay low for a few weeks....

We started counting the days. On the thirty-first day Jacob called me to ask if I'd heard anything. I hadn't, and neither had he. He let me know about his recent meetings with Darren and said Darren was just on his way to Sony for a meeting.

---

* At the time he had just been hired by Watchdog Management, a venture affiliated with music management greats Bruce Allen, Sam Feldman, and Steve Macklam. Darren is now the president of Watchdog. We've become good friends over the years. He still manages Jacob and the entire Hedley band.

Darren: Good news for me, good news for Hedley, good news for Universal Music — Sony decided that they wanted to put all their money on Kalan Porter, and they weren't interested in Jake or the Hedley band, so we were cooking with gas in no time ... things worked out as they were meant to. I'll never forget the day I was at Sony for the meeting and they said, "Yeah, you're free to go."

Almost exactly a year later, on September 6, 2005, Hedley's debut album was released on Universal Music, and the group has gone on to become one of the most successful recording and touring bands in recent Canadian history.

While Jacob Hoggard has primarily focused on music concerts and tours with his band Hedley, since our early connection through *Canadian Idol* he has appeared on television occasionally, including on *Degrassi*, and hosting and singing at *The Juno Awards*, as seen here in 2015.

Darren: We created a business around the opportunity that *Idol* presented, and you can do that when you have true talent. They're an unbelievably good band and he's an unbelievably good songwriter and front man.

Still, to this day Jacob remains very grateful for his time on *Canadian Idol.*

Jacob: I was a carpenter and I was looking to carve out a life for myself as a builder. I was thrust into an alternate universe and it really whipped me into shape in a lot of ways. The big thing for me is the relationships. So many of the people involved with that show — the producers, the directors, the CTV staff, the Insight staff — we've become long-term creative partners. Years later I hosted the *Junos* with them — it felt like a reunion. It was so special to know that out of that situation the real prize for me was the gift of the friends and the relationships and the people I can call family, like Stephen.

So for Jacob, clearly winning wasn't everything, it was to him an impediment to what he really wanted in his heart.

As for me, well, something else was stirring as a direct result of my own experience with *Canadian Idol.*

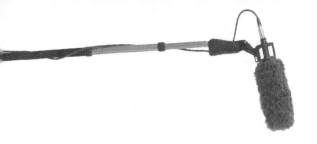

27
ALEXZ JOHNSON AND
INSTANT STAR

Not only is winning not everything, but success isn't always what you think it should be.

In each season, the first ten or so episodes of *Canadian Idol* were pre-taped; they followed the search for competitors across Canada and showed the audition process, replete with hopes and dreams, laughter and hugs, and lots of tears.

In early June the format switched to two live episodes per week — the first being an hour-long show featuring performances by each of the remaining competitors; the second being a half-hour show revealing the results of the voting, namely (in drawn-out dramatic fashion) who was being eliminated from the competition.

On the date of the first televised show in Season 1, Linda and I were seated with the live audience, proudly looking up at the eleven finalists I'd come to know over the past weeks and wondering which one of them would make it to the end. Linda leaned over to me and asked, "Do any of them really know what it will be like if they win?"

We both knew that while the competitors were fixated on the huge challenges of winning the grand prize, in many ways winning was the easy part. A flurry of publicity and record sales would follow the win, but could the winner sustain their career and their art after that? Some things were inevitable: the drama with record companies and managers; the need to keep feeding their fans while at the same time maintaining their own artistic and personal integrity; the battle between art and commerce — do they move in a particular direction because it would likely make them more popular, or do they focus on the purity of their art? "That's real drama," Linda added. "It could make a great TV show."

"Yes!" I replied enthusiastically. "We could explore the challenges that the winner would start facing, in their career, and in their personal life, and [this was where my love of the music side of things really shone through] we could create a new song every week, put out an album each year of new material, create a band featuring the star, do touring, and sell merchandise."

We were both getting excited. After the broadcast we went backstage to congratulate all the competitors and to wish them luck in the voting, but then we couldn't wait to get home and start exploring our story idea.

Over the next few weeks we narrowed our concept down and came up with a name for it: *Instant Idol*. We knew the name wouldn't stick — we'd never be able to use the *Idol* name in our television show — but we could come up with a real title later.

Once we had the concept pretty well formulated, my first call was to Bill Mustos, then CTV's vice-president and head of development. CTV was not only the broadcaster for *Canadian Idol*, it was also the Canadian broadcaster for *Degrassi: The Next Generation*, then in its third season, so CTV deserved the first pitch.

"Bill," I said, "We've got a show in development that is not right for CTV, but I wanted to call you first so that you could give me a 'no' before I go to other broadcasters." I was being completely sincere. I really didn't think our show would fit CTV's schedule. We were projecting *Instant Idol* as a half-hour drama, while most of CTV's offerings were either half-hour sitcoms or one-hour dramas. Our show was aimed at a youth audience, while CTV generally aimed for a sweet spot on the twenty-five to fifty-four-year-old demographic range. After I described the premise, there was a long silence. Then Bill said, "Don't go anywhere. I think we want this show."

He went on to explain that they were looking for a show that could follow *Canadian Idol* in the schedule. The *Canadian Idol* results show was only a half-hour long, so following it with a half-hour drama involving very similar subject matter seemed like it could work nicely.

Suddenly we were moving forward on a new series. We started refining the characters and the overall structure of the show in a document the industry calls the "bible," and at the same time engaged writers to create a draft pilot episode. The lead character would be a singer/songwriter named Jude Harrison (a nod to the Beatles song "Hey Jude" and to Beatle George Harrison),* and in the first episode she would win a singing competition, opening the door to a series of career and personal challenges. In every episode, we would feature an original song from Jude.

As writers generated more scripts, we needed to cast the show, particularly the lead actor who would play Jude, and we needed to start creating the original songs for each episode.

Before we started the audition process for the Jude Harrison role, I found myself discussing the concept for *Instant Idol* with a long-time friend and client, Belinda Metz. Belinda is a singer/songwriter herself and had released a full-length album, *Electric Splash*, with the hit single, "What About Me," but she was also an accomplished actor, including appearing as a series regular on David Carradine's *Kung Fu: The Legend Continues*.

She stopped me halfway through my explanation of *Instant Idol* saying, "I know who must play the lead role. She lives in Vancouver, and I'll help get her on tape for you."

---

* There were a number of Beatles references in the series, my favourite being the "Us and Them" episode in Season 4, which featured Jude performing at a charity event, leading to a closing shot that reimagined the cover of the *Sgt. Pepper's Lonely Hearts Club Band* album.

Belinda had worked with Alexz Johnson on a Disney series called *So Weird*, and she knew Alexz both as an excellent actor and as a singer with a beautiful four-octave range. On top of that Alexz was a songwriter. On Belinda's own initiative, she helped create a videotape of Alexz acting and singing, and they sent me the resulting tape along with some pictures and other background info.

The moment I viewed the tape I was immediately convinced as well. In my mind there was no need to even hold auditions for the lead role.

However, we did hold auditions. Linda was very persuasive that we owed it to ourselves to make absolutely sure we had the right actor playing Jude Harrison. Over the course of several months, we and our casting personnel auditioned over six hundred potential actors to play the Jude Harrison role. In the end, who won the part? The very first person we had considered, Alexz Johnson.*

Linda and I had learned from the *Canadian Idol* songwriting experience, and we asked Christopher Ward if he would organize the songwriting camps for our new show. We wanted to be sure the camps would be truly creative experiences and avoid some of the pitfalls of the early *Idol* camps.

Along with Alexz, her brother Brendan, and Christopher, the first camp included some great writers like Damhnait Doyle, Fred St-Gelais, Chin Injeti, Marc Jordan, James Robertson, Andrea Wasse, and Rob Wells. In later camps others like Lights, Luke McMaster, Chris Burke-Gaffney, Emm Gryner, Greg Johnston, and Jeen O'Brien joined us.

Christopher: After the *Idol* experience, I had been reluctant to venture back into the writing camp waters, but this was a unique challenge, and the chance to work with Stephen in a collaborative way was very exciting.

---

* The first season cast rounded out with an abundance of extraordinary talent: Tim Rozon, Laura Vandervoort, Kris Turner, "Maestro Fresh" Wes Williams, and later Tatiana Maslany (who went on to win an Emmy Award as Best Actress for her role in *Orphan Black*).

We started by reaching out to a much smaller group of writers. Stephen asked me to set up the collaborations based on what I knew to be each writer's strengths. I called many of the writers that I had connected with at the first *Idol* camp and assured them that this would be a very different experience. We started each camp with a Monday morning roundtable meeting in the boardroom at Epitome Pictures. The scriptwriters gave us themes, characters, and storylines that they understood and believed in. We asked questions and made notes. Their excitement was contagious and sent us rushing to the writing rooms to get started.

Of course, we had an advantage that *Canadian Idol* did not. Before the songwriters started writing, we would know who our star singer would be. The songwriters could meet with Alexz, get to know her, and understand her likes and dislikes, her vocal range (which was enormous), her strengths (which were many) and weaknesses (few), and they could co-write with her.*

> **Christopher:** Alexz was fully involved from the start and was very clear about what worked for her and what didn't. As with any kind of creative process, the songwriters responded to these well-defined parameters, and the songwriting was truly inspired.

> **Alexz:** Being able to be a part of writing music for that show was never taken lightly. It was a dream, and to this day I feel so lucky that I was given so much responsibility to work with such great writers. I learned so much about writing, and it started me off in such a great direction.

---

* In the first season, five of the featured songs were written or co-written by Alexz.

Rob Wells: It was really intimate — it wasn't forty-plus writers plus managers and the label and people working at the studio. It felt more like family; we were all together in one small space. It's really important when you have a camp like this — talent has to be there, but personality is key. When you run across people that you really get along with and can have a laugh with at the end of the day, you can write something really good.

Those songwriter camps created some very fond memories. Each camp lasted a week. They'd start on a Monday with a meeting between all the songwriters and scriptwriters and end on a Friday with a barbeque at Linda's and my home.

During the week the songwriters would split into teams of three — different teams each day — each team having a songwriter who was particularly strong in melody, one who was particularly strong in lyrics, and a "track guy," meaning a songwriter/music producer who was really adept with computer music programs and could create great-sounding demo versions of the songs. Some of the songwriters — like Lights or Damhnait Doyle or Jeen O'Brien or Alexz herself — were singers also, so they would sing on the demos.

Marc Jordan: In every group I was in, there was a music producer, and that was invaluable, too. You'd do something, and *Bing!* you were hearing what you were thinking so quickly. Sometimes you write a song in the real world, and it might be two weeks before you hear it come back to you ... but we had the luxury of doing everything so quickly, which is not normally my thing either, but I really enjoyed it. You could get it done immediately because of how the groups were put together. A couple of songs that Dav [Damhnait] put vocals on are some of my favourite songs I've ever written because she just killed them. She brought a slightly more vulnerable context to what I'd written. She did a beautiful vocal on "Time to Be Your 21."

On Friday evening at around 10:00 p.m., after we'd all had several glasses of wine or beer and eaten our hamburgers and hotdogs and vegetarian fare, and the last of the "track guys" had straggled in after making last-minute tweaks to their demos, I'd stand by our sound system and start playing the CDs handed to me by each team.

It was a perfect audience for the songs: everyone listening was either a songwriter, a scriptwriter, or part of our production team, and all had a vital interest in what they were hearing. Everyone would be completely silent while each song played and then erupt into applause and cheers at the end of the song.

Inevitably, I would cry.

Rob Wells: It is so rare in this industry to have people who really, really appreciate what you've been doing, and who created these amazing listening parties. You felt like a movie star on Stephen and Linda's property, with the infinity pool and the lake right there. I don't know any other place where that happens.

I remember everybody had to be very quiet, and we gave each song its time. The writers spoke about the song before it got played. I remember the joy on Stephen's face. He'd be standing right beside the CD player. He'd close his eyes and smile and, if it had rhythm, clap his hands, moving around doing a little shuffle. And if it was really emotional, he would start to cry. That never happens — an industry person that's really connected to the music. He let the lyric take over his whole soul and rip his heart out.

In each camp, and thus at each Friday barbeque, about fifteen brand new songs had been created. All of them were works of art. None of them had existed five days earlier. And a third to half of them would end up being featured in an episode of *Instant Star*.

Some of the songs even had a life beyond *Instant Star*. "Time to Be Your 21" was featured in an episode of *Pretty Little Liars*, causing Alexz and the song to trend worldwide on Twitter for three straight nights. And "There's Us" was recorded by the Backstreet Boys and others.

Rob Wells: We went down to the grand piano in the hallway at Centennial College [where we were holding that particular camp], and Christopher put the lyrics down on the piano, and instantly I was reading through them, getting excited, almost being moved to tears as I read the chorus. Christopher went for coffee for us, and in the time it took till he came back, I had the bulk of the music written for it. That was the easiest write I've ever had in my life. There was a stream of students and teachers flowing past us at the piano. I'm surprised we didn't get kicked off that piano 'cause we were being loud, singing away and playing heavily. Classes were going on. Another wonderful thing was having Jeen O'Brien available to sing the demo for us. I don't know if it had been anybody else if it would have been right. She brought every bit of emotion that was in that lyric to the table.

There are so many people that are up in arms that the Backstreet Boys recorded "There's Us." They're livid! I've seen pieces of artwork that show Alexz Johnson and the Backstreet Boys with a big "X" going through the Backstreet Boys. They feel that's Jude's song, and it shouldn't have gone anywhere else!

We had our scripts, we had our cast, we had our songs, and Linda and I were headlong into production of the first thirteen-episode season of our new series. CTV was keen to air the first episode in September, immediately following the final results show for Season 2 of *Canadian Idol*. We still didn't have a title, though.

At the last moment we decided to change the name slightly; rather than *Instant Idol*, we would call it *Instant Star*. That's one of the problems — and joys — with titles. Once you choose one, even if no one is particularly enthusiastic about it, over time everyone gets used to it and falls in love with it. It's like the Trent University student newspaper that I named *Arthur*.* Everyone knew it was a crazy name for a newspaper and would never last, but it's still called *Arthur* fifty years later. Even the title *Degrassi: The Next Generation* was meant to be replaced. It started as an homage to *Star Trek: The Next Generation*, and we all agreed we'd change it later — except we never did.

Instant Star was a title I'd fought against, feeling that it sounded like a reality show not a drama. I'd lobbied for the title *Hey Jude* — a short, punchy title capturing the name of the lead character in a quirky musical way, and clearly a drama (or at least a comedy or a drama). But to no avail. Everyone, including most importantly CTV, had fallen in love with the title *Instant Idol*, so if they couldn't have that they wanted *Instant Star*, and that was that. Truth be told, I kind of love it now.**

Instant Star premiered on CTV on September 15, 2004, immediately following the *Canadian Idol* final results show. It drew over a

---

* Many believed that I came up with the name because the Trent University crest appears to depict Excalibur rising out of the water, as in the King Arthur legend. In fact, it arose from my love for The Beatles. In the Beatles' film *A Hard Day's Night*, George Harrison is asked what his hairstyle is called and replies, "Arthur." Likewise, when a friend asked what our student paper would be called, I quipped "Arthur," and the name has carried on to this day.

** But because I'm the one writing this book, I get the last word: *Hey Jude* would have been better!

Me with the cast of *Instant Star* in 2007: Tim Rozon ("Tommy"), Alexz Johnson ("Jude"), "Maestro Fresh" Wes Williams ("Darius"), Kris Turner ("Jamie"), Mark Taylor ("Kwest"), Cory Lee ("Karma"), Craig Warnock ("Paegan"), Laura Vandervoort ("Sadie"), and Tyler Kyte ("Spiederman").

million viewers, excellent for a debut Canadian drama, and set us off on a four-season run that ultimately saw *Instant Star* air successfully in over 120 countries worldwide.

It never rolled out in the full way I had hoped it would, though. Once again, the issue of art versus commerce raised its head, in a way I hadn't been expecting.

You'll recall that the initial dream for what became *Instant Star* had involved putting out an album of new material each year, creating a band featuring the star, touring the band, and selling lots of records and merchandise. Alexz was initially on board with all of this, but as the show progressed, she became more and more uncomfortable with the notion of promoting music that was not the kind of music she would normally write or perform. She was fine with acting in *Instant Star*, fine with portraying the character Jude Harrison, but not fine with being personally identified, separate from *Instant Star*, with its music, particularly the music she did not create.

She spoke with her acting agent at the Characters Talent Agency about all this, and together they decided to bring in a music manager from one of their affiliated companies to help sort it all through. That manager turned out to be Darren Gilmore, who was soon to also become Jacob Hoggard's manager.

> **Darren:** Alexz had some very good songs that she'd created with her brother Brendan. She felt as an artist she was more like Kate Bush, whereas the Jude Harrison character she played on the show was more like Avril Lavigne. Hence the internal conflict of "who am I" versus "who I am on the show," and "what's the perception of me in the marketplace." She felt strongly that what her heart was telling her to do musically wasn't what she was doing on *Instant Star*. I think it was a real battle for her — in terms of wanting to be true to herself creatively, to do what her heart was telling her to do artistically, and at the same time wanting to move her career forward.

Bottom line, Alexz was not comfortable with touring to perform the *Instant Star* songs, nor was she keen to help promote any albums from the show. And after the first season, she wasn't keen to participate in writing the songs for *Instant Star*. She didn't have an issue with our releasing the music from the show, but she preferred that it be associated with Jude Harrison, not with Alexz Johnson.

> **Alexz:** I never wanted to be the Avril Lavigne, and I don't know why. I don't mean that in a bad way. The biggest thing for me was respect from creators that I admired, the artists I loved like Peter Gabriel and Paul

> Simon and Kate Bush. It was never power, money, or
> fame; it was always respect. I wanted Sting to come
> up to me one day and go, "I loved your record." It
> made me make a lot of decisions that made other
> people think, "You're crazy." But my spirit fought
> against it — against the mall concerts playing Jude,
> against this Miley Cyrus commercial success. Was it
> a mistake? Probably. But at the end of the day I can't
> help it. It's just ingrained in me.

I couldn't really fault her. In fact, I could only admire her.

I believed strongly that the *Instant Star* music was of excellent quality. I think Alexz did, too; that was not the issue. Simply put, she had a drive deep down inside of her to be associated only with music that was directly hers, that reflected her own authentic art: her own writing, her own world view, her own musical choices.

> **Darren:** To this day she believes so much in the path
> that she wants to take musically, she's still living it, try
> ing to do it her way. I give her full credit for that, for
> believing in what she's doing and believing in the kind of
> music that she wants to make.

When I had initially dreamed about creating a recording and touring star through what became the *Instant Star* television show, I'd also dreamed that the star of the show would have her own career, tied into but separate from the show, a career that would undoubtedly involve her living out in real life many of the same issues and dramas she'd be acting out on the show. Alexz was doing exactly that. In effect, she was struggling with exactly the same issue that Jacob Hoggard had struggled with on *Canadian Idol*: do you take a path that doesn't reflect your authentic art, but that may lay a foundation from which you have a much-improved chance to eventually pursue your authentic art? Or do you choose to be authentic from the start, knowing that choice may preclude you from being as "successful" as you otherwise might be in a popular or commercial sense?

That same core issue Alexz was dealing with in real life was also being faced by her character Jude Harrison on *Instant Star*. In that sense, both Alexz and *Instant Star* were being authentic and true. I think that's something to be proud of. Not only was art imitating life, but life was also imitating art … which was imitating life … which was imitating art….

> **Alexz:** As the show progressed it really did mirror itself. It was kind of bizarre. It was very authentic when I was experiencing these episodes and experiencing the same things in my life. I was able to act it so easily 'cause that was my life.
>
> There was a scene I did in the final episode of *Instant Star* where I tell Tommy, the man I love, I have to leave, and I choose my career over him … and I look to him onstage, and I say, "I need to fly. I need to go and do this to discover who I am." That resonated very true to what was happening in my life. I was very much in love at the time, and yet I did choose my career. I couldn't balance both. Choosing my love for music, that was powerful.

Others in our producing team, and among the broadcasters of *Instant Star*, were definitely not as magnanimous as I was (and am) on this. They expressed in blunt terms their strong desire for Alexz to tour and otherwise promote the *Instant Star* music and their disappointment when she proved firm in her resolve. She fulfilled all her contractual commitments to act and record the music, but she just didn't feel comfortable going beyond that.

The "Us and Them" episode in Season 4 of *Instant Star* included a performance by Jude (played by Alexz Johnson) at a charity event, which melded together into a final shot that paid homage to the cover of the Beatles' *Sgt. Pepper's Lonely Hearts Club Band* album.

Darren: I think that, ultimately, the path that I hoped she would've taken would've been finding a middle ground toward her musical identity and commercial success. I believe that you could have both.

Did her resolve make her own music career path ultimately more difficult? Yes. Was it frustrating and disappointing for me not to have the opportunity to build a music star's career in the same way that the producers of *Hannah Montana* had helped build Miley Cyrus into a star? Yes. But at the end of the day, was Alexz being a true artist? Absolutely, yes. She defined her success, and she lived it.

As I said at the beginning of this chapter, success isn't always what you think it is. Alexz came to realize that her definition of success was different from other people, and she was good with that.

Alexz: I always wanted the best of both worlds, which sometimes can be impossible. Stephen understood that when others didn't, and I still think of him as a true mentor in my life. I'm proud that my journey has been authentic. At least I have that. People who listen to my music go, "Wow, she really kept her word."

In the end, I have an amazing man in my life, who I just married. I have a hundred bucks in my pocket. I have a beautiful guitar, and I have my health, and I have good relationships with my family and my friends, and I'm successful. And then we die. What do you bring with you? Love. Your impact on people. That's it. That's more than enough.

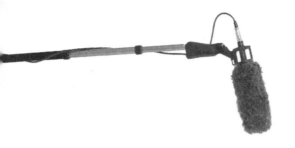

28
PULLING A RABBIT
OUT OF A HAT

By this point, you will have correctly surmised that I am one of those people — one of those potentially very annoying people — who manages to find something positive about almost any situation. It's not even the "glass is half full" thing. It's worse than that. It's "if you look at it from a right angle, namely from underneath looking directly up through the bottom, it pretty much looks like the glass is completely full" thing. Even when things look completely bleak, there's still a way to pull a rabbit out of the hat — if you can just find that way.

Case in point: I am extremely proud of our series *The L.A. Complex.*

Largely the invention of the brilliant showrunner Martin Gero, *The L.A. Complex* followed the lives of aspiring young actors, dancers, musicians, and comedians, all living in a rundown motel in Los Angeles, hoping to make it big. Really, it was about what sacrifices people will make to achieve their dreams and, in the end, what success really is.

> **Martin:** It was not *Glee.* It was not *Melrose Place.* It was not *Entourage.* I said, "Let's lean in to the fact that all these kids are poor and the motel is old and dirty." To me that's the more interesting take on L.A. because those people are desperate. I'd just turned thirty at the time and I was finding, even at that point, being around twenty-year-olds

to be insufferable, and the thought of doing a whole show with twenty-year-olds … what am I doing? In your twenties, essentially you're operating purely on instinct and no wisdom. But, in fact, the twenties are a fascinating time because you are making mistakes that are going to make you the person you end up being. All these characters who have gone down there because they have some premonition about why they have to be in L.A. — they're hoping it's not a delusion, that it was ordained that they were supposed to be there. That struggle … I felt very close to it because I had just moved to L.A., and I had a job at a coffee shop for two years where I thought I was going to be able to quit every week.

The show was well written, well directed, and well produced. The cast was talented and very photogenic (and included Cassie Steele, who earlier had played "Manny" on *Degrassi* and "Blu" on *Instant Star*.)

If you haven't seen it, you should. It launched in 2012 in Canada on CTV and MuchMusic. In the United States it ran on The CW and received critical accolades. Recently *TV Guide* ranked all The CW shows of all time (there are eighty-nine in total) and placed *The L.A. Complex* in the Top 10 of the best The CW has offered.*

Martin: That show had such a huge critical following. My next show was *Blindspot*, a massive NBC hit, a blockbuster once-in-a-career thing. All the press I did for it, everyone was going "Man, I gotta tell you, *The L.A. Complex* was one of my favourite shows of all time." There isn't a TV critic in the world that doesn't love that show. We were getting insane reviews.

---

* It ranked just ahead of *Gilmore Girls* and behind *Jane the Virgin*, *Crazy Ex-Girlfriend*, *iZombie*, *The Vampire Diaries*, *Veronica Mars*, and *Supernatural*.

Me on set with Alan Thicke during the shooting of *The L.A. Complex* in 2012. He was saying I should check out the new material his son Robin was working on — turned out to be "Blurred Lines," which was released the following year.

Entertainment Weekly did a three-page spread, calling it "summer's hidden gem." Now that I've got shows on network television, I've found out it's really hard to get three pages of *Entertainment Weekly*. We were getting crazy mentions in the *New Yorker*. It was a phenomenal time.

But.

Commercially, *The L.A. Complex* was not a success story. We can blame it on "being ahead of its time," or "the wrong time slot," or "not enough promotion," as we producers always will, but for whatever reason *The L.A. Complex* never measured up ratings-wise. In fact, "never measured up" is being very kind. The headline in the April 25, 2012, edition of *Entertainment Weekly* was succinct: "CW's 'L.A. Complex': Lowest-rated broadcast drama debut of all time."

It went on to reiterate, "The CW's new midseason effort, the imported sexy soap *The L.A. Complex*, set a new benchmark Tuesday night: according to network research analysts, *The L.A. Complex* is the lowest-rated in-season broadcast drama debut on record (tracking back to the start of the current ratings measurement system)."

Now, any producer worth his or her salt has produced a show that didn't work. That's part of the entertainment world: sometimes you win, sometimes you lose. But how many have produced a drama that had the #1 lowest-rated debut in the history of U.S. television? Only one. Yours truly, Stephen Stohn.

Of course, it wasn't just me — there were others on our producer team — but I'm happy to give the others credit for all the good things about *The L.A. Complex* and take responsibility myself for the bad.

"The lowest-rated broadcast drama debut of all time." It's absolutely unique. In some ways it's hard not to be proud of it. Furthermore, *The L.A. Complex* actually got ordered for a second season. And a third (although the third never ended up being produced). There's something to be said for producing the lowest-rated drama of all time and then having it ordered again and again.

In fact, everything about the way *The L.A. Complex* was ordered by the broadcasters was … weird.

Ivan Fecan and Susanne Boyce at CTV in Canada loved the concept and had ordered an initial six episodes, which we produced in 2011 at our Toronto studios — or, I should say, largely at our Toronto studios. We did a few days of filming in Los Angeles, mostly consisting of "beauty footage" Martin took from a helicopter, zooming into local landmarks. We edited the show in such a way that when we cut to the close-up shots, which had actually been shot back in Toronto, they appeared to be in Los Angeles.

When The CW saw those six episodes, they were so pleased they ordered thirteen episodes (the initial six, plus seven more than CTV had initially ordered). We couldn't shoot the additional episodes right away, though, as snow was coming in Toronto.

A few months later, in February 2012, CTV ordered thirteen more episodes — meaning that they had committed to a total of nineteen episodes, while The CW had committed to only thirteen.

Then in April, as you now know, the initial six episodes debuted to worse-than-miserable ratings on The CW, so we were not expecting The CW to order any more. They would still receive and broadcast the first seven of the thirteen new episodes we were starting to produce, but that would be it. The final six would be up for grabs in the United States though The CW still retained first dibs.

It was an extremely disappointing development, but on the glass-half-full side, we were still producing more episodes of a series we loved. There was no time for tears. There was work to be done, and not just work — really good, creative, and satisfying work.

By June we were part way through shooting when I got a very surprising call from Mark Pedowitz, the president of The CW. We loved working with Mark. He and Thom Sherman, Michael Roberts, and the others on the team at The CW were all bright, motivated, and no-nonsense, and they still managed to be eminently likeable.

> **Mark:** Stephen, I've got a hole in my schedule, and I want to fill it with the other six episodes you are producing.
>
> **Stephen:** Wow, fantastic!
>
> **Mark:** Wait a minute, there's a small catch. I have to run the episodes back to back, two hours at a time, over three consecutive Mondays in early September.
>
> **Stephen:** Mark, that's impossible, we won't be finished shooting until mid-September. You can't air shows that haven't even been filmed yet! And then there's all the editing, the music, the sound, and colour correction … it can't be done. Can't you buy us more time?
>
> **Mark:** I've got this hole that's come up in my schedule, and I can't push it later — after then we start running

into season premieres of our returning shows. This is all I can do. What if you double-shoot. Hire an extra crew, and shoot at twice the rate you are now?

I started some quick calculations. "Well, that is conceivable, in theory, but that would mean we'd have just…." I finished the calculations. "Just twenty-one days from the end of filming to get the shows to air. With all the editing and music and post-production we need to do, we can't make it. No one could."

"Ah, Stephen," said Mark, suddenly sounding very expansive. "I remember back in the days when I was at ABC Studios … we used to *dream* of having as much as twenty-one days to get to air."

He was completely bluffing me. I knew that. But it's like when two twelve-year-olds are in the schoolyard, and one triple-dog-dares the other. Mark Pedowitz had just triple-dog-dared me.

I responded in the only way a responsible, mature, seasoned producer could — or at least, a responsible, mature, seasoned producer with, evidently, the brain of a twelve-year-old. "We'll do it."

When the rest of our producing team initially heard the news, they were dumbfounded, uttering lots of exclamations like, "It can't be done," but after a short while everyone rallied around.

> **Martin:** I think Stephen and I both love unsolvable problems, and I'm sure that's his legal mind coming in to work there. We don't like to say no, and it was going to be best for the show. Maybe it's a sad thing, but I think I'm at my best when there is chaos. We both enjoy being the calm eye of that storm. Taking a breath, looking around, being reasonable … it may cost more money, but we'll end so much earlier.

It was chaotic, but it was controlled chaos. We were also in the midst of shooting Season 12 of *Degrassi*, so we had one *Degrassi* crew and two *The L.A. Complex* crews all jostling each other at the same time in the studio. We shifted schedules to work seven days a week, and every department buckled down to make it all come together.

> **Martin:** We had to be continuously shooting on top of one another. I would edit all night and all weekend. I've never worked harder. It was a seven-day-a-week job. A show that we were supposed to finish the last day of post-production in mid-January, we had to finish the third week of September. How can you take four months out of a production schedule and have it just work? Stephen and I would sit in his office very late at night trying to figure how do we do this.

I won't dwell on the incredible hard work, even heroism, that our writers, suppliers, cast, and crew exerted over the next weeks. I'll just say that it was a remarkable team effort. There's no question that it was very difficult. Tempers flared, but they flared in the best possible way. Some people stopped talking to each other, except as totally necessary, but everyone had the identical goal: working as hard as they could, and as inventively as they could, to meet the deadline at The CW.

> **Martin:** I did not leave Epitome Studios for basically four months. It's a cool place, but not for four months, twenty-four hours a day. There was a bit of cabin fever there, but there was a real moment when it looked like the whole thing was going to cave down around us because some of us weren't getting along. Stephen helped though — usually when somebody's trying to handle you, there's nothing more infuriating, but Stephen does it in a way that you know you're being handled, and somehow it's still very comfortable. You know he's treating you like a child, and that should be

infuriating, but he does it in a way where you're like, "I am being childish. He's right to talk to me this way." I was young, and it was my first show, and I put a lot of pressure on myself, and he was a great sounding board for me, telling me, "That *is* something you should get upset about," but also saying at times, "You need to let that go, you're hurting the show."

On a sunny Thursday evening later in August, I took a moment to acknowledge what had been happening. On the coming Monday, in just four days, we would complete shooting of the final two episodes. Our team would then work around the clock for the ensuing twenty-one days, and delivery to The CW was going to be made on time — probably not with even hours to spare, but on time. Yes, we had received some very bad news in April, then some good but seemingly impossible news in June, but now we were on the verge of meeting our deadlines, and we were making and delivering some great television. It made me smile.

Then the phone rang. It was Martin Gero on the line. "Joe is in the hospital. It's appendicitis." Joe was Joe Dinicol, a hard-working and very talented actor who played the part of neophyte stand-up comic Nick Wagner. I immediately went on-set to meet Martin and find out where things stood.

At first, things didn't look so bad. We've had actors suffer appendicitis before, and as long as it's caught in time and the appendix hasn't burst, they've been able to return to work fairly soon. If we could figure out a way to minimize Joe's workload and rejig the schedule so all his scenes were shot on the final day — or even a few days later, while we carried on with post-production on everything else — he could likely recover enough to act.

Luckily, we had already shot all the storylines in which Nick appeared, except for a major one in the second-last episode. (As is the case with all television shows, we had been shooting scenes out of order and, indeed, had been "block shooting" the final two episodes, meaning that we were shooting scenes from the final two episodes over the same time period.)

But then the phone rang again.

The appendix had burst. It was very serious, and Joe was one sick puppy. He would be in the hospital for at least another couple of weeks, and certainly far too weak to act. With tubes down his throat, he couldn't even speak. Joe was devastated, but there was nothing he could do.

We were devastated as well, but somehow both Martin and I remained convinced that we would somehow pull a rabbit out of a hat and make it all work.

It was primarily up to the writers, led by Martin, to come up with a solution. Here's the storyline dilemma they faced: Nick has been hired to perform at a network executive's house. He and his comedian girlfriend, Sabrina (played by Georgina Reilly), realize this could be a big break for him. It also creates frustration in their relationship as Sabrina feels left behind. But when Nick arrives at the network executive's house, he finds it's not his big break at all. He's not performing for the network executive, but rather at a bat mitzvah for the network executive's young daughter and dozens of her friends. At first Nick feels he can't go on, and not just because he's disappointed: his comedy material is very adult-oriented and not suitable for preteens. In the end, he rises to the occasion and adapts his material on the fly to turn it into a successful performance, if success is measured by appealing to a gaggle of preteen girls.

All the later Nick Wagner scenes in that episode and the final episode had already been shot. Could the writers rewrite such a major scene and still have all the scenes before and after make sense?

"We've solved it." Martin had arrived in front of my desk and was gesturing for me to come down the hall into the writers' room to hear the new pitch.

It wasn't one of the writers, but our extraordinarily insightful editor, Mike Banas, who'd come up with the solution while chatting with the writers over lunch: "Nick arrives at the network executive's house. We only see him from behind. First thing, he's handed a bunny suit and told

That's ostensibly Joe Dinicol playing the part of Nick Wagner in *The L.A. Complex* in 2012, but Joe was in the hospital with acute appendicitis, so it's actually Aaron Abrams inside the bunny suit.

to put it on, that the young daughter loves bunnies, and he has to remain in the bunny suit for the rest of his time there."

> **Martin:** We had no margin for error. There was a whole day, which comprised most of the episode. I had a terrible idea — clown makeup and a wig. And then our editor, who had worked more hours than anyone toiling away on the show, said, "Bunny suit, man, bunny suit!" We made all these ridiculous rules, like "You can never take the head off, it will startle the children!"

It was a perfect solution, and so elegant and funny that it made the entire storyline even better than as originally written.*

And the person who would be inside the bunny suit pretending to be Nick? One of the actors, Aaron Abrams, was about the same height

---

* It's worth downloading the episode to see for yourself. If you go to iTunes, just search for *The L.A. Complex*, Season 2, Episode 12.

and build as Joe, so he filled in, and we later re-dubbed his voice with a Joe Dinicol sound-alike (which we got away with since the voice was muffled anyway.)*

I'm happy to say that Joe ultimately survived his appendix episode very successfully, and he has gone on to act in many major series since then, including *Grey's Anatomy, Blindspot, Halt and Catch Fire, Saving Hope*, and *Arrow*.

As for us, The CW was so pleased with the final six episodes that they ordered a third season of *The L.A. Complex*.

Management had changed at CTV in the interim, though. Ivan Fecan and Susanne Boyce were no longer in charge, and the new management team wasn't keen on the low ratings we were still generating on *The L.A. Complex*. They cancelled the show, despite its critical accolades.

Without CTV's financial support we couldn't move forward. It was odd to have a Canadian-content show that was ordered by a U.S. network, but not by a Canadian one. On the other hand, low ratings are low ratings — and I guess there are only so many times you can pull a rabbit (or a bunny suit) out of the hat!

Or are there? *The L.A. Complex* may not have been a huge success, but, as they say, every ending is really just another beginning.

---

* Aaron had been a writer and co-executive producer in the first season of *The L.A. Complex*. In the second season he had also acted, playing the part of has-been actor Ricky Lloyd. IMDb.com correctly lists Aaron as acting in Episode 12 but notes beside his name "(credit only)," meaning that he was edited out and didn't end up appearing in the episode. In fact, he did appear, but inside the bunny suit.

29
WE SELL THE COMPANY

I have a bobblehead doll of Mr. Burns from *The Simpsons* on my desk, partly because *The Simpsons* is one of my favourite shows, and partly because Michael Donovan, the head of DHX Media, bears a remarkable resemblance to Mr. Burns.*

Michael is one of those rare people who is both a genius and a magnificent dinner companion. If I had the choice of anyone to have dinner with, outside of immediate family and friends (and of course outside of my hero, Elon Musk), Michael Donovan would be at the top of the list. The only thing that would make it better would be if his brother Paul, who — if possible — is even more of a genius, were to tag along.

In the winter of 2012 Michael asked to meet with me at the Windsor Arms Hotel in Toronto. Though DHX Media was relatively small at the time, it was already a public company with its shares traded on the Toronto Stock Exchange. Michael's vision was to grow it further

---

* My favourite episode is "Homer at the Bat," in which Mr. Burns makes a million-dollar bet that his Springfield Nuclear Power Plant baseball team will win. Mr. Burns brings in nine ringers from the big leagues to make it so — but the winning run arises not from any of the nine, but from Homer being hit by a pitch when he is distracted by Mr. Burns's signals from third base.

into the largest independent producer and distributor of children's and youth television shows in the world.

As part of his growth strategy, at our meeting Michael pitched the idea of DHX Media buying Epitome Pictures from Linda and me — not just the production company, but also our studio, and all rights in our catalogue of *Degrassi* and other television shows.

My reply was to express sincere thanks for his thinking of us, but I added, "I don't think it's a good idea. Not because we wouldn't love working with you, but because I just don't think a production company like ours is a good fit with a public company."

I went on to explain that Linda and I had always shied away from the idea of going public, that we felt there was too much emphasis that the stock market placed on short-term thinking. Linda and I just wanted to make great television over the long-term, not to be marching to the demands of shareholders who would want ever-increasing revenues and profits with every quarterly financial report.

Michael was not easily dissuaded, however. He talked glowingly about what we had accomplished over the years and said that Linda and I would be shielded from the short-term expectations, that *Degrassi* would be like a coral reef — we could carry on producing it as we always had, and DHX would not interfere in any way. He added, "We would be crazy if we did. The two of you know what you are doing!"

With that, we agreed to explore the notion further, and over the next couple of months we exchanged financial information and entered into some preliminary negotiations. Then things stalled. The financial terms were not really to our liking, and we decided that rather than negotiate further, we would simply withdraw and not negotiate at all. Michael was disappointed, but he accepted our position.

A year later Michael invited me to another meeting, this time over lunch in Cannes, on board a boat that DHX Media had leased during the MIPCOM television festival. DHX Media had grown larger in the meantime, having acquired some other companies such as Cookie Jar Entertainment, and by then Michael had indeed fulfilled his vision of

DHX becoming the world's largest independent owner of children's television programming.

We had also grown somewhat. At the request of our bankers, we had switched our method of accounting to be more comparable with that of a public company. And in addition to the forty new episodes of *Degrassi* and thirteen new episodes of *The L.A. Complex* that we had produced that year, our catalogue of older *Degrassi* shows was becoming quite popular on services such as Amazon.

Michael got straight to the point. He was still interested in acquiring Epitome, and as we talked he ripped a sheet of paper from a notebook, asked me to help project our most recent revenues, cash flow, and EBITDA* (a fancy acronym for profits). Then he jotted down a "back of the envelope" calculation of what he thought the purchase price should be, arriving at $33.6 million. I immediately pulled out my iPhone and took a picture of his calculations.

This figure was more to Linda's and my liking. Also to our liking was Michael's outline of plans to expand the use of our studio by bringing in other live action DHX Media television shows. This would mean more work for all the crew who had been loyal to us over the years, and it satisfied us that our Epitome family would be on a good footing after the sale.

Over the next six months we engaged in long and detailed negotiations with DHX, ending up with a purchase and sale agreement the size of a phone book.** Over those months, we weren't negotiating with Michael, but rather with the accountants at DHX, who kept trying to lower the purchase price. We kept insisting that the price be maintained.

At one critical juncture we were still about a million dollars apart in

---

* EBITDA is "Earnings Before Interest, Taxes, Depreciation, and Amortization."

** For those of you who are members of Generation Z, a phone book is a very thick, bound volume — distributed free of charge by telephone companies in the pre-internet era — consisting of thousands of thin pages on which were printed all the telephone numbers and addresses of people in a local calling area.

Picture I took with my iPhone, on the DHX Media boat in Cannes Harbour in 2013, of Michael Donovan's "back of the envelope" calculations for the DHX purchase of Epitome.

the negotiations, and Linda insisted that she was going to call Michael to ask him to step back into the fray and get the price increased. I was hesitant because we didn't really have any solid arguments at that point that we hadn't already made over and over again with the accountants, other than our feeling that a higher figure was better.

Linda said she was going to call Michael anyway, and I countered with a different suggestion: not asking for a million dollars more, but rather asking for $2,222,222.22 more.

Linda was puzzled, but I explained that we were beyond negotiating rationally, we were negotiating based on feelings, and the number twenty-two had a very special significance for Michael. He had been integrally involved, since its beginnings decades earlier, with the ongoing and hugely successful sketch comedy show *This Hour Has 22 Minutes*, and twenty-two was his lucky number.

Linda thought my suggestion was crazy, but to her great credit she agreed anyway, and dialed Michael's cellphone. He was in England at the time, shopping in Harrods department store, and when Linda made her pitch for the additional $2,222,222.22 Michael just roared with laughter, as I knew he would, causing odd stares among the patrons at Harrods. He was so taken by the notion that he promised to call his people and get the price increased. A few days later he called back to say that while he couldn't talk the accountants into the full amount, he could get us an extra million dollars. We just grinned.

On April 3, 2014, the deal was announced: DHX Media had bought Epitome and its associated entities for $33 million, almost exactly the figure that Michael had scribbled down in his "back of the envelope" calculations. With adjustments for cash reserves and receivables, the amount paid to us ended up being even a bit higher than what he had scribbled.

In effect, the agreement the size of a phone book, which took six months of negotiations, simply codified the few lines of calculations that Michael and I had arrived at over a two-hour lunch on a boat in Cannes Harbour.

The final days before the April 3 announcement were harried, though. Tempers were getting short. There is a period of time in such transactions where the acquiring party undertakes "due diligence" — namely going through all the agreements, financial records, and other files of the company being acquired — making sure that everything meets their expectations. The due diligence period had gone on and on, for far longer than we thought was warranted. I remember saying to one of the DHX Media executives that if I was asked one more time for a copy of the agreement for my writer's share of the *Degrassi* theme song "Whatever It Takes," copies of which I had already supplied to them five times, the deal was off.

It was all made more complicated by the need for strict confidentiality. Since DHX Media was a publicly traded company, no information about the existence of the transaction could be allowed to leak out. On our side only Linda and I and three other confidantes had any idea what was happening, and in our conversations and internal emails we used code words — such as "Carlaw" instead of "DHX Media" — so that no one would inadvertently happen upon a revealing conversation.*

---

* The head office of DHX at the time was located on Carlaw Avenue in Toronto.

The date for closing the transaction was continually pushed back until finally, on Wednesday, April 2, it looked very possible that we would be signing all the documents in the early evening. We set a timetable for a press release the next day, to be followed immediately by a "town hall meeting" of all our employees, cast, and crew at the Epitome Studios. The prime agenda for the meeting was to reassure everyone that not only were their jobs secure, but also it was our strong hope that the acquisition by DHX would result in even more work. At that point, the timetable looked as follows:

10:00 a.m.	Toronto Stock Exchange to halt trading in DHX Media shares.
10:01 a.m.	Approved press release to be initiated; may take several minutes to become official. All must remain silent until confirmation has been received that the press release has "crossed the wire" and become official.
10:05 a.m.	Immediately upon the press release becoming official, approximately fifty personalized emails to be released directly by Linda and Stephen to funders, suppliers, and others who have a direct connection with Epitome.
10:15 a.m.	Meeting for all employees, cast, and crew in the Epitome boardroom.
10:30 a.m.	Toronto Stock Exchange to resume trading in DHX Media shares.

I don't know if you've ever imagined what it would be like at the completion of a purchase and sale of this type. I certainly had my own preconceived notions from more than twenty years earlier when I was a partner at McCarthys. Everyone would gather in a large boardroom.

There would be representatives from both companies, of course, but there would also be scads of lawyers, many of them very junior, reading the documents carefully and then running about making last minute corrections. The documents would then be signed, in a silence so hushed you could hear the pens squeak, followed by a brief round of applause, and a short speech of congratulations, and then flutes of fine champagne would magically appear.

I guess things have changed dramatically over the past twenty years. First, we weren't in a large boardroom, and second, we were all alone. There was nobody from DHX Media with us. There were no lawyers (well, technically I was there, but I was not acting as a lawyer — we had engaged McCarthys to act on our behalf). There weren't even any documents to sign, at least not yet. There were just Linda and I, and our three confidantes, waiting in the otherwise empty Epitome studios. Waiting. And then waiting some more.

It wasn't until after midnight when the first documents started to arrive, sent as PDF attachments in emails from McCarthys to me. And they weren't even the full documents — they were only the signature pages. We were to print them, sign them, and then email them back to McCarthys whereupon they would be sent on to the DHX Media lawyers, who would arrange a similar procedure for counter-signature by DHX Media executives.

There were about twenty such signature pages to sign. It was when she signed the first one that Linda started to cry. And she couldn't stop crying.

It wasn't that she had any regret. We'd been negotiating for six months — much longer if you included the first negotiations that we'd had two years earlier — and Linda absolutely knew that it was all for the best. It was just that she'd spent most of her adult life building up *Degrassi*, and all our other shows, and the studio we'd created, and the friendships we'd made through it all. She knew we'd still be working on *Degrassi* and other shows and that we'd still be working with our friends. But it was a moment of pivotal change — all for the best, but things would never really be the same.

Oh, and there were no flutes of champagne. We did have some wine that someone had sent us as a present two Christmases ago, and some cold pizza from earlier in the evening. So we simply drank the wine, I comforted Linda through her tears, and we signed the pages.

The next morning we arrived back at the studio at 7:00 a.m., ready for our big day, only to find that there was a problem. DHX had its own cash reserves but also a credit line provided by a syndicate of large banks. All the banks needed to sign off on a transaction of this size, and one of them hadn't. We were assured they would sign in the end, but there had been some kind of miscommunication between that bank and DHX Media that needed to be corrected.

In and of itself, waiting for one bank to sign off was not a huge deal; if the transaction was delayed for a few hours, it was delayed. But we had already arranged for the town hall meeting at 10:15 a.m. In our nearly twenty years of operating the studio, we had never called a meeting of this sort. Everyone knew something was up, and we were aware that speculation was rampant, but we could do or say nothing, other than to postpone the meeting.

We sat in our offices, avoiding everyone other than our three confidantes, and waited for a phone call.

It was early afternoon when the call came in. Everything was now in order, and the Toronto Stock Exchange had halted trading in DHX Media shares. The press release was initiated, we sent out word that everyone in the studio should head for the town hall meeting in fifteen minutes, and we stood by, waiting for confirmation that the press release had "crossed the wire" and was official.

The phrase "crossed the wire" is a throwback to the days when the only trusted method of transmitting news was via a "wire service," which could be relied upon to undertake the simultaneous distribution and disclosure of press releases and material news to media, investment systems, regulatory services, and websites. Wire services are still relied upon, but these days news travels in many different ways.

We were still awaiting official confirmation that the press release had crossed the wire when people started showing up at our door asking

The animated Epitome logo featured a torch as the middle letter *t*, casting a shadow that reveals the name "Epitome," as an homage both to early forms of film — shadows on the wall — and to Plato's "Allegory of the Cave," in which Plato posits that what we perceive in our lives is only an imperfect shadow of the ideal (or what we might call the "epitome").

what was happening: they had received Google Alerts on their cellphones that DHX Media had purchased Epitome. I yelled to Linda, "Release the hounds!" — meaning that we should immediately release the personalized emails to funders, suppliers, and others.

A few minutes later we entered the town hall meeting. Half the people in the room knew what was going on because of the Google Alerts, and the other half were taken by surprise. We tried to answer questions as best we could, mostly to assure everyone that production of the current season of *Degrassi* was completely unaffected, that for the rest of the year it was business as usual, that their jobs were secure, and that Linda and I were not going anywhere. While we had sold the business, we would be carrying on as executive producers for this season and at least a few more to come, so future seasons of *Degrassi* would proceed very much the same as they always had. On top of that, we shared how hopeful we were that many of them could be part of the new productions that DHX would be bringing into the studio.

Everyone applauded as Linda ended by saying, "Now let's get out of here. There's work to be done!"

Finally in the early evening, after the town hall meeting and numerous phone calls and email exchanges, Linda and I were able to head home and sit on our front porch, just the two of us. As we looked out over Lake Ontario, we clinked glasses of chilled 1996 Dom Pérignon champagne and offered up toasts to *Degrassi*, to the past, and to the future, whatever it brought.

And a special toast to Michael Donovan, who had put in motion this profound change in our careers.

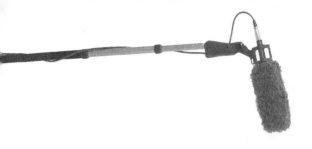

30
THE TIMELESS MIND

This is the philosophy chapter — not philosophy in the Aristotle or Plato sense, though I love them both, but philosophy in the sense of what drives me, Stephen Stohn, and gives meaning to my life. This chapter doesn't have any celebrities, behind-the-scenes revelations, stories of me making a fool of myself in court, or tales of writing songs or going on adventures. This chapter combines the different beliefs and practices that drive me.

The year 1964 was important not just because I saw my first rock concert, The Beatles; at least one other seminal event in my life occurred that year.

My best friend's uncle and I hit it off immediately when we first met. He was a remarkable man who rarely ventured outside as he suffered from what was then called "manic depressive reaction." He was extremely bright, having retired early from a distinguished career as an inventor and engineer for a large chemical company. We immediately found some common interests, among them a mutual love of cryptic crossword puzzles.

It's not that we spent a long time together — I had at most a half-dozen relatively brief visits with him — but in one of our final interactions he had a gift for me. Before revealing the gift, he told the following story:

When I was much younger, I had an odd dream that repeated itself over several nights. In the dream I entered a large library building and made my way to a stack of books, specifically three stacks along the left side. I walked to that stack and sought out the last shelves near the wall, and I was attracted to a thin book with a yellow cover standing on its own on the very bottom shelf. There my dream always ended.

A few days later I found myself walking along a street I rarely walked along, and I looked up to find myself in front of a library building that I had never noticed before. On impulse I entered the building and was immediately struck with a strong sense of having been there before. I felt a bit foolish and almost turned around and left, but I decided to walk slowly to exactly the third stack of books on the left, and I sought out the bottom shelf nearest the wall. Astoundingly, there I found a thin book with a yellow cover standing on its own.

Needless to say, I signed up at that library and took the book home with me. It turned out that the book was called *An Experiment with Time*, published in 1927 and written by an English aeronautical engineer named J.W. Dunne. It is a copy of that very book that is my gift to you today.

He went on to explain the central theory of the book, namely that events humans perceive in our waking hours as occurring over forward-moving periods of time are, in fact, occurring simultaneously — that there is no past and future, only the present — and only our human perceptions impose a sense of elapsing time onto events.

But Dunne's theory was more than that. He believed that our dreams are not encumbered with the imposition of elapsing time. In other words, he believed that we dream in a jumble of past, present, and future events.

To demonstrate his theory, Dunne asks us to cast aside our suspicions and disbeliefs and undertake a very simple experiment: to write down our dreams in detail as soon as possible upon awakening each morning. A few days later we are to look back over the dreams and compare them — not in their totality, but rather in individual small details — with events that have actually transpired since the dream occurred. Dunne gives a number of examples in the book.

Dreams, other than the most vivid ones, tend to dissipate very quickly. But with some discipline (particularly required to immediately write the dreams down upon awakening), it does become easier to recall them.

Within a week or so of reading *An Experiment with Time* I had the knack of writing my dreams down, the most vivid being a nonsensical one in which I was sitting in the front row of chemistry class. In the class our chemistry teacher introduced our headmaster as his assistant to demonstrate an "amazing" scientific principle, namely that hot water can be poured from a kettle into a pure white coffee cup.

I woke up and dutifully scribbled the dream down.

Two days later I was unexpectedly called out of class to the head-master's office, an office I had never entered during my three years at the school. In fact, I had never even met the headmaster; he was to me only a distant god-like figure who hovered above the lives of us mere students. I was quite agitated as I approached his office, assuming I had done some-thing for which I was to be punished.* His secretary apologized that the headmaster had just stepped out for a moment but would be right back, and she asked me as to sit in his inner sanctum until he returned. Of course, I obliged and, while sitting nervously, noticed just inches in front of me a simple object that had great significance: a pure white coffee cup filled with hot water. Just like in the dream.

Could it be a coincidence? Well, maybe. The odds of my having an interaction with the headmaster for the first time in my school life were

---

* It turns out our interaction was benign. He was pleased to congratulate me as the recipient of the history prize.

very small, but not zero. And it's unusual to have hot water in a coffee cup, though hardly impossible. However, the confluence of the headmaster, the hot water, and the pure white coffee cup, all taken together as they were in the dream, was enough to convince me that there was definitely something to J.W. Dunne's theories, and that the subconscious mind maybe did have access to timeless information.

In the years following I would have other dreams that could seemingly only be explained as dreams of future events. But at the time, in 1964, I didn't need any further proof. I simply accepted the proposition that there was something wonderful and almost magical about the human mind, and recognized that at least small elements of the immediate future could become known. The question was how to make use of this proposition in some practical way.

In a way I've spent the rest of my life testing and exploring that question.

Actually, there are many more questions than that. If the future can be accessed now, does that mean there is no such thing as free will? That our actions are predetermined in some way? In which case, what is the point of deliberating on choices if the end result is already set? Or are there several different possible futures and different probabilities attached to each of them (akin to what is now called the multiverse theory proposed by some leading physicists, including Stephen Hawking)? Does this mean we have some free will, but perhaps it is more limited than we believe? And so on. Each question spawns even more questions.

To a sixteen-year-old boy, the practical question was the most tantalizing. Yes, the follow-up questions later led me to study philosophy in university, and to make a hobby of reading books on quantum physics. Most immediately appealing, though, was figuring out if there was any way to access even a tiny portion of the hidden power of what I have come to think of as our "timeless mind."

Even back at age sixteen it was immediately clear that trying to actually predict the future out of a jumble of seemingly random scenes in a dream was out of the question. There would be no magically foretelling the price of IBM shares the next day, or the next winner of the Kentucky Derby. But at the very least, the old adage of sleeping on difficult decisions seemed very wise, giving a chance for the subconscious mind to come to solutions guided by some possible awareness of future tendencies.

Was there anything else that could be done?

Later the same year I chanced upon a magazine article that suggested writing down your goals. I immediately wondered what would happen if you did exactly that, but in vivid enough detail to allow your subconscious mind to work with you, using its ability to know future tendencies to help subconsciously guide your actions in a way that helped fulfill the goals.

The results were subtle for the longest while, but ultimately astonishing.

You know from the earlier "Cowboy Junkies" chapter that I have come to believe strongly in the power of writing down exactly what you want. This has been a lifelong belief that started when I read that magazine article so long ago.

When I first tried writing down what I wanted myself, it seemed easy enough. My list started out: "I'd like to make $250,000 a year. I'd like to have a #1 song on the Billboard charts, win an Oscar, and an Emmy, and have a #1 book on the *New York Times* bestseller list."

There's nothing wrong with starting out by aiming high, but my list was completely imbalanced. There was nothing about health. While I wanted a beautiful wife, there was nothing about real love or friendship. No mention of respect or honour or compassion. All in all, it was a limited and narcissistic list (hardly surprising, perhaps, for a boy growing up in a North American culture that so strongly worships fame, money, and physical beauty).

Still, I kept at it over the ensuing weeks and months, asking myself why I wanted a particular thing, and what was behind it. And the list kept evolving, becoming deeper. As I said in that earlier chapter:

The more you think about it, the money, the fame, the lifestyle aren't all that much of a driver. You start to realize health is important. And the love and respect of friends, family, colleagues, and even people that you don't really know all that well, are all tremendously important....

I find it an absolutely, overwhelmingly, powerful exercise because if you can actually get through all the layers of self-deceit and rationalization and wish fulfillment, and actually get down to the core of it all — then fix the core goals in abundant detail in your mind — something amazing can happen. Your mind knows clearly what it is you are focusing on, what you are really reaching toward. And all aspects of your conscious and subconscious mind can work together to move you toward your goals.

Probing and finding your core goals requires effort, but it is not essentially a complex exercise. Anyone can do it. It doesn't require any special insight or intelligence; it simply requires persistence and an open, questioning mind.

Is that all there is to it?

At first I thought so. I seemed to be making concrete progress, and new pathways seemed to be opening up for me. Believing in the timeless mind and fixing in that mind authentic, detailed goals were two important foundations. It wasn't until my late twenties that I realized something else was needed.

There were successes, all right, or at least viable inroads that could result in successes. By the age of twenty-nine I had already helped found the Trent University radio service and the Trent newspaper, *Arthur*, partaken of the many adventures through Europe and Turkey with Christopher Ward, produced two feature films, written songs, completed a law degree, and started an entertainment law practice with George Miller.

But there was a frantic quality to what I was doing. There seemed to be so many things going on at once in my mind, so many thoughts competing for attention, that I started to wonder if the whole process of arming the timeless mind with clearly defined goals was actually being sabotaged by the mind's own frantic activity to achieve the goals.

I was achieving some intermediate goals, but the deeper goals were still elusive. Looking back now, I realize that while I accomplished a lot, it was for entirely the wrong reason. I wasn't striving for true inner satisfaction, but rather flailing away as if there was some inner pain or loss — perhaps arising from the early years of feeling bullied and alone — that could be assuaged by accomplishments.

Then I discovered meditation.

I had heard of meditation years before. My heroes, The Beatles, had travelled to Rishikesh in northern India to study transcendental meditation (TM) with Maharishi Mahesh Yogi, and later on The Beach Boys had done the same.

Notwithstanding that it had attracted celebrities, it sounded pretty weird — interesting, but weird — until one day a friend came into my office and breathlessly announced that she had taken a TM course and it had changed her life. She seemed buoyantly happy and energized and couldn't stop talking about how different and wonderful she felt, to the point that I was very skeptical about what she was really feeling. Still, she was insistent that I try the TM course, and I figured, why not? It couldn't hurt, and maybe it would help.

That was almost forty years ago, and I've been meditating every day since.

The big thing that I discovered about meditation is that it helps filter out the franticness and the distracting thoughts that had become inherent in my mind at that time. The incessant silent talking to myself was significantly reduced. I didn't find the euphoria that my friend had found,* but I did find that peaceful feelings came easier and irritations came less.

---

* Unlike me, she actually stopped practising TM a few months later.

I'm not here to sell TM itself. There are many different methods of meditation (and mindfulness, as it is sometimes called), and I have no knowledge that any one method is superior to any other. But I'll describe a bit about the TM experience so that you can get a feel for what it is.

You practise TM twice a day for fifteen to twenty minutes. During each session, you sit in a relaxed way with your eyes closed and focus your attention on a mantra. Your mantra is given to you by a TM instructor, and you are requested to keep the mantra confidential.* If your attention is drawn away from the mantra, as it inevitably is, you don't try to force it back, but rather gently return to the mantra and allow the competing thoughts to drift away.

That's it.

There is an official TM course that teaches the nuances of the practice, and I do recommend that course, but what I have described is really the essence: you give your mind a relaxing vacation for fifteen to twenty minutes, twice a day.

There are lots of other books, articles, and studies on the benefits of meditation and mindfulness, so I'm not going to proselytize. I simply assert that it changed my life profoundly, enabled me to accept adversity and challenges much more positively, and helped me to concentrate on my priorities much more clearly.

I've been asked a number of times whether meditation makes you boring, accepting everything as it is and just zoning out from the real world. Of course, the answer is a resounding no! I've been more energized, challenged, intrigued, and passionate since I started meditating. Yes, I now just let go of small stuff that previously might have made me irritated or distracted, but that leaves more time to focus on the big stuff.

---

* I have honoured that request by never revealing my mantra, but I will describe it for you, simply, as a word of two syllables that doesn't seem to mean anything, at least not to me, and not in the English language.

Since I began meditating, life settled down for me. I got married, had a son, became a partner in a large law firm, and then started my new life as an executive producer for *Degrassi*, *The Juno Awards*, and other shows and ventures. And on top of it all, I had a great time doing it.

I credit meditation with making that all possible, for helping my dreams become reality while keeping me from burning out in the process, for keeping it all in perspective, and keeping it all tremendous fun.

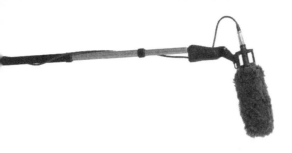

31
DR. STOHN

Many of the dreams set nearly fifty years ago in Europe and Turkey during Christopher's and my travels, and certainly many of the real goals behind those dreams, have come to fruition, though not always in the ways we had originally intended.

I had the chance to reflect on this when I was asked to give an address to the graduating students at Trent University on the occasion of being awarded an honorary doctorate, and this is what I had to say in its entirety:

> Mr. Chancellor, Mr. President, Mr. Mayor, members of the graduating class, faculty, family, and friends:
>
> I'm told it is traditional in a convocation address for someone like me, of advanced years and supposed advanced wisdom, to pass along a nugget of inspiration to assist you on the road ahead. Often this inspiration consists of some variation on the theme, "follow your heart; follow your dream." But I don't actually think that is quite the best way to go. Let me explain.
>
> I was fortunate enough to be a student here at Trent nearly fifty years ago, at a time when many of its institutions were still being created. So it was up to the

relatively small group of us to found — and establish the first guiding principles for — a series of important extracurricular activities, such as the student government (including the balance between university-wide and individual college governance), the student newspaper, Arthur, Trent Radio, and the folk club and other music and social institutions while at the same time earning a degree.

Behind the scenes in 1969 during the time Christopher and I helped found the radio station at Trent University.

As it was for me in the 1960s, I have come to real-ize that the degree being conferred upon you today is not just a degree, it is a confirmation of a life and learning experience that is unique. Many other students will be graduating this month from various colleges and universities elsewhere in Canada, and around the world, but the degree you are receiving today is unique because Trent University is unique. Trent embodies, as it has since the early days, a multidisciplinary approach (what we called back in my day a "renaissance" approach) to learning; that is, the encouragement of different think-ing patterns evolving from a variety of different areas of study and of extracurricular activities. In the former regard, I majored in a combination of philosophy and economics — two disparate fields whose language and thought patterns are in many ways polar opposite — but combined together in the unique Trent sauce, these subjects turned out to be an incomparable foundation for a career as a lawyer, entertainer, and producer.

Now, let us return to my promised nugget of wis-dom — a nugget that is, I suggest, particularly appro-priate for those like yourselves who have spent time embraced in the Trent University renaissance mode of thinking. I said before that the theme of convo-cation addresses is often a variation of "follow your heart; follow your dream." But my exhortation today is not to "follow your dream," but rather to "know your dream."

Know your dream. For following a dream that you only partially understand creates obstacles and frustra-tions. And the unique learning that you have experi-enced over your months and years here at Trent gives you a special ability to engage in more varied processes of authentic introspection — sometimes parallel, sometimes conflicting processes — to unlock the layers of self-deception to which we are all prone, and to discover what your real dream is. I have no doubt that your real dream is not what you initially thought it might be. For when we ask ourselves "why" — what is behind my thinking that I would like to have a certain trait, or to be free of a certain perceived problem, or to engage in a particular career or lifestyle or relationship — we start discovering that what we initially thought was a dream is often merely a means to an end. And it is the end we must discover. It is the end that is the real dream.

I was lucky enough to discover the kernel, the starting seed, of my real dream at 4:30 p.m. on September 7, 1964. I was attending my very first rock concert, at the old Maple Leaf Gardens in Toronto, and before the main act came on there were several warm-up acts that played two or three songs each with the house lights still up.

Back in those days there weren't the huge stacks of sound equipment and arrays of guitars and drums on stage that we're used to now. I remember each group had their own logos on their drum kits, names like Brenda Holloway, King Curtis, and Cannibal & the Headhunters. They'd play their two or three songs, and then roadies would quickly switch the equipment and the next warm-up act would race on. Near the end was a group called Sounds Incorporated, who had an international hit at the time. They sang their three songs and then left the stage. Their equipment remained, so we figured they would come back to do another few songs. But they didn't come back. It seemed like fifteen or twenty minutes went by with nothing happening. The crowd was getting more and more restive, and started chanting, almost to the point of anger and frustration.

Then every light in Maple Leaf Gardens went out. Total blackness. The entire crowd screamed in pandemonium, and suddenly a single spotlight shot onto the Sounds Incorporated drum kit. A roadie raced across the stage and ripped off the front of their bass drum to reveal a new name — The Beatles — and the four lads ran out on stage. We heard almost nothing after that with all the screaming that accompanied their show.

So it was that afternoon I knew what my dream was. I was destined to be a rock star.

Well, of course, that was what I *thought* my dream was. Over my years at Trent and beyond I realized more and more that what I really wanted was to work with talented and creative people, helping projects move forward, particularly projects that impacted people's lives positively. As I delved further, I started to realize that for my dream to be worthwhile, I'd have to be healthy and have the respect and trust of loved ones ... and I came to realize how many other aspects of personal, physical, emotional, and career health were vital to what I wanted in life, and must become part of the dream....

And so, over time, my real dream started to become evident in a very vivid and detailed way. And while my initial dream never did come true, I am happy to say that the real one is very much happening and, indeed, part of it is culminating here and now on this podium.

So I encourage each of you to engage in ongoing self-questioning to find your dream, and when you think you have found it, to keep asking, "Why is this my dream? What is behind my thinking this is my dream?" until at last you truly find your authentic, real dream. And once you know what that dream is, you won't need exhortations to follow it. You'll likely find that you are already a substantial way down the path toward achieving it.

So that is what I leave you with today: know your dream. Know your dream, and you will be that much closer to realizing it.

In closing I would like to now further applaud and congratulate each of you on your many accomplishments that are being specifically memorialized here today. And in that regard, I would like to speak as one of, and on behalf of, the Trent students who have graduated before you, and welcome you into the special ranks known as Trent University alumni. From all of us, we applaud you, we congratulate you, and we wish you every good fortune on your road ahead.

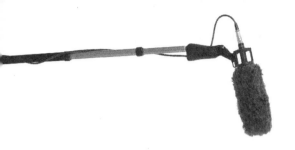

32
PUTTING IT ALL TOGETHER

There is a story about a Zen teacher who faced a number of different life events. He was in a car crash, and his friends talked about how sorry they were, and how bad he must feel, but his response was, "It is neither good, nor bad; it just is." The car crash had a twist: while recovering in the hospital he met a nurse, they fell in love, and they were subsequently married. His friends talked about how wonderful this was, and how happy he must be, but his response was still, "It is neither good, nor bad; it just is."

The story goes on, revealing different happenings that appeared to be happy but in fact turned out sad, and vice versa, with the Zen teacher always making the same neutral response.

I like that story, but only to a point. It does speak powerfully to how our view of events is necessarily framed by our own individual patterns of perception — patterns that we can choose to change. But there is an element of passivity in the story that doesn't appeal to me. Where is the passion in the man? Hello? He's in the hospital! He's fallen in love!

It is the same passivity that some people fall back on when they say, "Well, I guess it was just meant to be." No. Not right. That's victim talk. It wasn't "just meant to be." It just was. And this day is a new day, and we can choose to move forward with whatever has been handed us, with power and vigour and strength … and passion.

As I look back over my life to date, there have been plenty of failures, plenty of moments it would be easy to look back on and say, "Man, I wish that had never happened." But do I really wish those things had never happened? Take, for example, our devastating failure to mount the *Killing Ground* feature film? Would we have been able to go forward on so many other productions without having gained years of experience on that one? I don't think so. Or think of the cancellation of *Riverdale*. Would we ever have brought back *Degrassi* for another four hundred episodes if *Riverdale* had not been cancelled? I don't think so. There are many other examples like those, big and small, set out in this book.

What I keep going back to is the openness to life's twists and turns epitomized in the adventures that befell Christopher and me when we were travelling about Europe in a Volkswagen van, an openness and adaptability that I am blessed to say has carried on for the rest of my life. Those qualities and the goal setting and questioning have been a part of my life for decades.

As you'll have gathered through the course of this book, I think that authentic goal-seeking, combined with embracing what I've been handed, has led me to where I am today — sitting in front of a Mac computer, writing this book, with some (I hope you agree) pretty amazing stories to tell. Even more amazing: there are dozens of stories that I haven't included in this book, not because they weren't compelling enough, or funny enough, or behind-the-scenes enough, or made-me-look-like-an-idiot enough, but just because they didn't easily fit into the central themes I've tried to pursue.

I have one final story that I think embodies all this, a fitting conclusion, but a story that started way back at the very beginning of this book. You may recall, in the prelude, the phone call cancelling *Degrassi* that I had just received.

It was mid-March 2015 when I received that fateful phone call from Viacom. My first reaction of surprise had turned to anger. How could they do this to us after fourteen years as the top original series on their TeenNick channel? And if they were going to cancel us, couldn't they have given us the courtesy of more notice, rather than dealing the dirty news to us on the eve of shooting the new season?

But surprise, anger, frustration, and all other emotions had necessarily been quickly put into abeyance. We needed a plan.

I immediately put in a "Houston, we have a problem" phone call to Steve DeNure, the president and chief operating officer of DHX Media, the company that had purchased us earlier that year. Steve, in turn, had tracked down Josh Scherba, head of the distribution arm of DHX Media.

Josh had previously been connecting with Netflix, Amazon, and Hulu to test the possibility of entering into streaming arrangements for past episodes of *Degrassi*. He immediately undertook to change those discussions to focus on orders for brand new episodes comprising the upcoming season.

It was one thing to talk with those services about licensing past episodes that had already been aired many times — the licence fee for that would have been a relatively small amount — but quite another to talk with them about commissioning brand new episodes, where they would be paying enough to cover most of the costs of production. These would be very difficult and complex discussions, and time was definitely not on our side.

However, we had an ace in the hole, and it arose directly from a very clear goal we had set for ourselves at the beginning of that year. I had been aware for some time that television ratings on *Degrassi* had been declining (though no more so than all other shows aimed at the youth audience). More and more teens and young adults were switching from cable to the internet to watch television shows, and most often they were turning to Netflix.

So months before, when we met with our head writers Sarah Glinski and Matt Huether, I'd had an interesting challenge for them. "We will be on Viacom for another season," I'd said (we were convinced that was the case), "but we need to change things up. We need to make *Degrassi* even more accessible to our audience, to keep them tuning to us on television instead of turning to the internet. When you create the stories and scripts for the new season, we want you to pretend that the

Linda and I kneel beside a cake celebrating the shooting of the five hundredth episode in the *Degrassi* franchise in 2015, joined by cast and crew. That's Amanda Arcuri ("Lola") with the clapperboard between us. Visiting for the day, and on the far left, are Netflix executives Tamara Rotenberg and Andy Yeatman, as well as DHX executive Josh Scherba.

audience is watching us on Netflix. Change how you think about the series, drop any preconceptions you have been following, ignore the rules for traditional television, and make this new season one that you feel passionate about, one that in your hearts you want to make … one that would sparkle on Netflix."

The writers responded enthusiastically, energetically, and brilliantly. They created a brand new approach to the series, which they referred to as becoming the unique authentic voice for the new generation of teenagers called Generation Z* — whose first memories are all post 9/11, who grew up as digital natives, and who are determined to save the world.

Over the first months of the year the writers had filled out their vision, creating story arcs for a truly new season, script outlines for all the episodes, and actual scripts for the first couple of episodes.

---

* That's what sociologists call it, but I like to call it "Generation Netflix."

One of my favourite places in the world — the recording studio — in this case at the Orange Lounge in Toronto, where I'm a part owner. Some of the most famous musicians in the world have recorded here, including Katy Perry, Amy Winehouse, OneRepublic, Imagine Dragons, Kanye West, Annie Lennox, Nelly Furtado, Justin Bieber, and Drake.

When we pitched all this to Viacom, the reaction had been immediately positive. We didn't have a confirmed order from them, but we thought it was just a matter of deciding how many episodes they would order, not if they would order at all. For the next weeks we worked away on the new season and made preparations to begin actual shooting.

It was a total shock when Viacom about-faced by saying they would not continue with *Degrassi*.

But in the process of creating a new direction, an authentic direction that we were all very passionate about, we had actually simultaneously created a very well-planned and detailed pitch exactly suited for Netflix.

Only one week had passed since that phone call from Viacom when Linda, Sarah, and Matt boarded Air Canada flight 799 to Los Angeles to attempt to sell the new *Degrassi* season. Josh had arranged a series of three meetings for the following day, one meeting each with Hulu, Amazon, and, at the end of the day, Netflix.

All three services were very receptive, but by the time Linda, Sarah, and Matt were boarding the plane back to Toronto, Netflix had called to say they were ordering the show.

Without really being aware of what we were doing all those months earlier, we had set a goal — an authentic goal — and we had achieved it.

It took a couple of months to have a final signed deal with Netflix — lots of negotiating and back and forth was required — but on June 8, 2015, we started shooting the first season of what we now call *Degrassi: Next Class*. Since then we've produced a total of four seasons of *Degrassi: Next Class* for Netflix, and we are working on the fifth. These seasons have been made available in seventeen different languages, everywhere in the world except China, Crimea, Syria, and North Korea.*

When I was starting out, did I have any idea I'd ultimately be involved with a television show that would be seen around the world? The short answer is, of course, no. When Linda was in my law office in 1979 getting help with the rights to what became the first of *The Kids of Degrassi Street*, neither of us had the slightest clue that thirty-eight years later *Degrassi* would still be thriving.

But I think the better answer is, yes. A qualified yes, perhaps, but long ago I'd visualized being deeply involved in the entertainment worldand having lifelong projects to immerse myself in. And it's happened. It's not how I visualized it happening, but it's happened.

Even better, it's still happening. I've got to sign off now: I have a meeting to attend on some new *Degrassi* storylines; then I have an apology email to write to my editor for being late in delivering this book; and then I'm heading over to the legendary Orange Lounge recording studio, where I'm working with my friend Aubrey Winfield on some new recordings for an up-and-coming musician.

All in all, I'm really just carrying on. And having some fun. And doing … whatever it takes.

---

* China is in the works. We actually deliver episodes subtitled into Mandarin and Cantonese, but the other three are restricted due to U.S. government regulations.

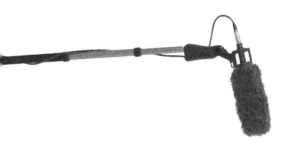

ACKNOWLEDGEMENTS

Like most Canadian boys growing up, my hero was a hockey player: in my case, the moody left winger for the Toronto Maple Leafs, Frank "The Big M" Mahovlich. He was a worthy hero, not only entering the Hockey Hall of Fame after twenty-two seasons in the NHL, but also going into politics after his hockey career ended, becoming a senator in the Canadian Senate. He also had a complex personality, having to be hospitalized for depression after years of mistreatment by his coach, Punch Imlach, in an era when mental illness was not generally spoken of.

I've had other heroes in my life. In the music world, Brian Wilson of The Beach Boys and Paul McCartney of The Beatles head the list with, more currently, Elon Musk.

But there are also everyday heroes who are just as important, if not more so. Some of them will never have known how important they were to my life, people like Phil Lind, Doug Bassett, and Stuart MacKay, who each took the time when I was just starting my career to meet with me to discuss the future of the television industry, even though they had never met me before. I've tried to pay forward their kindness by always meeting with young people — whether I know them or not — when they ask for any advice I can give.

I've written about how important George Miller and Peter Grant have been as mentors to me. Another I've mentioned in this book, but who has no idea what a role model he has been, is Ivan Fecan. His ability to express a grand vision one moment and then plunge into minute detail the next has been an inspiration. And Jack Richardson, best known for producing the biggest hits of The Guess Who, has also been an inspiration not just for his talents and insights, but also for his extraordinary generosity to me and so many others.

One very important person I haven't talked about, but must, is Tom Symons. Tom was the president and vice-chancellor of Trent University when I attended. He had a grand vision for Trent becoming an "Oxford on the Otonabee River," creating a sanctuary where renaissance thinking could flourish and interdisciplinary study would be commonplace. During my years as a student under his leadership I helped to found the student newspaper, *Arthur*, and the Trent Radio station, and I got involved in rock bands and folk music. Oh yes, and I majored in philosophy and economics. All of these elements formed a vital and perfect foundation for my career.

As I've mentioned earlier, there are dozens of stories I haven't included here because they didn't easily fit into the central themes I've tried to pursue. For a similar reason, I've deliberately kept this book focused mostly on the professional side of my life, so while a number of friends and family have been mentioned in this book, many have not. Maybe in another decade or so I'll write a sequel, have the chance to introduce some of these other wonderful people, and tell some of the stories they star in — stories that absolutely should be told.

My literary agent Sam Hiyate was quick to encourage me to write this book and has always been there to give much-needed advice (most of which I've taken). Melinda Downie and Iain Christiansen have been invaluable in their help organizing this book (as they always are in helping organize my life!). And I've met many new friends at Dundurn Press, like Dominic Farrell, Margaret Bryant, Elena Radic, Kate Unrau, and Michelle Melski, whose guidance has been appreciated more than they will know.

Finally, there are three people to whom this book is primarily dedicated.

First is Christopher Ward, who is not only a lifelong best friend, and my co-author, but also a key player in many of the adventures. We collaborated in the past writing songs, and now we've had the chance to write a book together. Ironically, in the songs it was Christopher who wrote the words, and I mostly just wrote melodies. Here, I have written the words, but that became possible only because of the tireless hours Christopher spent interviewing me, transcribing the interviews, debating with me, editing me, encouraging me, and then interviewing dozens of others (and once again transcribing those interviews).

My son Max has been more of an inspiration than he knows from the very beginning: he was born via Caesarian section, and I was in the room, on the verge of fainting. To keep myself conscious, I babbled on to him about important things — namely the positives and negatives of the Toronto Blue Jays pitching rotation. He just looked up at me with big eyes, seemingly taking it all in. He is an author himself now and has an M.B.A., and I am so proud of him.

And my wife, and love, and business partner, and co-creator of everything *Degrassi*, Linda Schuyler. People wonder what it's like to work together for so many years while also being married. Part of what makes it work — oddly perhaps — is we quite often disagree on things. All of the people we work with know we disagree, so they understand it would be useless to try and be a "Yes person" since they would be cozying up to one but disagreeing with the other. So our colleagues quickly learn to speak whatever is actually on their minds — and in the end we take it all in, appreciate everyone's honesty, make decisions, and move forward. Linda is always very supportive, notwithstanding our disagreements, of my weird sense of humour and many foibles. She knows my early goal in life was to be a rock star, so I'm going to give her the last words in this book:

Linda: He's a rock star in my mind!

PHOTO CREDITS

Courtesy of the authors: 26, 29, 35, 46, 89, 129, 131, 297, 314, 323

Courtesy of Biserka Livaja: 194

Courtesy of CARAS/iPhoto Inc.: 113, 171, 266

Courtesy of DHX Media (Toronto) Ltd.: 148, 187, 192, 196, 204, 208, 213, 216, 218, 225, 229, 235, 236, 243, 244, 277, 281, 285, 292, 302, 322

Courtesy of Warner Music Canada Co.: 78